3ds max™ 5

FOR

DUMMIES®

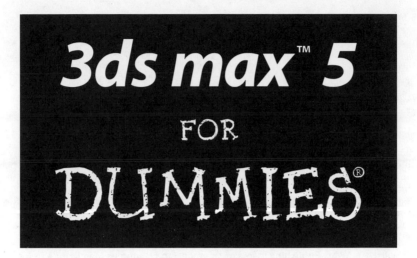

3ds max™ 5
FOR
DUMMIES®

by Shamms Mortier, PhD

WILEY

Wiley Publishing, Inc.

3ds max™ 5 For Dummies®

Published by
Wiley Publishing, Inc.
111 River Street
Hoboken, NJ 07030
www.wiley.com

Copyright © 2003 by Wiley Publishing, Inc., Indianapolis, Indiana

Published by Wiley Publishing, Inc., Indianapolis, Indiana

Published simultaneously in Canada

For general information on our other products and services or to obtain technical support, please contact our Customer Care Department within the U.S. at 800-762-2974, outside the U.S. at 317-572-3993, or fax 317-572-4002.

Wiley also publishes its books in a variety of electronic formats. Some content that appears in print may not be available in electronic books.

Library of Congress Control Number: 2002112136

ISBN: 0-7645-1676-0

Manufactured in the United States of America

10 9 8 7 6 5 4 3 2

1B/RV/RS/QT/IN

ⓦWiley Publishing, Inc. is a trademark of Wiley Publishing, Inc.

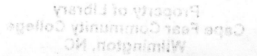

About the Author

Shamms Mortier, PhD, has been involved in computer graphics and animation since its inception in the 1980s. Beginning as a traditional pen and ink illustrator and animator, he entered the realm of 3D modeling and animation beginning with 3ds max version 1. He has maintained a working relationship with 3ds max through its various incarnations, developing graphics and animation for government, academic, and professional broadcast clients through his studio in Bristol, Vermont, Eyeful Tower Communications and Earful Tower Productions (a soundtrack and audio FX production facility). He has authored more than 25 books on computer graphics and animation topics for the world market and teaches various classes on media and creative pursuits at colleges in his area.

Dedication

For Diane, Mic, and Ania

Author's Acknowledgments

Thanks go out to a number of individuals whose efforts and support helped in the production of this book — to Bob Woerner and Christine Berman at Wiley Publishing, Kevin G. Clark and David Marks at AutoDesk, and to David Fugate and Maureen Mahoney at Waterside Productions.

Publisher's Acknowledgments

We're proud of this book; please send us your comments through our online registration form located at www.dummies.com/register/.

Some of the people who helped bring this book to market include the following:

Acquisitions, Editorial, and Media Development

Project Editor: Christine Berman

Acquisitions Editor: Bob Woerner

Copy Editor: Barry Childs-Helton

Technical Editor: Jim Robb

Editorial Manager: Leah Cameron

Media Development Manager: Laura VanWinkle

Media Development Supervisor: Richard Graves

Editorial Assistant: Amanda Foxworth

Cartoons: Rich Tennant (www.the5thwave.com)

Production

Project Coordinator: Kristie Rees

Layout and Graphics: Amanda Carter, Sean Decker, Stephanie Jumper, Jackie Nicholas, Jeremey Unger

Proofreaders: Laura Albert, Tyler Connoley, David Faust, TECHBOOKS Production Services

Indexer: TECHBOOKS Production Services

Publishing and Editorial for Technology Dummies

Richard Swadley, Vice President and Executive Group Publisher

Andy Cummings, Vice President and Publisher

Mary C. Corder, Editorial Director

Publishing for Consumer Dummies

Diane Graves Steele, Vice President and Publisher

Joyce Pepple, Acquisitions Director

Composition Services

Gerry Fahey, Vice President of Production Services

Debbie Stailey, Director of Composition Services

Contents at a Glance

Table of Contents

Introduction

· ·

*W*elcome to the world of virtual 3D design and animation, as crafted and presented in 3ds max — no less than the world's largest-selling 3D application. 3ds max (insert the trumpet fanfare here) is used all over the world by thousands of designers to develop 3D interactive games and realistic 3D effects for movies and television, and to create astounding 3D content for display on the Web. Purchasing and working through this book will give you an enhanced introduction to 3D design and animation in general — and some hands-on experience with 3ds max itself — to bring your 3D ideas to life.

About This Book

For folks unfamiliar with the way 3D software works, using 3ds max can be a daunting task. Just hefting the weighty documentation that comes with the software can be frightening. The documentation is thorough and detailed enough, but it's not quite as welcoming as your grandmother waiting at the door with fresh baked cookies to soothe your fears. When you first open the software on the screen, you may get another shock. The complexity looks overwhelming to many beginners, so much so that it may cause you to stare at the 3ds max interface in a wide-eyed slack-jawed fashion. This book, on the other hand, is designed so that your introduction to 3ds max will be as warm and fuzzy as possible, while at the same time presenting all the information you need to know in order to dive into the realm of your own 3D visions.

How to Use This Book

How you use this book depends somewhat on who you are and the level of your previous encounters with the general concepts of 3D design, and any experience you may have had with other 3D software. The book is not designed like a novel, with the requirement that you read it from start to finish, but rather as a reference and an encyclopedia of interactive information to help you understand various facets of how 3ds max functions.

If you're a novice to 3D design and know very little about 3D concepts and nothing about 3D software, don't be embarrassed. Everyone has to start somewhere.

As a 3D novice, pay special attention to the terms used for various 3D operations and tools. Picking up the lingo not only gets you quickly into 3ds max, but imagine the fun at parties when you 3D-speak with others. (Impress your friends! Astound your peers! Dumbfound total strangers!)

You may want to read any parts or chapters in the book that totally overwhelm you the first time through more than one time. Using 3D, however, is a bit like learning to skydive. It isn't until you're in the air and screaming that what you've discovered really kicks in. The object is to read a little and then play around with 3ds max on your computer.

The mouse is the primary tool you use to bridge the gap between the real world you move in and the virtual world of the computer, no matter what type of software you use. 3ds max is a Windows-only application, meaning that it runs only on computers with the Microsoft Windows 2000 or XT operating system installed. This is important as far as the mouse is concerned, because a mouse attached to a Windows system is either a two-button or three-button mouse. The two-button mouse is by far the most common, so I refer to it throughout the book. Because the Mac remains the platform used by a good many 2D and 3D designers, I'm dismayed that Discreet doesn't support the Mac with 3ds max, restricting max magic to Windows-only users.

Distinguishing between the left mouse button and the right mouse button is important. In most cases, you click or click and hold the left mouse button to select items from a list. You right-click when you want to open a menu and possibly a sub-menu of choices, in order to bring up a list of actions in a separate window.

To create the 3D content you dream about in 3ds max, you have to remain the master of your mouse, using it to access the needed tools and menu options. I alert you when you need to right-click as opposed to left-click.

As you read through the text, you'll come upon statements like this:

XXXX⇨YYYY⇨ZZZZ

This isn't secret government code, but rather a statement that tells you to go to a specific place in a 3ds max menu as a step to either activate a command or to bring up a specific command window. The previous statement, for example, means "go to the menu named XXXX, and then down to the submenu YYYY. Under YYYY you will see various listings. Go to the one named ZZZZ." As you get into the text, you'll recognize these directions and zip right through the instructions. . . . I promise.

What I Assume About You

I assume that you have some basic knowledge of computers that includes turning on the computer and interacting with your keyboard and mouse. I further assume that you know how to install the 3ds max software from the CD-ROM.

You need at your personal disposal a system that runs 3ds max Version 5 or above and one of the following operating systems: Windows 2000 Professional or Windows XT. 3ds max doesn't work on Windows ME or Windows 95 or earlier, though it may work on some Windows 98 Second Edition systems. Your computer should be using a Pentium III or IV chipset, have a CD-ROM drive and at least 512MB of RAM, and be running at a speed of 512 MHz or better. You should also have a color monitor capable of millions of colors and a screen size of at least 1024 x 768 pixels. If any of these tech terms are new to you, check the documentation that shipped with your computer that defines what these specifications mean.

How This Book Is Organized

Each part of this book builds upon previous ones and improves your 3ds max expertise in a cumulative step-by-step fashion. However, this book is also an encyclopedia of information so that you can always return to any part or chapter of the book that is helpful in refreshing your memory about specific topics. If you already have a basic knowledge of 3D software, you can begin by going immediately to the part or chapter that most interests you.

Part I: First Things First

This part introduces you to general 3D concepts, tools and command locations, and ways that you can customize and personalize the look of the 3ds max environment on the screen.

Part II: All About max Models

You find out all about models in this part — how to create and customize them using the wealth of 3ds max tools. Models are to a 3D designer what images are to a 2D designer. Everything you see in the room you are sitting in and in the world outside of your window, including both man-made and natural objects and creatures, is a potential model to a 3D designer.

Part III: Applying Modifier Alchemy

In 3ds max terms, the potion that Dr. Jekyl drank was a *modifier* that transformed him into Mr. Hyde. Modifiers are devices that alter the geometry and other aspects of a model, and learning what separate Modifiers do and how they can be controlled is a big step in the direction of mastering the magic of 3ds max. This part of the book takes a look at a number of 3ds max Modifiers and how they're used to alter selected 3D models in various ways.

Part IV: Trees of Fur and Fish of Wood

When traditional painters create objects in a scene, they paint their shape and texture qualities at the same time. For the digital 3D artist however, the form of a 3D object is created separately from its textural qualities. This part of the book looks at the art of 3D texturing, and the understanding and use of a range of specific texturing methods, tools, and processes.

Part V: Lights, Camera, Action!

Placing lights and manipulating camera controls are necessary prior to animating models in a scene. This part describes how to create captivating effects using light and shadow in a scene and how to position a camera for animation.

Part VI: Animation at Its Best

Although you can use 3D software to create some unbelievably photorealistic images, everyone associates 3D with animations. If you've never been exposed to computer animation before, or to the terms used to point to its elements, this is a must-read part of the book. If you've had some experience with either 2D or 3D animation, this part still will be helpful to you. 3ds max gives you warm and friendly access to its state-of-the-art animation tools, and animation is a big part of what computer graphics are all about. A careful read of this part not only gives you a sense of ease when animating in 3ds max, but also gives you the necessary understanding to take on any additional animation software out there.

Part VII: f/x Are Us

Computer animation effects (f/x) have become an accepted part of the movie-going experience. Some films rely on special f/x so heavily that there seems to be little character development or acting in between. 3ds max is bulging with special f/x potential, and finding out how to control f/x magic is one of the most exciting parts of a 3D journey.

Part VIII: Pictures Perfect

If you never discover how to render your 3ds max images and animations, nobody would be able to appreciate your efforts. Your rendered images and animations are the jewels in the crown of your 3ds max work. Whether your renderings are shown in a major Hollywood film, on broadcast television, on your Web page, or just recorded to a CD for distribution to your friends, you'll be able to share your creations beyond the walls of your workspace.

Part IX: The Part of Tens

This part gives you some suggestions for making your 3ds max sessions more fun, and delves into a number of 3ds max add-ons that are guaranteed to maximize your max interactions even more.

Icons Used in This Book

If you flip through the book, you'll see icons in the margin next to a block of text. These icons are designed to alert you to some nugget of information.

When you see this icon, pretend I'm whispering in your ear about a sure bet at the racetrack. Just kidding. I pass along this information to make your experience with 3ds max quicker and more efficient.

This icon points you to a tidbit that you'd be wise to keep in mind as you work with 3ds max.

Skip this text at your own risk! Ah well, some folks like to live dangerously.

When you see this icon, it means that the information goes a bit deeper into some relevant technical information about a topic. Skip it if it gets too deep.

This icon alerts you to some really cool examples of animation contained on this book's CD-ROM.

Where to Go From Here

Well, at this point you've got pretty much the whole story. Use this book however it best serves you. Write notes in the margins. Highlight helpful sections. Step through the doorway into this book and your date with destiny — or at least a feast of creativity with 3ds max.

Part I
First Things First

The 5th Wave By Rich Tennant

"Well, it's not quite done. I've animated the gurgling spit-sink and the rotating Novocaine syringe, but I still have to add the high speed whining drill audio track."

In this part . . .

Most of the professional 3D artists and animators I know didn't go to school to learn their craft — at least they didn't get a degree in computer art or animation. Instead, realizing that their attraction to electronic art was overwhelming and incessant, they purchased a computer and some suitable software and taught themselves the basics.

When I decided to approach 3ds max, back in version 2, I had some experience with other software. When I first received the huge heavy package however, my heart sank. I think I spent about a week just lifting up the documentation and putting it down again, hoping that this effort would somehow cause the instructions to soak into my hands, and from there make its way into my brain. No such luck. Without anything like this book to guide me, I had to go through the documentation a page at a time, sweating and grumbling each step of the way. It was pure torture. Reading software documentation, especially when it arrives in two volumes of almost a thousand pages each is, to put it mildly, a challenge.

This book was created out of a sense of empathy for other new 3ds max users. Knowing what has to be learned in order to remove the blocks between creative ideas and the tools that bring those ideas to life, makes it possible to guide you through the 3ds max maze of necessary preparations for your own pursuits. Not that you can avoid the documentation, but after going through this book, you should be able to use the docs as a valuable reference, a kinder and gentler approach to learning.

Chapter 1

Reading the Roadmap

A whole world of wonder opens up to your exploration when you discover how to navigate in 3ds max. You're using the same software used to create all kinds of effects in major Hollywood movies and on broadcast television. It all starts with the basics of 3D creation, and this book walks you through each step, so fasten your seatbelt and get ready for a great adventure!

Before you can start creating 3D scenes in 3ds max, you have to know how to navigate the GUI (Graphical User Interface). The GUI appears when you start 3ds max, and at first it may look overwhelmingly confusing. But don't worry. It's really not that scary. The GUI is your interactive window into 3ds max, loaded with all the tools and commands you'll need to bring your 3D creations to life.

The chapters in the first part of this book show you where to find max's controls and menu selections, present some needed definitions, and provide an overview of what specific tools and controls do.

Uncovering the Multidimensional

I'm certain that many world-class painters in history would have jumped at the chance to explore the tools offered by 3D software if they were alive today. Just think of it. Imagine being restricted to a 2D canvas, where all you can do is to fake your 3D image by using the rules of shade and shadow and perspective — as opposed to moving into the canvas to see your image from any 3D camera angle. After you create a 2D painting, the image remains in whatever view you have assigned to it. When you work in 3D, that isn't the case. After all your objects are in place in your 3D world and the lights and textures have been calculated and temporarily set, you're free to move around and snap images from any angle you like. Each traditional 2D painting is a one-shot deal, whereas each 3D composition can be a doorway to infinite illustrative snapshots.

Until film came along, the artist was limited to capturing a single snapshot of movement from a series of possibilities. With film, the artist can create a series of motion sequences that bring all image elements to life. Movement in a 3D space is a four-dimensional activity (the fourth dimension being time). Using today's blazingly fast computer hardware and processors, coupled with state-of-the-art tools, the artist's dream can move in three dimensions of space and come alive.

Starting 3ds max

To get 3ds max up and running, do the following:

1. **With your computer turned on, locate the 3ds max icon.**

   It's located in the directory where you installed 3ds max, or you may have placed a copy of it on the desktop.

2. **Double-click the icon.**

   Loading takes a few seconds, and then 3ds max appears on your screen.

Figure 1-1 shows what 3ds max looks like.

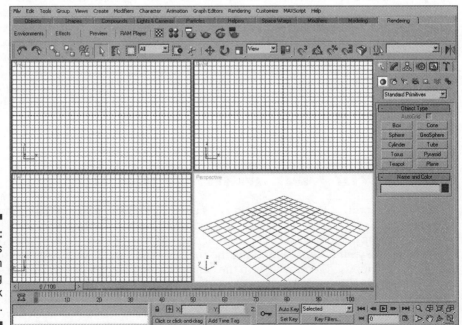

Figure 1-1:
Eeeek! 3ds max is open and looking right back at you.

Meet the 3ds max tools

If you try to use a wrench as a hammer, or attempt to turn a screw with a toaster instead of a screwdriver, you might be described as tool-challenged, at the very least. Technology has led to the development of a huge assortment of tools, each designed with a specific purpose. The tools and commands in 3ds max are also used for specific operations, so you have to know where to find them and have some idea of what they are meant to do. It's a bit more complex than swinging a hammer, because 3ds max presents you with a large series of hammers, each designed with a specific task in mind. I get to the specifics of tool usage in later chapters.

Locating the right tools and menus

Before you can use any of the 3ds max tools, you have to know where they're located. A group of 3ds max main menus and toolbars appears at the top of the opening screen (see Figure 1-2).

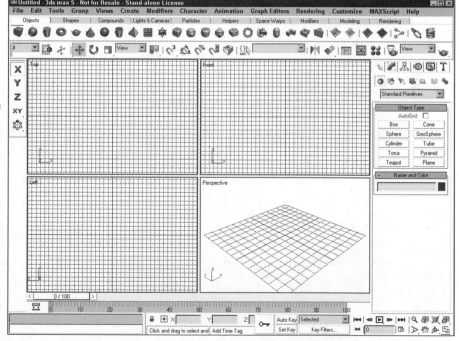

Figure 1-2:
A dark border has been placed around the items at the top of the 3ds max interface to show you where the main menus and toolbars are.

If you don't see the Tabs Panel and/or the Main Toolbar on your 3ds max interface, then you have to make sure they are turned on. Choose Customize⇨Show UI⇨Tab Panel and if needed, Choose Customize⇨Show UI⇨Main Toolbar.

The menu bar

The list of named items that run across the very top of the 3ds max interface is the menu bar, shown in Figure 1-3.

Figure 1-3:
The menu
bar at the
top of the
3ds max
interface
contains a
list of menu
options.

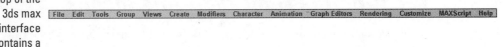

Clicking any option in the menu bar reveals the menu selections under that heading (see Figure 1-4).

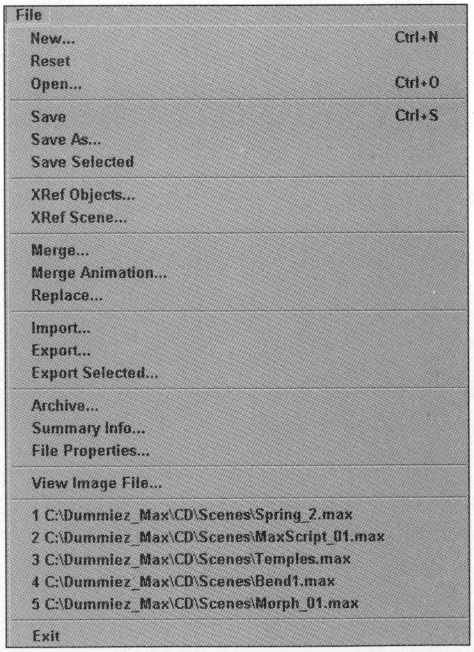

Figure 1-4:
Click an
option on
the menu
bar to open
a menu of
choices.

To close a menu, simply click any other part of the screen. Think of the Menu lists as a selection of menus brought to your table at a restaurant, each one for a different classification of delectable possibilities — meats, salads, breads, insect delights, all manner of selections to please your 3D palette.

After you open a menu with a left-click, it remains open until you close it. When it is open, you can move the mouse over any selection, and click again. This selects that option. Selecting different options in different menus initiates various actions. A command in this book that asks you to take an action that targets a specific menu item is written as follows:

> Go to AAA⇨BBB

AAA represents the name of the menu, and BBB represents a selection in that menu. For example

> Go to File⇨Export

means to left-click the File menu to open it, and then to click the Export option in the open menu to select the Export command. This convenient shorthand has become a standard way for software documentation and books to guide you through specific actions without getting bogged down in words.

> Go to Kitchen Cabinet⇨Cookie Jar⇨Cookies.

Working with tools

You can access various tools in 3ds max by choosing menu options, pressing key combinations from your keyboard, or clicking tool icons on a toolbar. The easiest way to access tools is by clicking toolbars. The following sections provide details on how to access the tools you're likely to use most.

The Tab Panel

If I tell you that I love the Tab Panel in 3ds max, you'll probably think I've spent too much time in front of the computer — but I do. The Tab Panel is at the top of the 3ds max interface, as shown in Figure 1-5.

Figure 1-5:
This is the Tab Panel, with the leftmost tab (Objects) selected.

Clicking any tab in the Tab Panel brings up all the tool icons associated with that tab. I cover each of these tabbed topics in later chapters in the book. Explore the icons associated with each tab by clicking separate tabs. Figure 1-6 displays the Tool icons associated with each of the tabs in the Tab Panel.

Figure 1-6:
From top to bottom, the graphics display the Tool icons in the Objects, Shapes, Compounds, Lights & Cameras, Particles, Helpers, Space Warps, Modifiers, Modeling, and Rendering tabs.

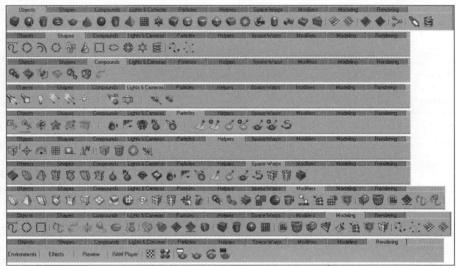

The number of tool options may look overwhelming, but by the time you finish this book you'll be breezing through these tools. For now, don't sweat the details. As high-end 3D software goes, 3ds max is one of the most user-friendly and clearly designed.

The Main Toolbar

The Main Toolbar, shown in Figure 1-7, is where you find all of max's basic tools. The Main Toolbar is located just below the Tab Panel at the top of the 3ds max interface.

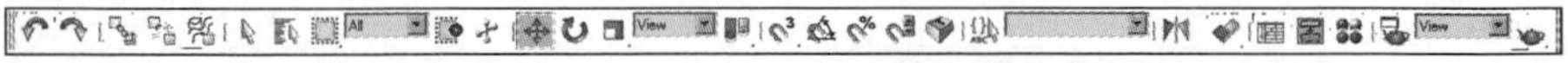

Figure 1-7:
The Main Toolbar.

The Main Toolbar icons displayed in Figure 1-7 may not all be visible on your screen. If not, you can slide the toolbar left and right by left-clicking and dragging any empty part of the toolbar. When your mouse pointer turns into a hand, it's in position to drag the toolbar.

The icons displayed in the Main Toolbar are used to select, transform, and organize models and other objects already in a 3ds max scene. They differ from the icons in the Tab Panel, which *create and modify* scene content.

When you perform actions that require selecting a tool first, this book tells you to "go to the Tab Panel" or "go to the Main Toolbar" first. That should make those pesky tool icons a lot easier to locate. The more familiar you become with 3ds max, the less you'll need to be reminded where to find the tools you need for any particular purpose (but I include reminders anyway, throughout the book, just in case you aren't reading it straight through). Each tool in the Main Toolbar gets its share of attention and content; each chapter in the book invites a closer examination of these tools.

The viewports

Viewports enable you to perceive the contents of a scene from different angles. Figure 1-8 shows the standard default viewport arrangement that 3ds max opens with.

Figure 1-8:
This four-part viewport arrangement is the one that 3ds max opens with unless and until you customize the viewport arrangement.

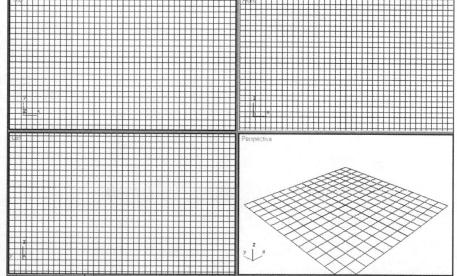

As you can see in Figure 1-8, the default viewport arrangement uses four separate viewports unless directed otherwise. From upper-left to lower-right, the viewports are Top, Front, Side, and Perspective. The grid you see is used to place objects in a scene at definitive distances from each other, and is also used as a measurement device when creating the sizes of 3D models. Right-click in any of the viewports to activate that viewport. A yellow outline indicates the active viewport.

The Command Panel

At the right of your 3ds max interface is a separate panel of options called the Command Panel, shown in Figure 1-9.

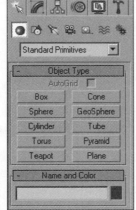

Figure 1-9:
The 3ds max Command Panel.

The row of tabbed icons at the top of the Command Panel determines what options are displayed in the area below the row of tabs. There are six tabs at the top of the Command Panel. Left to right, they are Create, Modify, Hierarchy, Motion, Display, and Utilities. As you need to know more about how to use these commands throughout the book, I supply the details.

Options at the bottom of the 3ds max interface

At the very bottom of the 3ds max interface is another control area, shown in Figure 1-10.

Figure 1-10:
The control area at the bottom of the 3ds max interface.

This control area has two separate parts: Animation controls and Viewport Manipulation controls.

Animation controls

As shown in Figure 1-11, the larger section that starts from the lower-left corner of the lower Control area and continues about three quarters of the way across the interface encompasses the 3ds max Animation controls. (Other 3D software sometimes calls this area the *Timeline*.)

Figure 1-11:
The Animation controls.

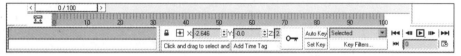

For more about using the options in the Animation controls, skim the chapters in Part VI.

Viewport Manipulation controls

The Viewport Manipulation controls are on the far bottom-right of the 3ds max interface, as shown in Figure 1-12.

Figure 1-12:
The Viewport Manipulation controls.

There are two rows of icons representing the Viewport Manipulation controls. Left-top to right-bottom they are: Zoom, Zoom All, Zoom Extents, Zoom Extents

All, Region Zoom (Field of View — for the Perspective Viewport), Pan, Arc Rotate, and Min/Max Toggle. Each of these options gets a more detailed treatment in the section "Getting around in the 3D GUI Viewports" (which follows).

Gooey Max: Navigating in a 3D Graphics User Interface

A GUI (pronounced "Gooey") is a techno-abbreviated term for *Graphics User Interface*. Every piece of graphics software has its own GUI. 3ds max has a 3D GUI, which in many ways resembles other 3D GUIs. If you learn how to navigate in 3ds max's GUI, you can more easily learn how to navigate in any 3D GUI (not that you'd want to of course!).

Getting around in the 3D GUI Viewports

A few paragraphs ago (we all seemed so much younger then), a peek at the lower-right part of the 3ds max GUI revealed Viewport Manipulation controls. Each of these eight controls has its own function — but none of them can do anything until they have some content to work on. To take care of this essential business, follow these steps:

1. **Click the Objects tab on the Tab Panel.**
2. **Select the sphere object (the second object from the left) to highlight it.**
3. **Place your mouse pointer at the center of the Front Viewport and then click and drag to create a sphere that measures half the size of the viewport.**
4. **Release the mouse. Right-click to end the creation process.**

   You see a visible sphere in all viewports, resembling the one shown in Figure 1-13.

   Little does this innocent sphere know what's in store for it: The Viewport Manipulation controls are about to change the way you see the sphere in the viewports. Follow the instructions given here for each tool to see how these controls work.

Zoom

When you activate the Zoom control over any viewport, it zooms the view in or out. Click the Zoom icon, and then click and drag (either up or down) in each of the four viewports. As you can see in Figure 1-14, each viewport can have its own separate zoomed view.

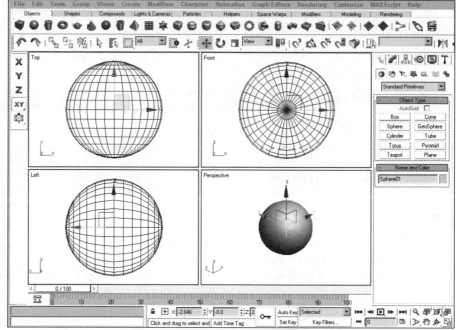

Figure 1-13: Congratu-lations! The sphere you created should look like this in all viewports.

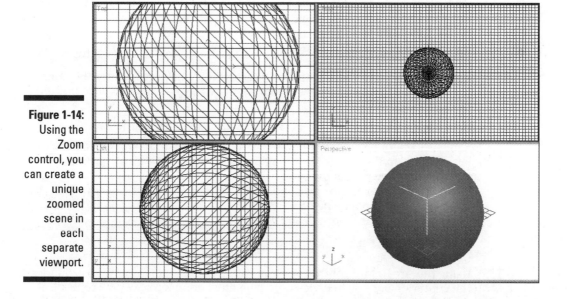

Figure 1-14: Using the Zoom control, you can create a unique zoomed scene in each separate viewport.

Zoom All

 Click and drag up or down in any viewport when the Zoom All control is selected to zoom all viewports in or out at the same time, as in Figure 1-15.

Zoom Extents

 Clicking the Zoom Extents control icon once zooms out to show all the objects in any selected viewport, centering the object(s) in that viewport.

Zoom Extents All

 Clicking the Zoom Extents All control icon once creates a default zoom on all viewports at the same time, centering the object in all viewports.

Region Zoom

 The Region Zoom control introduces you to an important concept . . . the *marquee.* You probably know what a marquee is in the real world. An old theater may have a marquee out front — the lighted area over the front entrance that displays the names of the films that are showing. Film titles may be encircled by a band of lights that seem to move in a line. It's this aspect of the movie marquee that gives the marquee option in 3ds max (and other software, like Photoshop) its character. A marquee in 3ds max is a way of selecting a defined area of a viewport, or a part of an object. Clicking the Region Zoom activates the Region Marquee. When the Region Zoom is active (it lights up after you click it), you can use this in the Front, Side, or Top Viewports to draw a marquee around a part of the scene in that viewport that you want to zoom into by simply clicking and dragging out a marquee around that area. The default marquee that defines a region is a rectangular dashed line, but there are fancier marquees that I cover in other parts of the book. The Region Zoom appears to be unavailable when the Perspective Viewport is active, but it's hidden under the Field of View Flyout.

Pan

 Pan is a camera term that originated in film meaning to move the camera left/right or up/down without changing the direction the lens is pointing to. Panning in a viewport allows you to see parts of the scene normally not visible in that view. In all graphics and animation software, the standard icon used for the Pan tool is the hand. Click the Pan control to highlight it, then click and drag your mouse in any viewport to pan the scene.

Arc Rotate

 Using the Arc Rotate control, you can rotate the camera (your eye) around the center of any selected viewport. The most common viewport to use this control on is the Perspective Viewport. Click this control and then click in the Perspective Viewport and you'll see a circle with four rectangular control points superimposed over the view, as shown in Figure 1-16.

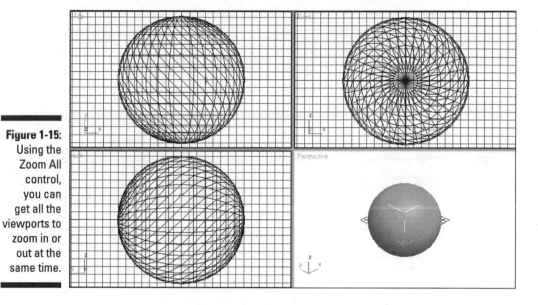

Figure 1-15:
Using the Zoom All control, you can get all the viewports to zoom in or out at the same time.

Figure 1-16:
Clicking in the Perspective Viewport when the Arc Rotate control is active super-imposes a circle with four control points over the scene.

While the Arc Rotate control is still active, clicking and dragging over these four control points will rotate the view either left/right or up/down. If you use the Arc Rotate inside of the circle, the rotation will be freeform. If you start outside of the circle, the view will tilt, Batman style.

Other options are associated with the Arc Rotate control. One is a tiny, downward-pointing triangle at its lower right corner. This triangle is called a Flyout. Many controls have a Flyout, which indicates that there are more controls hidden underneath. If you click and hold over this triangle, the Arc Rotate control shows three separate options. If you select the middle option and then go through the rotation process, you rotate the viewport around. Try it.

TIP

Tool Tips don't work when choosing a control within a Flyout. If you look at the bottom center of the GUI as you are holding down the mouse button, you see the name of the control displayed there.

Min/Max Toggle

 Clicking this control with the left mouse button will enlarge the currently selected viewport so that it fills the screen, blotting out the other viewports. Use this control when you need to work on parts of a scene that need up-close viewing. Clicking this control again returns the viewports to your default arrangement.

How the GUI design influences your work

As you read and work through this book, take a look at the room you're sitting in. You may have spent a good bit of time moving furniture around in the room, adjusting the lighting, making sure your computer keyboard is at a convenient height, and making your environment as comfortable as possible. As you work in 3ds max and adjust various viewport settings to suit your needs, you're also maximizing your *virtual* working environment. That's why your familiarity with the Viewport Manipulation controls is so important. The viewports are your window into a virtual workroom, and being comfortable in that environment leads to better and more friendly 3D design work. It takes some time to find the right virtual working environment, just as it took you a little time to find the right configuration for the placement of the items in the room you're working in. In Chapter 2 I show you additional ways you can customize the look and personal comfort of your virtual 3D design environment.

Now You See It, Now You Don't

3ds max is a visual workplace. Because of the number of tools and controls that are present on the interface, you're forced to customize the screen so that you can see everything, yet remain in an uncluttered workspace. The following sections detail two things to keep in mind.

Changing your screen's resolution

The Windows display screen has a defined number of pixels (picture elements) horizontally and vertically. The more pixels your display addresses, the smaller the data on the screen, but the more data that can be displayed. If the display is set too high, then you will suffer eyestrain trying to see what you're doing. If the display is set too low, a program that provides a lot of display data — such as 3ds max — won't fit. As with so much else in life, you can get it to work by configuring a happy medium.

To set the pixel resolution of your display, do the following:

1. **Double-click the My Computer icon on your Desktop.**

   A window appears, displaying all the drives on your system (plus an icon labeled Control Panel).

2. **Double-click the Control Panel icon.**

   The Control Panel window opens.

3. **Double-click the Display icon.**

   The Display Properties window opens.

4. **Click the Settings tab at the top of the window.**

   On the Settings tab, you can set your screen resolution by moving the slider left or right. Make sure you set the Colors to 24 or 32 bit for 3ds max, by choosing from the list under Colors. I suggest moving the slider so that your screen resolution is at least 1024 x 768 pixels.

5. **Click OK to apply the settings and then close the window.**

   Your system is now set to display all the toolbars and functions of 3ds max.

Improving visibility

Sometimes your 3ds max interface feels too cluttered with tool options and controls. You may not need to display certain parts of the interface at a specific point in a project. If that occurs, choose Customize➪Show UI and see what's checked. Selecting a checked item removes the check and removes that element from the 3ds max GUI. To get it back, just select it again and *voilá!* — it reappears.

1 Know It's Here Somewhere

When you have added all sorts of objects, lights, cameras, and other 3ds max elements to a scene, it may be difficult to select the item you need when you want to modify it. Never fear! 3ds max has a perfect answer for that situation. If that happens to you, go to Tools⇨Selection Floater to bring up the Selection Floater window. Everything in your scene is listed. Click on the name of the object, choose the Select button, and close the Selection Floater window. The object or objects are now selected for any desired modifications.

Chapter 2

Customizing Your Workspace

• •

In This Chapter

▶ Customizing the default space

▶ Moving stuff around on-screen

▶ Altering your viewpoints in 3D space

• •

*H*ere's a scenario: You're in a strange city, looking around for an apartment to rent. Apartments you can afford are scarce, but you are diligent in your search, and finally find one listed in the paper. Feeling the urgency to get settled, you rush to the address, and thankfully, it's not rented yet. The landlord answers your knock, and agrees to show you around. The apartment seems to have a pleasant view of the city, and it's fully furnished. "There's one thing," the landlord cautions, "if you want to live here, you are not permitted to move anything around. Every piece of furniture, every lamp and knick-knack, everything down to the smallest item, has to remain exactly where it is. We check once every couple of days." This apartment might be described as a *default space* in that it comes prearranged with no options for personal design input; de fault (ahem) is yours if you move anything. How difficult would it be for you to live somewhere that forbids you to place any personal stamp on the arrangement of the elements? Could you be comfortable in this situation?

To do your best thinking, and by extension your best work, you must be able to work in a comfortable environment. Everyone has some definition of *comfort*. That means that a *default* environment you find yourself in may have to be customized, or reorganized, to fit your needs. When you first open 3ds max, the GUI is presented to you in its default condition. The GUI appears the same way to all new users, but the 3ds max developers were very wise. Recognizing the need for personalizing your design space (moving things around in your apartment), they provided the tools to do just that. It's like the landlord saying, "go ahead . . . move the furniture around any way that makes you comfortable." Even if you like things the way they are in 3ds max, you know you can change them if you want to; go ahead, breathe a sigh of relief.

Changing Things Here and There

Most of the personalized changes you can make to the GUI in 3ds max won't become a need for you to explore until you spend some time with the software. Initially, you may decide that the default UI look is okay for now, and you just want to get on with the business of creating 3D models and placing them in scenes. The personalization of your 3ds max environment will be based upon your experience with the software over time. When the time does arrive, however, you'll want to know how to navigate to the right menus and controls that can help you achieve the GUI environment you want.

Color is first

The first time 3ds max pops up on the screen, the GUI looks like Figure 2-1. Pay special attention to the color of the viewports.

Personally, I find the dull gray of the default viewports kinda depressing. Like many of you whose eyesight is challenged already, I also find it hard to distinguish the viewport grid from the background color. Why force more eyestrain upon yourself? Might as well change the viewport background color. The following steps do the trick:

1. **Choose Customize⇨Customize User Interface.**

   The Customize User Interface window appears.

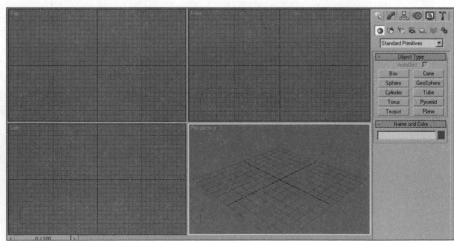

Figure 2-1: This is the default 3ds max GUI, as it appears when you first start the software. Note the dull gray color of the viewport backgrounds.

2. **Left-click the Colors tab at the top of the window.**

   Make sure Viewports is selected in the Elements list at top left.

3. **Select Viewport Background from the list below Viewports.**

4. **Click inside the rectangular color swatch at the upper right.**

   The Color Selector appears.

5. **Select a color from the Color Selector, and then click Close to accept the color change.**

   You can make the color anything you like. (I select white for the viewport background to make anything placed in the viewports easier to see.)

6. **At the bottom right of the Customize User Interface window, click Apply Colors Now.**

   You should see the viewport background color change immediately. See Figure 2-2.

Now take a look at the GUI to appreciate the change you made. Quite a difference, eh? See Figure 2-3.

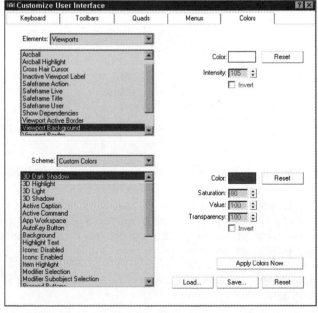

Figure 2-2:
The viewport background color is altered under the Color tab in the Customize User Interface window.

Figure 2-3:
Changing
the viewport
background
color to a
lighter color
or to white
makes
everything
much more
visible.
Compare
this image
to Figure 2-1.

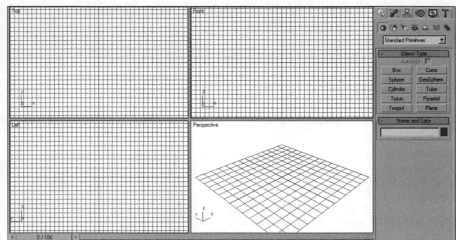

Return to Customize⇨Customize User Interface again. Under the Colors tab, select Viewport Label from the Elements⇨Viewports list. This is the color of the labels that show you what view you are in. Change the color to black. Now the labels can be clearly distinguished from the viewport background color.

If you have loads of free time, you can make hundreds of alterations to each element in the GUI. This chapter covers only the most needed and useful ones. When you have exploration time, look at the listings under each tab in the Customize User Interface window. Until you accumulate experience using 3ds max, many of the terms will seem like gibberish to you. When the time comes to alter some 3ds max features, however, you'll know exactly where to go and how to get the job done.

To grid or not to grid

The grid lines that you see in each viewport are very helpful when you want to move something to an exact place, or when you want to use them as measuring guides. At other times, however, their presence can be quite annoying. When you want to remove the grid, follow these steps:

1. **At the upper left of a viewport, right-click the label of the viewport whose grid you want removed.**

   A menu of options opens. About halfway down the list, the Show Grid option has a check mark next to it.

2. **Click the Show Grid option so the check mark disappears.**

   This action shuts the grid off for that viewport. To turn it back on, click the option again. Figure 2-4 shows the configuration I use when I start a

3ds max project: I remove the grids from the Top, Front, and Left Viewports but keep the grid in the Perspective Viewport.

You can always switch the grid on or off for any viewport.

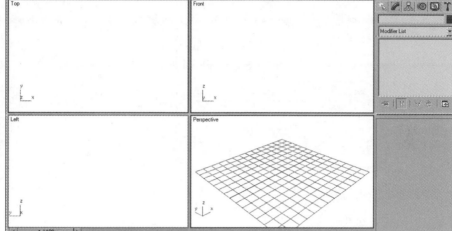

Figure 2-4:
If you open other viewports, all grids are removed.

Machiavelli's caution and the grid

Machiavelli, the Italian philosopher and advisor to royalty, cautioned that the first way to subjugate a people was to forcibly alter their measurement system, thereby throwing the populace into chaos. Good old Machiavelli would probably go into spasms if he were alive today, when the world uses two main measurement systems to do business: the U.S. Standard (feet and inches) and the Metric System (meters, centimeters, and so on). The conversion to one common measuring system doesn't look as if it'll happen any time soon, so the two competing systems will just have to continue getting along.

The grid in the 3ds max viewports can be configured as a measurement device for either system, which is one reason why 3ds max has such a large worldwide audience of users. To set the grid to your needed measurement system, follow these steps:

1. **Choose Customize⇨Units Setup.**

   The Units Setup window appears, as shown in Figure 2-5.

2. **Click either the Metric or US Standard radio button.**

   Click the down arrow that opens the respective list and set the measurement system details that will determine how each of the grid boxes in your viewports measures distance.

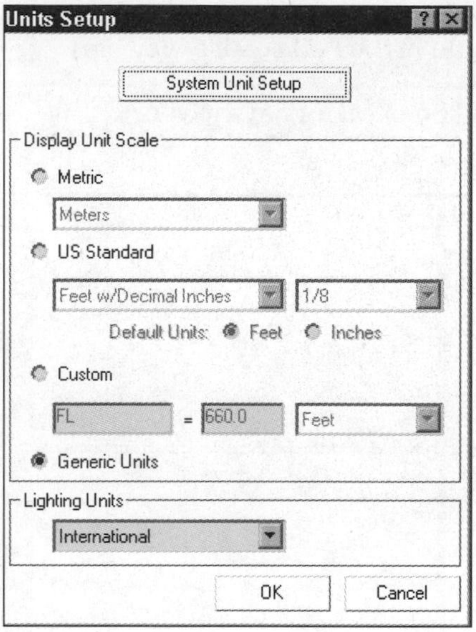

Figure 2-5:
The Units
Setup
window.

3. **Go to Customize⇨Grid and Snap Settings.**

   The Grid and Snap dialog box appears.

4. **Click the Home Grid Tab. Set the Grid Spacing to your desired value (that is, 1' or 1m). Click the X icon to dismiss the dialog box.**

As you zoom out, the grid will simplify to larger units to reduce clutter. As you zoom in, the grid will subdivide. At the bottom of the GUI to the right of the Z value box is an indicator of the current grid size. If you can't see the Grid=xxxx box, you must resize a portion of the GUI. Click and drag with the left mouse button on the vertical divider (to the left of that Padlock tool). Drag to the right to reveal the Grid size indicator. (Whew!)

Exploring Viewport Options

Chapter 1 covers how viewport data can be zoomed, and how the point-of-view can be rotated in any selected viewport. But how about altering the sizes of the viewports, or perhaps deleting one or more viewports to create another arrangement entirely? Using our rented-and-furnished-apartment analogy, the first case would be like magically making a room larger or smaller; keeping the overall space the apartment takes up the same as it was. In the second case, it would be like tearing down walls between rooms to create a more suitable living space. In either case, you would pray that the landlord wouldn't raise the rent or evict you!

Moving viewport borders

If you look carefully at the default viewport arrangement, you'll notice dark borders around each viewport, with spaces between viewports. If you move your mouse pointer (which by default is a large arrow) over a border, something wonderful happens: The pointer becomes a smaller, double-pointed arrow that goes vertical when you place it over a horizontal border, and horizontal when you place it over a vertical border. When this change happens, it's a signal that you can move the viewport borders by left-clicking and dragging — thereby reconfiguring the viewport layout. Don't take my word for it, give it a try! Figures 2-6 and 2-7 give you an idea of what to expect.

Viewport layout presets

Moving the viewport borders is okay when all you need to do is to emphasize selected viewport space, but what about the times when you really need a faster way to configure the viewport layout, and even may need to delete one or more viewports. As you may suspect, 3ds max has an answer for that too. To see what it looks like, follow these steps:

1. **Right-click one of the viewport labels at the upper left of a viewport.**

   The Viewport Options menu appears.

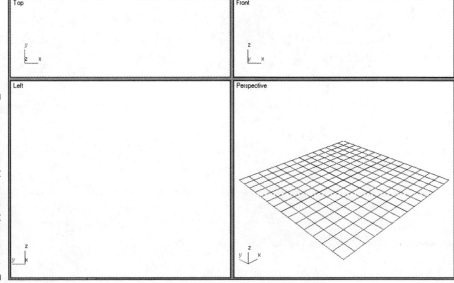

Figure 2-6:
When you move the horizontal viewport borders, the viewports contract and expand at the top and bottom.

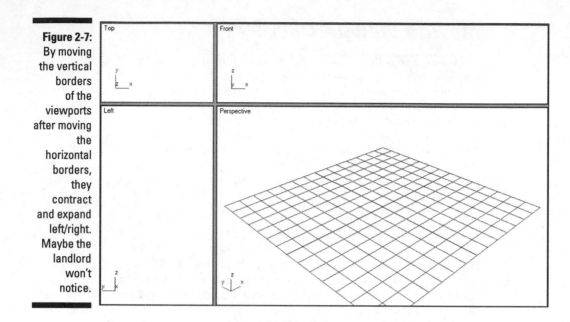

Figure 2-7:
By moving
the vertical
borders
of the
viewports
after moving
the
horizontal
borders,
they
contract
and expand
left/right.
Maybe the
landlord
won't
notice.

2. **Select the Configure option, which is the bottom option on the list shown in Figure 2-8.**

The Viewport Configuration window opens, as shown in Figure 2-9.

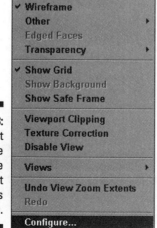

Figure 2-8:
Select
Configure
from the
Viewport
Options
menu.

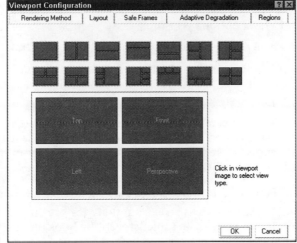

Figure 2-9:
The
Viewport
Configuration
window.

3. **Click the Layout tab from the top of the window.**

   The optional layouts appear.

4. **Click one of the 14 Layout presets (shown at the top of this window).**

   The chosen preset is highlighted.

5. **Click OK.**

   The viewport layout changes to the one you chose.

There is nothing to prevent you from customizing any one of these presets further by moving the borders as shown previously.

Selecting desired views

When it comes to manipulating objects, 3ds max has to know which viewport you want to work in. By left- or right-clicking in a viewport, you tell the program which viewport you're working in. When a viewport is active, a colored line surrounds its border.

If you look at the labels of each viewport, they tell you what the viewpoint associated with that viewport is (Top, Front, Left, and Perspective). But what if you are working on a project that demands a duplication of one view or another, perhaps so the same view can be zoomed in for one and zoomed out for the other? How do you decide what the label of any selected viewport is to be? Simple — just follow these steps:

1. **Right-click any viewport label.**

   The Viewport Options menu appears.

2. **Move the mouse pointer down until it sits on the Views option.**

   A submenu of Views options pops up.

3. **Move your mouse pointer over one of the options and click to select it.**

   Your viewport is now configured with whatever option you chose.

Strange viewport choices

The bottom five view options may look a bit strange to you (ActiveShade, Schematic, Grid, Extended, and Shape). Selecting any one of these options alters how that viewport is used as a window to display different information than simply a standard view. Briefly, here's what each option does:

- ✔ **ActiveShade:** This option provides you with an instant rendering of the selected object in the scene as seen from that viewport angle. Because I cover Rendering as a separate topic later in the book, no further detail on the use of ActiveShade is provided here.

- ✔ **Schematic:** Selecting the Schematic option presents you with a flow-chart view of all elements in a scene, and how they are interconnected.

- ✔ **Grid:** This option gives you fast access to the position of the grid in a viewport. You can create a custom oriented grid, and the Grid View will align to that custom orientation.

- ✔ **Extended:** Asset Browser and MaxScript Listener are the two sub-options here. Selecting the Asset Browser gives you instant access to all the 3ds max content files on your system or on the Web. MaxScripts are essentially small programs that automate the creation of 3ds max content of different types. This book does not cover 3ds max scripting, which is an advanced topic for computer programmers.

- ✔ **Shape:** Selecting the Shape option transforms the selected viewport to orient to a selected shape, such as a Line object.

Viewport rendering options

You have control over the way objects and other scene elements appear in each separate viewport. Objects can be viewport-rendered in a range of ways, from simple boxes that give you a basic sense of their volume all the way to textured models that display all the details down to the way light is reflected from surfaces. These options are not really rendering options per se; they have more to do with viewports. That's why I touch on them here.

3ds max is not alone in allowing you this deep level of viewport control, but 3ds max is unique in the way each separate viewport can display separate viewport-rendered choices. But why have all these options at all? Why not just force all viewports to render everything super-realistically? The answer has to do with time. It takes longer to render a screenful of super-realistic data than to render basic box proxies *(wireframes)* of the same objects.

The term *wireframe* indicates a model that is visible only in its most skeletal sense. Not only does it take less time to render a wireframe in a viewport, but the wireframe gives you a clear view of the structural elements that are at the root of building models . . . polygons.

Follow these steps to specify how a viewport displays its contents:

1. **Right-click the viewport's label.**

   The Viewport Options menu opens, showing both Wireframe and Other as available options.

   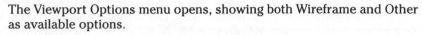

   In Non-Perspective Viewports, Wireframe is checked as a default.

2. **Place the mouse pointer over your preferred option.**

   • Placing the mouse pointer over Wireframe highlights that option.

   • Placing the mouse pointer over Other displays a sublist of options.

   Figure 2-10 shows the viewport display options.

Figure 2-10:
The list of viewport display options appears.

The list of display options that appears is structured with the most realistic but processing-intensive selection at the top, and the least realistic but most friendly processing-intensive option at the bottom. The default selection for the Perspective Viewport is *Smooth + Highlights;* the default display option for other viewports is *Wireframe.* You can elect to change the viewport display for each viewport to its own display option, as shown in Figure 2-11.

Figure 2-11: In this illustration, each of the four viewports has been set to a different display option. Top-left to bottom-right: Facets + Highlights, Lit Wire-frames, Facets, and Smooth.

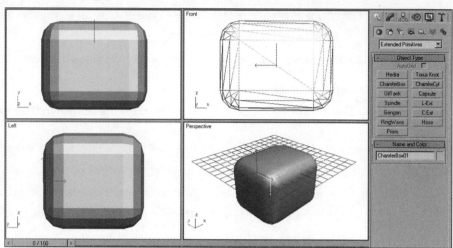

When you find viewport layouts and configurations that seem to fit the way that you work, don't forget to save them. You can save as many as you like, loading specific ones that match the projects you are working on. To save a viewport layout, follow these steps:

1. **Choose Customize➪Save Custom UI Scheme.**

2. **Name the file something that reminds you of how you configured it (for example,** MyBestRender.ui**).**

3. **Choose Customize➪Load Custom UI Scheme to access your saved viewport layout.**

   You can select the saved layout from the list that appears.

Part II
All About max Models

"I can't really explain it, but every time I animate someone swinging a golf club, a little divot of code comes up missing on the home page."

In this part . . .

There you are, sitting at a work table, ready for the master sculptor to enter the room. The door creaks open, and the sculptor appears, his legs wobbling under the heavy load in his hands. With a frightening crash that almost knocks you off of your chair, he drops a 50-pound mound of clay on the table in front of you. He removes a packet of sculpting tools from his lab coat pocket, and throws them down next to the clay. "OK", he shouts, "Make something!".

What a nightmare! The mound of clay sits there, ready to become a masterpiece worthy of display in any world museum, waiting for your touch to release its potential, but nothing is happening. The tools look like strange alien implements, and you have no idea how to use them. What you need is some guidance in order to set about shaping the clay.

3ds max has all of the virtual clay you will ever need to sculpt your 3D masterpieces, and it has an array of professional tools ready to do what your ideas command. This part of the book walks you through the use of max's sculpting tools and processes, so by the time that mean sculptor returns to the room, your work table will display 3D models that will astound all onlookers.

Chapter 3

Polygons, Properties, and Transformations

*T*his chapter looks at the types of models you can create in 3ds max. Included are methods based on loading preset or saved models, locations, and procedures. Models have properties, which are aspects that define their form. For example, a sphere has a curved surface and a diameter. Models are made up of smaller polygonal units. The form of any model in 3ds max can be infinitely transformed into other forms by using specific tools and commands on polygons and surfaces.

Introducing 3ds max Primitive Models

The basic element of a 3D scene is a *model* (also called an *object* in 3ds max, although there are other objects that are not models). The basic element of a model is a polygon.

Because confusion can be the spice of life, here's a spicy tidbit: Some model elements are not strictly polygons at all — but they get dissected later in the book. For now, consider polygons as the basic elements of the models that inhabit this part of the book.

Polygon? Say what?

No, *polygon* does not mean the parrot flew away. In math-speak, a polygon is a surface created by connecting three or more points in space. Because math uses a lot of definitions that put things in purely imaginary space, a polygon has no depth dimension.

In 3D techno-talk, the points that generate a polygon are called *vertices* (the fancy plural of *vertex*). The lines that connect the points are called *edges*. If the polygon has three vertices, its surface is called a *face* (no nose or eyebrows required). If you called the piece of paper on your desk a quadrangular, four-point polygon (such language!), you'd be pretty nearly correct. (A piece of paper actually has a tiny thickness, or depth dimension.) If you attacked that quadrangular polygon with scissors, you could cut it into any number of triangles (three-point polygons). And because a three-point polygon is what 3ds max considers a face, a quadrangular polygon can have a variable number of faces. Figure 3-1 shows just such a situation.

In the figure, a quadrangular polygon at the upper left has no faces; the rest (upper-left to lower-right) have 2, 4, 6, 8, and 16 faces, respectively. The more faces a polygon has, the more complex it becomes. But there's a practical reason to pay attention to that complexity: Such a polygon takes more information to describe — so it takes up more storage space when you save it to disk.

Figure 3-1:
If you split a quadrangular polygon into triangles, each triangular surface becomes a face.

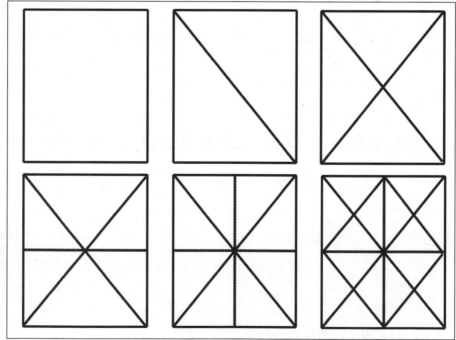

Poly, are you normal?

Triangular polygons — those created from three vertices — are consistent to a fault: They always have a surface that exists in a flat plane. Polygons created from more than three points are more wishy-washy; they may or may not have a perfectly flat surface area. This is because one of the points may be lurking above or below the plane in which any of the other three points exist — and if that's the case, you've got a three-dimensional object.

Because any three-sided *poly* (that's a nickname for *polygon*) always has a perfectly flat surface, you can draw a line perpendicular to the face of the poly at any point, and that line will be perpendicular to any other location on the poly's surface or face. I know, this may bring back nightmares of high school geometry for some of you. In 3D tech-speak, an imaginary perpendicular line drawn from the center of a three-point polygon's surface is called a *Normal.* It's important to introduce the concept of a Normal here; some later chapters refer to Normals for different reasons. For the moment, think of a Normal as a TV tower built at the center of the polygon. And not to worry, a polygon's Normal has nothing to do with making it act just like all the other polygons. (For that matter, the author of this book is under no illusions that he is normal, supernormal, or subnormal — he's just *different.*)

A polygon's Normal is an imaginary perpendicular line drawn from the center of the polygon (as shown in Figure 3-2). A poly's Normal has everything to do with the *visibility* of the polygon.

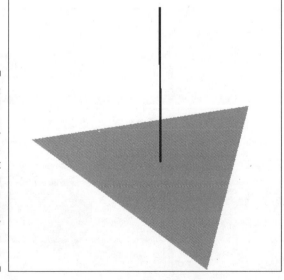

Figure 3-2:
A Normal is an imaginary perpendicular line that originates from the center of a (usually triangular) polygon.

Using Transformations on Models

In 3ds max, three main operations are known as *Object Transformations*: Positioning, Rotating, and Scaling. To *Position* an object is to change the XYZ space coordinates that describe where it is. To *Rotate* an object is to turn it around an X, Y, or Z axis. To *Scale* an object is to increase its size along any X, Y, or Z axis, or along two or more axes at the same time.

Importing a model

You have to have set up a 3D model in a 3ds max scene before you can explore transformation operations. Later in this chapter, you find out how to create 3D models from scratch; for now, a ready-made model (from the huge model library that comes with your 3ds max software) is all that's needed. Here's how to get one on-screen:

1. **Choose File➪Open➪Scene➪Characters to open a folder with various modeled content.**

   This collection of scenes was installed when you installed the software.

2. **Search the contents until you find a model you want to use for exploring the Transformation options.**

   In Figure 3-3, I use a sphere to represent the model you select.

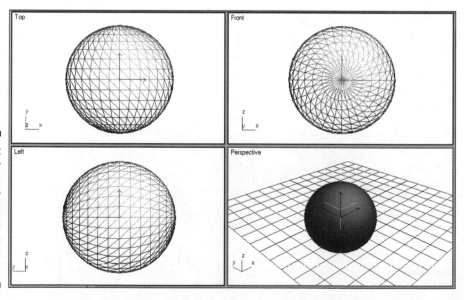

Figure 3-3:
Your imported model (for example, this sphere) appears in all viewports.

3. **Click OK to load your chosen model into a 3ds max scene.**

   After you have imported your selected model, it appears in all the viewports.

The Pivot Point

Every model in a 3ds max scene, whether imported or created on the spot, has a Pivot Point — the point used as the center when you rotate or size the model. Knowing how to make use of the Pivot Point is (ahem) central to understanding how to transform and animate objects in scenes. To see the Pivot Point of a model, follow these steps:

1. **Select a viewport that shows the model in Wireframe display.**

2. **Use the Min/Max Toggle control to make the viewport take up the entire screen.**

   The faint axis arrows you see at the center of the wireframe model emanate from its Pivot Point, as shown in Figure 3-4.

   For more about the Min/Max Toggle control, see Chapter 2.

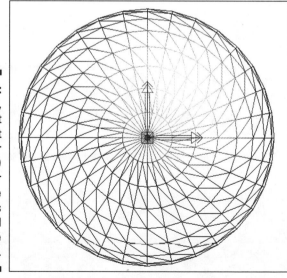

Figure 3-4:
By default, the Pivot Point sits at the center of your 3D object or model; the faint axis arrows tell you where it is.

The Pivot Point isn't stuck in its default position. You can move it to any other point in 3D space, even outside the object itself — honest. That's a legitimate choice. For example, what if the model you were working with was a character's arm? If the Pivot Point were at the center of the arm, the arm would rotate from its center. But an arm does not rotate from its center. It rotates from a point nearer to the shoulder of the character. If the Pivot Point were placed at the center of a model of an arm, you would have to move it. Here's how to move a Pivot Point:

1. **From the Command Panel at the right of the 3ds max GUI, click the Hierarchy tab.**

   The Hierarchy commands appear.

2. **Choose the Affect Pivot Only command.**

   The Pivot Point shows up more prominently on-screen. Now you can move the Pivot Point.

3. **On the Main Toolbar, click the Select and Move tool.**

4. **Click and drag the mouse pointer over the top vertical arrow of the Pivot Point to pull it upward.**

5. **Release the mouse button when the Pivot Point is at the very top of your imported model (as shown in Figure 3-5).**

   Your object now uses this repositioned Pivot Point as its center for transformation operations.

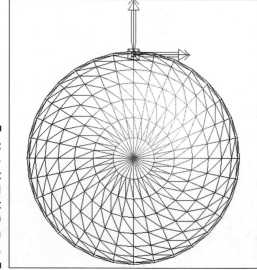

Figure 3-5: Congratulations! Not only did you get the (Pivot) Point, you moved it.

6. **When you're satisfied with the new placement of the Pivot Point, return to the Hierarchy Panel and click the Affect Pivot Only command again.**

   The Affect Pivot Only command switches off.

Moving selected models

The first transformation I look at is repositioning a selected model, moving it in 3D space. You can accomplish this task in two ways — manually or numerically.

Moving models manually

I will illustrate this method with a sphere, but you may wish to use the model you imported previously, or another imported model. In most circumstances, this is the method you will probably select when you need to move an object to a new position in a 3D scene.

1. **With your model visible in the scene, click the Select and Move tool in the Main Toolbar.**

2. **With the Select and Move tool active, click and drag over the object in any viewport.**

   As the object moves in one viewport, the same movement is reflected in all the other viewports (see Figure 3-6).

3. **Explore the movement of the model on all three axes.**

Moving models numerically

If you want to position a model at an exact point in 3D space, manual movement by itself just can't do the job. You can move the model manually to a general area, but if you need a more exacting process to nudge it into its final destination, follow these steps:

1. **With the model selected in the scene, right-click the Select and Move tool in the Main Toolbar.**

   The Move Transform Type-In panel appears (as shown in Figure 3-7), with the model's present XYZ coordinates listed in the Absolute World column.

2. **Enter numbers in the Absolute World column to match the position you want the model to occupy.**

3. **Place your mouse pointer over the up/down arrows next to each coordinate; then click and hold until the correct coordinate shows.**

If you have seriously specific coordinates in mind, type them into the XYZ areas.

4. **Click the X at the upper right of the panel.**

   The panel closes and the new position takes effect.

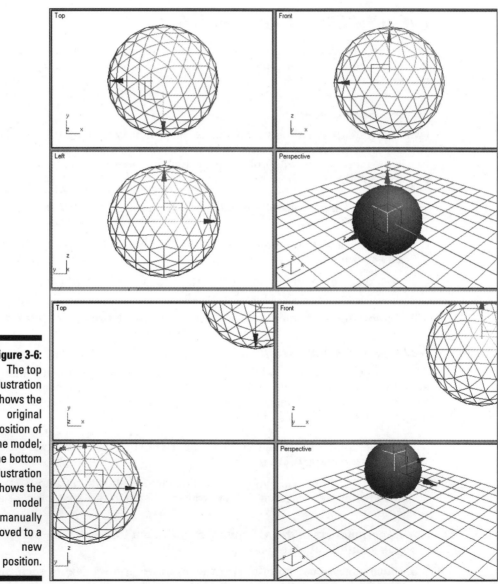

Figure 3-6:
The top illustration shows the original position of the model; the bottom illustration shows the model manually moved to a new position.

Figure 3-7:
Use the
Move
Transform
Type-In
panel when
you want
the model to
move to an
exact
position.

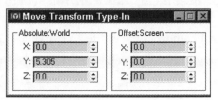

Rotating selected models

Rotating a selected model in 3D space doesn't put it anywhere else. This operation simply puts it on an imaginary rotisserie, whether manually or numerically.

Rotating models manually

As any basketball player can tell you, a sphere is a handy object for illustrating the manual method of rotation. The manual method is also the usual way of rotating an object to a new XYZ angle in a 3D scene — like this:

1. **With your model visible in the scene, click the Select and Rotate tool in the Main Toolbar.**

2. **With the Select and Rotate tool active, click and drag over the object in any viewport.**

   As the object rotates in one viewport, the same rotation occurs in all the other viewports.

3. **Explore the rotation of the model on all three axes.**

Rotating models numerically

You can rotate a model manually to an approximate degree, but to budge it that final hairsbreadth into its final orientation, you may find the numerical method does the trick. To rotate a model numerically, here's the drill:

1. **With the model selected in the scene, click the Select and Rotate tool in the Main Toolbar.**

   The Rotate Transform Type-In panel appears with the model's present XYZ angles listed in the Absolute World column.

2. **Enter numbers in the Absolute World column to match the angle you want the model to rotate to.**

3. **Place your mouse pointer over the up/down arrows next to each coordinate, and click and hold until you get to the correct angle you want.**

   If you prefer, you can type in a new angle in the XYZ areas.

4. **Click the X at the upper right of the panel.**

   The panel closes and the new angle takes effect.

Scaling models

Scaling models (no, you won't have to scrape their scales off) means making them larger or smaller along one or more axes. The process is similar to the movement or rotation transformations, though a bit more complex. You can change the scale of a selected model by clicking and dragging or by choosing a numerical option.

The Scaling tool in the Main Toolbar has three options. To get a look at them, click and hold down the left mouse button with the pointer on the arrow at the bottom-right of the tool to reveal the elements; Figure 3-8 shows what you see.

Scaling models manually

To manually scale a selected object, first choose one of the Scaling tools from the Main Toolbar. Then, with the mouse pointer on the edge of the selected object, simply click and drag the edge of the object outward (for a larger scale) or inward (for a smaller scale), as shown in Figure 3-9.

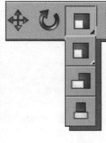

Figure 3-8:
The three Scaling tool options, top to bottom: Select and Uniform Scale, Select and Non-uniform Scale, and Select and Squash.

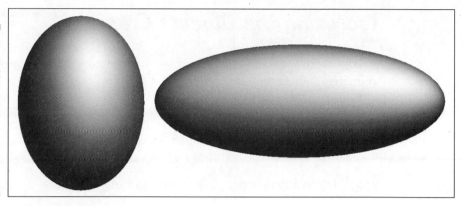

Figure 3-9:
The sphere on the left has been non-uniform scaled; the sphere on the right has been squashed.

Scaling models numerically

Numerical scaling is the way to go when the results need to be mathematically perfect. Follow these steps:

1. **From the Main Toolbar, select the Scaling option you want to use.**

   You can choose Uniform, Non-uniform, or Squash.

2. **Click the selected Scaling tool.**

   The Transform Type-In panel appears. Here you can input the needed scaling numbers for the X, Y, and Z axes.

Ye Olde Object Properties Panel

Any object you put in a scene, whether it's a 3D model or another 3ds max object, has specific properties (parameters) that describe its boundaries. In that way, it's much like any real-world object in a room; you can describe the object by referring to its individual properties. Unlike real-world objects, however, 3D models have uniquely controllable parameters — for example, how many *segments* are involved in the object's form, and what parts of the model are visible.

The next chapter digs into the process of creating and customizing basic (primitive) objects by working with nothing more than their parameters. If that sounds like parlor magic ("at no time will my hands leave my arms . . ."), then it's a good time to get to know the amazing Create Command Panel.

Accessing the Objects Create Command Panel

Parameters differ according to the model they represent — but they all have one thing in common: They show up in a Create Command Panel located at the bottom of the Command Panel (at the right of your 3ds max screen). Without an object or model in the scene, the Create Command Panel looks rather empty, as shown in Figure 3-10 — just a blank Name area and a lackluster color swatch.

Introducing an object should liven up the place. Here goes:

1. **Click the sphere icon under the Objects tab in the Tab Panel at the top of the screen.**

2. **Create a sphere in any viewport by clicking and dragging.**

3. **Take another look at the Create Command Panel.**

    Wow! Look at all the data displayed in there now! You'd think an object had just materialized.

Figure 3-10: The bottom part of the Command Panel is devoted to the display of object parameters. But you've gotta have an object first.

Customizing parameter options

Take a closer look at the Parameters of the newly created sphere, but don't click in any viewport. Notice that the sphere now has a default name (Sphere01) and some newly generated data — radius, segment count, and some other hieroglyphics. Figure 3-11 shows an example.

Now for the magical part: Without deselecting the sphere (don't click anywhere in a viewport), you can change its properties *just like that*.

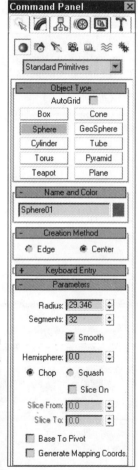

Figure 3-11: Suddenly there's more to know about the new sphere you created.

Tweak it!

Of course, the real world would get all bent out of shape if its objects went around changing their properties willy-nilly; that's why those properties are relatively hard to change. You can't, for example, twist some dial on a remote control to alter the shape or size of your favorite chair (at least not yet). But in the virtual 3D realm of 3ds max, you don't have to obey the (virtual) laws of physics. So go ahead — tweak that object to suit your whims:

1. **In the Segments area in the sphere's Create Command Panel, delete the default data and type in a new number.**

2. **In the Hemisphere option, change the 0.0 default value to 0.5, and then press Enter.**

Look at the altered object you have created from the basic sphere, visible in all the viewports. Can you feel the creative power surging through your veins, making your eyes glow and your ears wiggle? This bit of magic is brought to you by the Create Command Panel — and you can use it to alter any form in a scene, as shown in Figure 3-12.

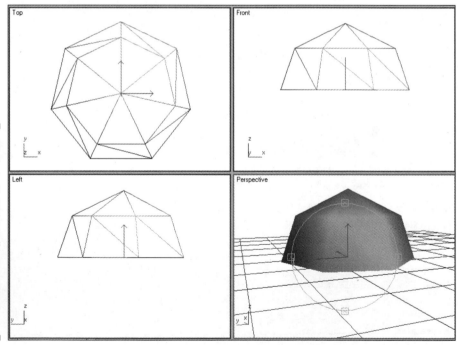

Figure 3-12: This diamond-like form with a flattened bottom is the result of just a little twiddling in a sphere's Properties Panel.

If you do mistakenly click somewhere in a viewport after an object is created in the scene, the parameter for the object disappears. It's not lost forever, however (more about that subject in Chapters 6 to 12).

Constrain it!

When you engage in Transformations (moving, rotating, or scaling selected objects), you can instruct 3ds max to limit *(constrain)* the operation to one or two axes in the selected viewport.

To put the kibosh on all this wanton transforming, follow these steps:

1. **Choose Customize⇨Show UI⇨Show Floating Toolbars.**

   A set of Floating Toolbars appears in midair. Well, actually on-screen. A toolbar is *floating* if you can move it anywhere on the screen.

2. **Choose the Floating Toolbar called Axis Constraints, as shown in Figure 3-13.**

   If you've worked with a previous edition of 3ds max, you may remember that the Axis Constraints tools were previously included on the Main Toolbar.

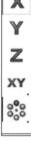

Figure 3-13:
The Axis
Constraints
Floating
Toolbar.

For now, pay attention to the first four tools: X, Y, Z, and XY. These tools affect transformation operations, especially if you're moving an object. If X is selected (for instance), you can move the object only along the X-axis of the selected viewport. XY is the one to use if you require free movement in the non-perspective viewports. (Note the Flyout symbol on the XY tool. Click and hold down the left mouse button to see to Flyout tools.)

3. **Explore the use of these options by selecting one of them and applying a transformation to an object.**

   Feel the thrill of power as the Floating Toolbars do your bidding. Bwahahha! (Pay no attention to the man behind the curtain. . . .)

Chapter 4

Model Movers and Shakers

. . . .

. . . .

*T*his chapter looks at the types of simple, off-the-shelf 3D models — *Primitives* — embedded in 3ds max for you to use and customize. Placing 3D Primitives in a scene and using the Command Panel to customize them is about as fast and fun as 3D animation techniques can get. These Primitives form a group of objects that you can use to create your own models by combining and altering their forms.

Primitive Objects in the Beginning . . .

Okay, pop quiz: *Just what is a modeling Primitive?* Please select from the following multiple-choice answers, and keep in mind that none of your grade depends on it:

1. Someone who is completely unfamiliar with the latest Paris fashions.

2. A person who is just beginning to learn how to create a clay pot.

3. The artist's model who sat for the first paint-by-number cave drawings.

4. None of the above.

That's right — none of the above (and everybody passes anyway). In 3D techno-terminology, a *modeling Primitive* is a simple model made readily available in 3D software so you can instantly create an object, place it in a scene, and modify it to look the way you want. Different 3D software packages contain a range of 3D Primitives, with the most common ones being the cube or box, cylinder, and sphere. 3ds max features a much wider variety than that. If you go to the Tab Panel and select the Objects tab, the icons that are displayed (as shown in Figure 4-1) show all the 3ds max 3D modeling Primitives at a glance.

Figure 4-1:
The icons in
the Objects
tab in the
Tab Panel
display
all the
modeling
Primitives in
3ds max.

You have already created a sphere and placed it in a scene using the sphere icon in the Tab Panel, so you have some idea about the modeling Primitive creation process. If you go to Create⇨Standard Primitives or Create⇨ Extended Primitives, you'll also find all the 3ds max Primitives listed there. This is an alternate way to select a modeling Primitive for creation and use in a 3ds max scene. In this chapter, you are going to create and modify the modeling Primitives by using another method altogether, by selecting and modifying the modeling Primitives from their listings in the Command Panel.

You are already aware that the Command Panel resides at the right of the 3ds max GUI. At the top of the Command Panel is a row of six tabbed icons that stand for Create, Modify, Hierarchy, Motion, Display, and Utilities. See Figure 4-2.

If you click the Create icon tab, all the Create options are displayed as icons below the Create tab. See Figure 4-3.

And behold! You can display everything you want to know about modeling Primitives (also called *object Primitives*) by choosing Command Panel⇨Create⇨Geometry.

Figure 4-2:
The Create,
Modify,
Hierarchy,
Motion,
Display, and
Utilities
icons at the
top of the
Command
Panel.

Figure 4-3:
Clicking the
Create tab
reveals the
seven
Create
options:
Geometry,
Shapes,
Lights,
Cameras,
Helpers,
Space
Warps, and
Systems.

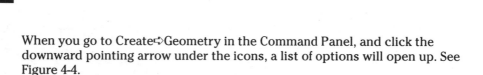

When you go to Create⇨Geometry in the Command Panel, and click the downward pointing arrow under the icons, a list of options will open up. See Figure 4-4.

In this chapter I focus on the top two items in this list: *Standard Primitives* and *Extended Primitives*.

Figure 4-4:
A list of
options
opens up.

Standard Primitives

Choose Create⇨Geometry⇨Standard Primitives in the Command Panel. The ten Standard Primitive buttons appear in the Command Panel. See Figure 4-5.

The ten Standard Primitives are Box, Cone, Sphere, GeoSphere, Cylinder, Tube, Torus, Pyramid, Teapot, and Plane. In the 3ds max Primitives creation process, these ten Standard Primitives can be separated according to the number of steps needed to create them. Among the Standard Primitives are one-step, two-step, and three-step operations.

Figure 4-5:
The ten
Standard
Primitive
buttons in
the
Command
Panel.

One-step Standard Primitives

You can create the following Standard Primitives in one step after selecting
them: Sphere, GeoSphere, Teapot, and Plane. Just click any one of them in the
Command Panel; then click and drag in any viewport and *shazam!* There's
your 3D object. The default viewport to use is the Top Viewport, as shown in
Figure 4-6.

> **You:** Hey! Whazzup? The Sphere and the GeoSphere look like the same
> object!

> **Me:** Ahhh . . . but not upon closer inspection.

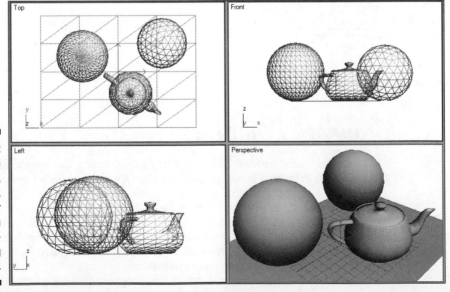

Figure 4-6:
Creating the
Sphere,
GeoSphere,
Teapot, or
Plane with a
single click-
and-drag
movement.

If you look at the Wireframe displays of the Sphere and GeoSphere, you see an important distinction in their polygon arrangements. The Sphere has quadrangular polys split into two faces each; the GeoSphere has triangular polys throughout. See Figure 4-7 for a closer look.

Figure 4-7: The polys in the Sphere on the left are bisected quadrangular polys; those in the GeoSphere on the right are triangular.

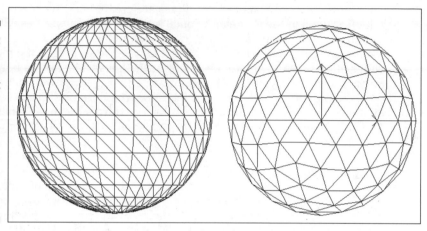

The polygonal difference between the Sphere and the GeoSphere may seem like a "so-what" difference, but it becomes very important when you modify and deform each of these 3D forms.

Using the one-step method detailed earlier, explore the creation of a Sphere, GeoSphere, Teapot, and Plane. Work in the Top Viewport. Apply various transformations to the objects after you have created them. When you are satisfied that you have a good grasp of this one-step creative process for these four Standard Primitives, select each object (with the Select, Select and Move, Select and Rotate, or the Select and Scale tools found on the Main Toolbar) in turn and press the Delete key on your keyboard to clear the viewports.

Two-step Standard Primitives

The following Standard Primitives are created in two steps after selecting them in the Command Panel: Box, Cylinder, Torus, and Pyramid. After clicking any of these Standard Primitives in the Command Panel, click and drag in any viewport to create the initial base of the 3D object. After that, release and move the mouse either up or down to create the height or thickness of the selected object. The default viewport to use is the Top Viewport. See the two-step Standard Primitive lineup in Figure 4-8.

Using the two-step method detailed earlier, explore the creation of a Box, Cylinder, Torus, and Pyramid. Work in the Top Viewport. Apply various transformations to the objects after you have created them. When you are satisfied that you have a good grasp of this two-step procedure for these four

Standard Primitives, select each object (with the Select, Select and Move, Select and Rotate, or the Select and Scale tools found on the Main Toolbar) in turn and press the Delete key on your keyboard to clear the viewports.

Three-step Standard Primitives

The Cone and Tube Standard Primitives are created in three steps after selecting them in the Command Panel. After clicking any of these Standard Primitives in the Command Panel, click and drag in any viewport to create the initial base of the 3D object. After that, release and move the mouse either up or down to create the height or thickness. Click when height or thickness is where you want it. Now move either up or down again to create the third parameter. In the case of the Cone, the third movement sets the dimension of the apex (tip); for the Tube, the third movement sets the height. The default viewport to use is the Top Viewport; Figure 4-9 shows you what to look for.

Using the three-step method detailed earlier, explore the creation of a Cone and a Tube. Work in the Top Viewport. Explore the creation of Cones with flat tops by adjusting your third mouse movement in different ways. Explore the creation of Tubes with different wall thickness and heights by adjusting your second and third mouse movements. Apply various transformations to the objects after you have created them. When you are satisfied that you have a good grasp of this three-step procedure for these two Standard Primitives, select each object in turn and press the Delete key on your keyboard to clear the viewports.

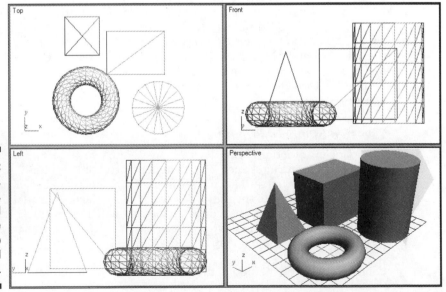

Figure 4-8:
The Box, Cylinder, Torus, and Pyramid are two-step Standard Primitives.

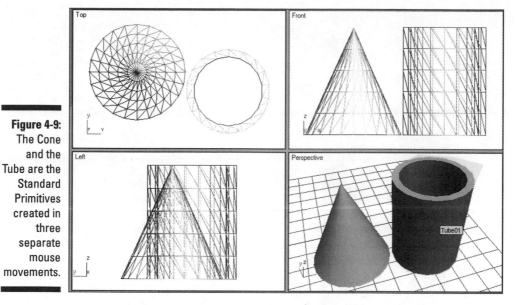

Creating Modified Standard Primitives

Here's where you can really get the most use out of creating Primitives from the Create Command Panel, as opposed to using either the menu selections or the icons in the Tab Panel. If you've been happily selecting object buttons in the Command Panel to create Standard Primitives, you've probably noticed that any selection you click gives you some choices: the object's parameters, in a menu of options that shows up in the lower part of the Create Command Panel (as shown in Figure 4-10).

Look Ma, no mouse!

There is an option in the Command Panel for each of the Standard Primitives called *Keyboard Entry*. You open this option by clicking its title; once inside, you can enter any values you care to in the input boxes, and then simply click Create. Instantly the object with the parameters whose values you just defined pops up in the scene. Using the Keyboard Entry method of Standard Primitive object creation is best when you need 3D objects to conform to specific dimensions and/or in specific XYZ locations. This removes any need to click and drag the mouse pointer in any viewports.

After you set the parameter values for a Standard Primitive in the Command Panel, those same values (except for size) are applied to additional objects of the same type that you create with the mouse by the click-and-drag method.

Figure 4-10:
If you select the Sphere Standard Primitive button in the Command Panel (for example), you gain access to all the Sphere's parameter options.

Slice and dice

The Cone, Sphere, Cylinder, Tube, and Torus parameters in the Command Panel respond to another command: *Slice*. Slice removes a set section of the selected object, just as a knife would cut an even slice of cheese away from a wheel. The Slice operation is activated by first placing a check mark in the box next to the Slice On option. Clicking in the box places — or removes — the check mark.

Two values determine the size of a slice: *Slice From* and *Slice To*. The values are measured in degrees. If you remember your geometry, 360 degrees equals the entire perimeter of a circle. When the Slice operation is activated, the 0 point at the very top of the Top Viewport that displays the object is considered to be both the 0 value and the 360 degree value. If you said "make the slice start from 0 degrees and go to 360 degrees," the entire object would be sliced away, so it would disappear from the scene. The From/To values are calculated counterclockwise in whatever viewport is active, which is usually the Top Viewport in a slice operation (but it can be any viewport).

Explore the creation of the Cone, Sphere, Cylinder, Tube, and Torus with Slice switched on and random values from 0 to 360 degrees entered into the Slice value areas in the Command Panel. See Figure 4-11 for an idea of what you see.

The Hemisphere command

Another neat customization that you can apply from the Create Command Panel parameters is the *Hemisphere*. This operation works only on the sphere, and you can do it all automatically, without doing anything in a viewport. Here's how:

1. **Activate the Sphere button in the Create Command Panel.**

2. **Go down to the parameter that is titled Hemisphere.**

   The input value box next to it reads 0.0, the default.

3. **Click and drag over the default value; while that value is highlighted, type in another value in the box (pick a number between .1 and .99).**

   Acceptable values range from 0 to 1; entering a 1 erases the sphere entirely.

4. **Click the Keyboard Entry control in the Command Panel, set a Radius value, and then click Create.**

   Voilá! Your partial-sphere object pops into existence.

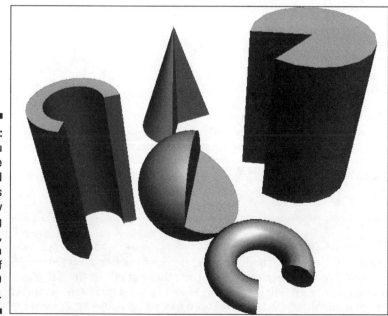

Figure 4-11:
When you Slice the Standard Primitives that allow the slicing operation, you get a series of varied 3D objects.

Take a look at the four variations of the sphere created by using the Hemisphere command in the Command Panel. See whether they resemble any object you may want to create in a scene. Perhaps you'd use the one at the upper-left for a radar dome, the one at the upper-right for a helmet, and the one at the lower-left for an upside-down bowl. The Standard Primitives, especially when they're customized a bit, can easily become identifiable 3D objects/models in a scene.

Extended Primitives

In the Create Command Panel, go to Create⇨Geometry⇨Extended Primitives. Your Command Panel should look like Figure 4-12.

As you can see from your Command Panel, 13 separate Extended Primitives offer their own individual sets of parameter controls in the Command Panel, just as the Standard Primitives do. Ah, but Standard Primitives simply stick to basics; Extended Primitives let you get a little wilder with more complex 3D forms. The Extended Primitives start out (demurely enough) in groups based on how many mouse movements it takes to create them.

Figure 4-12:
This is what your Create Command Panel should look like, displaying the Extended Primitive buttons.

Two-step Extended Primitives

Torus Knot, Capsule, and Hose are three of the two-step Extended Primitives. To create any of them (after selecting them in either the Tab Panel or the Command Panel), click and drag to form the basic shape — and then release the mouse button. Drag some more to give the object thickness or height, and click when you're satisfied with the dimensions.

Three-step Extended Primitives

Two steps away from the basics, the three-step Extended Primitives follow the same procedure used to create a two-step Extended Primitive. After you click the second time, however, you drag the mouse again — up or down — to create a third aspect of the form (like a chamfered or rounded edge). You get seven three-step Extended Primitives in 3ds max: ChamferedBox, ChamferedCylinder, Oil Tank, Spindle, L-Ext, C-Ext, and Prism. Sneak a peek at Figure 4-13, and then jump into creating each of these 3D forms.

One-shot wonder

The only Extended Primitive that can be classified as what I call a *one-shot wonder* is the Hedra. With one click-and-drag operation in any viewport, a 3D Hedra form is created. *Hedra* may sound like a good name for a heavy-metal band, but it's actually short for the classic term *Polyhedra*. The Polyhedra were considered classic forms by the ancient Greeks because of the way they filled space. To appreciate those Hedra parameters, click the Hedra option in the Extended Polygons list in the Command Panel.

Some historical investigators suspect that the many-headed Hydra monster from Homer's *Odyssey* could be a reference to polyhedral forms. Maybe Homer had to struggle with geometry just like the rest of us, and got his revenge by picturing the subject as a monster.

Figure 4-13: A collection of some three-step Extended Primitives in a 3D scene.

The most important Hedra parameters are the Hedra form options, the five Hedra choices listed at the top of the Command Panel Parameters:

- Tetra (Tetrahedron)
- Cube/Octa (Cubahedron or Octahedron)
- Dodec/Icos (Dodecahedron or Icosahedron)
- Star 1
- Star 2 (the special Starhedrons)

The circular selection areas at the left of each of the Hedra form options are called *Radio Buttons*. When you click a radio button, a small black dot appears, and you select the option it relates to.

After selecting a Hedra type, simply click and drag in any viewport to create the 3D form. See Figure 4-14.

Minding your Ps and Qs and Rs

When you face a fierce Hedra Extended Primitive and want to control its parameters, you can do so by invoking three separate Axis Scaling values: P, Q, and R. These three values push or pull on the faces that define the Hedra type. The best way to get a sense of their customizing potential is to explore the use of any Hedra. Simply replace the default values (set to 100 in each case) with your own values, press Enter on the keyboard, and watch how your new PQR values affect the selected Hedra in the viewports.

To conquer the other Hedra monsters, select each Hedra one at a time and then randomly alter its PQR values (in its PQR parameter settings, available in the Command Panel).

The Gengon Extended Primitive

The Gengon Extended Primitive is unique enough not to be grouped with other Extended Primitives, even though it is also created in a three-step process. The first click-and-drag movement creates the base, the second click-and-drag movement creates the height, and the third click-and-drag movement creates smaller sides that are woven between the larger sides. In many ways, you can think of the Gengon as a variation of the Cylinder.

The Gengon has two unique parameters that may be adjusted in the Command Panel after the initial object is created: *Sides* and *Fillet*. The Sides value adjusts the number of the larger sides of the Gengon, and the Fillet value adjusts the number of the smaller sides. Explore the creation of the Gengon, and adjust the Sides and Fillet values to create a variation of the Gengon theme. To enjoy a prepared Fillet of Gengon, take a whiff of Figure 4-15.

The special RingWave Extended Primitive

Beware sailor: Here be more monsters. The RingWave is the most bizarre member of the Extended Primitive family. It's about as much like the others as an extraterrestrial hanging out in a family of humans. It's the only Primitive that's preset as an *animated object* — and though you may find it hard to put to any practical use in a project, it has a seriously high "cool" factor as a virtual toy.

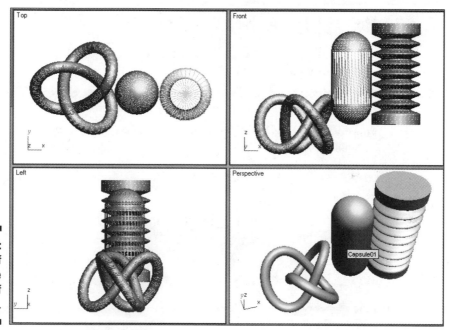

Figure 4-14: A display of the five types of Hedra.

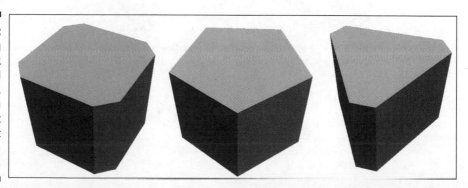

Figure 4-15: By using different Sides and Fillet values, the Gengon can exhibit different personalities.

Okay, I admit it — this weirdo Primitive has me doing something just as bizarre: a *positive* rant. I just love software that contains some fun-but-otherwise-useless elements. Part of what this is telling you is that 3ds max is so chock-full of professional features that it can afford to give you a neat techno-toy now and then.

You create the RingWave in a two-step process, just as you would any other two-step Primitive — but that's where the similarity ends. For this Primitive, you get a large array of adjustments and controls to twiddle in the Command Panel. Consider it a sneak preview; later sections of this book show you the brass tacks of creating animations. The RingWave gives you a taste of controlling an animation right now. (Who could resist that?) To watch the magical RingWave in action, follow these steps:

1. **Using a two-step click-and-drag process, create a RingWave in the Top Viewport.**

2. **Go to the bottom of your screen and click the Play button in the VCR control panel.**

3. **When you want to stop the animated playback, click the Pause button, which is in the same place that the Play button was.**

4. **Adjust the RingWave parameters to create RingWave variations, as suggested in Figure 4-16.**

Figure 4-16:
The animated RingWave.

Making a Scene

One way to use 3D Primitives is to build composite objects. In Chapter 6, I talk about ways you can glue objects together. The following steps describe how you can work with different Primitives to create a scene:

1. **Working in the Top Viewport, place any number of interesting Primitives in a scene.**

   These can be a mix of both Standard and Extended Primitives. Use any ones that you find of interest.

2. **Move them into place by clicking and dragging to create an object.**

   In order to get the positioning just right, it helps to work in first one and then another viewport. Make sure XY is active in the Axis Constraints panel.

After you create a complex 3D model in 3ds max and save it, you can use it as a component to create even more complex structures. Figure 4-17 starts you down that particular primrose path.

You can get unlimited use out of the Standard and Extended Primitives when it comes to creating elements for a scene. Here's how to create a scene with a table, with something interesting placed on the tabletop.

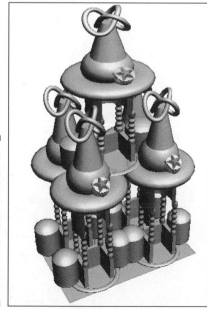

Figure 4-17: Large, complex structures can use smaller similar structures as building elements.

1. **Create a tabletop from a squashed box Standard Primitive.**

2. **Elongate the width so it looks like a long tabletop.**

3. **Add four legs to the table, each created from a Hose Extended Primitive, as shown in Figure 4-18.**

4. **Place some interesting Standard and Extended Primitives on the table.**

You can create thousands of interesting 3D scenes by using similar methods.

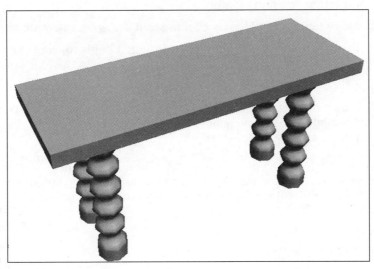

Figure 4-18:
The table.

Chapter 5

2D Shapes in Flatland

*T*his chapter walks you through using the 2D drawing tools to create shapes in 3ds max. 2D shape creation is essential in the construction of unique 3D models. 2D shapes are like ultra-thin slices of bread. They are a part of the loaf that shows the shape the loaf takes, but not the thickness. The 2D slice can be used to determine the 3D loaf by imagining it extended in space.

Creating Basic 2D Shapes

Before you master creating 2D shapes, you have to know where to find their controls. It's important that you first find out how to create 2D shapes so that you can convert them to 3D forms later. You can access 2D Shape tools from three places — on the Main menu by choosing Create⇨Shapes, by clicking the Shapes tab on the Tab Panel, and on the Command Panel, shown in Figure 5-1.

Common shapes

Eleven separate 2D Shape options are available: Line, Rectangle, Circle, Ellipse, Arc, Donut, NGon, Star, Text, Helix, and Section. This chapter looks at each of them. Because the Command Panel contains ways to customize 2D shapes, it's a more convenient approach than the Main menu or the Tab Panel.

Figure 5-1:
The
Command
Panel.

Line

The Line is the most basic 2D shape. You create Lines by click-and-drag movements in a viewport (usually not the Perspective Viewport). Two parameter settings in the Command Panel are especially vital in the creation of 2D Line Shapes:

✔ **Initial Type (Corner or Smooth):** Choosing Corner as an Initial Type creates a sharp corner when the line changes direction; choosing Smooth creates a smooth curve.

✔ **Drag Type (Corner, Smooth, or Bezier):** The three Drag Types set how the line behaves when it is dragged after clicking.

After a Line is created, and before you click anywhere else in a viewport, the Initial Type and Drag Type can be changed, and the Line will reflect the changes before your eyes. Create a Line using the Command Panel option by following these steps:

1. **Choose Create⇨Splines⇨Line in the Command Panel.**

   Spline is an interchangeable term for a 2D shape.

2. **Create a Line with Sharp or Smooth points (vertices) by choosing the appropriate Initial Type in the Command Panel.**

   Whatever viewport you work in, select the Smooth display so the line stays visible.

3. **Decide whether you want a Sharp, Smooth, or Bezier Drag Type, and click the appropriate radio button in the Drag Types section.**

A *Bezier* is a spline that has control handles at the points where it has been clicked — it's the best choice if you want to edit the Lines shape afterward.

4. **Select a Non-Perspective Viewport.**

5. **Lines are created by either or both click-and-drag or click-to-click operations, so try both.**

6. **When you want to determine the end of the line, simply click.**

You can constrain the direction in which a line is drawn by holding the Shift key down as you draw the line. If you want to remove a vertex, press the Backspace key on the keyboard.

Rectangle

The Rectangle is a closed Line with Sharp corners. The Rectangle is created in one click-and-drag movement. Holding down the Ctrl key on your keyboard while creating the Rectangle constrains the shape to a perfect square. When the Rectangle is the shape and size you want it to be, you simply let up on the mouse button.

Of all the Rectangle parameters in the Command Panel, Corner Radius is especially important. By default, it is set to 0 in the current units. Inputting other values up to about 5.5 will make the Rectangle's corners more and more round. Above that value, you will start to introduce loops into the shape, which is okay only if you want them. Very high values produce very wacky shapes, as shown in Figure 5-2.

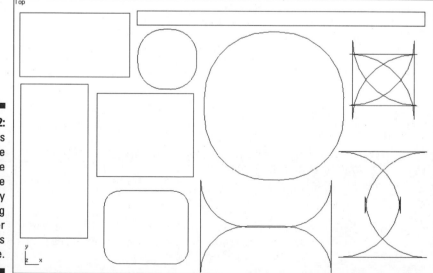

Figure 5-2:
Variations
of the
Rectangle
shape
created by
altering
the Corner
Radius
value.

Circle

The Circle is always a perfect circle, and is created in one motion by a click-and-drag movement. You release when it is the size you want.

Ellipse

The Ellipse is created in a single click-and-drag movement; you release when it's the size you want. Holding down the Ctrl key while you create the Ellipse constrains it into a circle, as shown in Figure 5-3.

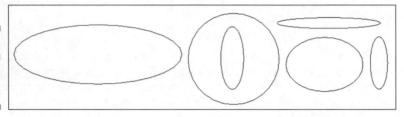

Figure 5-3:
Variations of
the Ellipse
shape.

Arc

The Arc is a curved segment of a circle. It is created by clicking to set the beginning of the Arc, dragging to the end point of the Arc, and then clicking and dragging to determine the size of the invisible circle that the Arc is a part of. (It may take a little practice to create exactly the Arcs you want; Figure 5-4 shows some examples.)

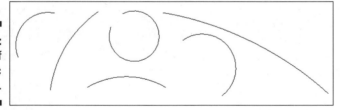

Figure 5-4:
Variations of
the Arc
shape.

Donut

The Donut is a circle within a circle, perfectly concentric. You create it by clicking and dragging to form one radius, and then dragging and clicking to form the second radius and to set the shape, as shown in Figure 5-5.

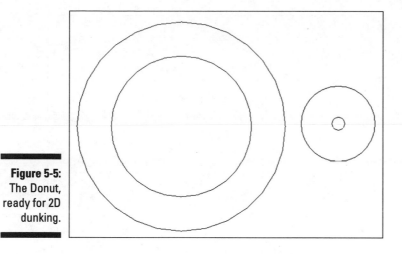

Figure 5-5:
The Donut,
ready for 2D
dunking.

NGon

The NGon is a polygon with N sides. You can set the value of N in the NGon's Command Panel. The higher the value of N, the more the NGon will approach the shape of a circle, as shown in Figure 5-6.

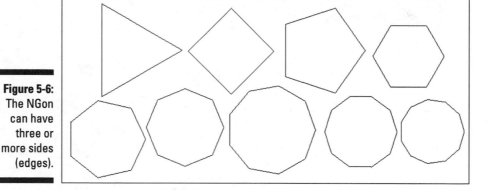

Figure 5-6:
The NGon
can have
three or
more sides
(edges).

Star

The Star shape is determined by its number of Points and by two radii that set how far those points are from the center. You can set all three parameters in the Star's Command Panel. One click-and-drag movement sets the overall size of the Star; a second click-and-drag movement sets the relationship between the two radii. Figure 5-7 shows three different Stars created this way.

Figure 5-7:
These Star
shapes
have
different
numbers of
points, and
also show
different
radii
relation-
ships.

Text

3D Text is one of the most requested features in any 3D software, and 2D Text shapes are the basis of 3D Text. When you click the Text option in the Command Panel, a number of parameters come into view, as shown in Figure 5-8.

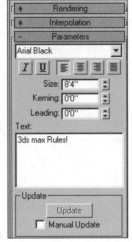

Figure 5-8:
The Text
parameters
in the
Command
Panel.

The most important parameters in the Text Command Panel are Font Name and Text Content. When you click the downward arrow next to the Font name, you can scroll down the list that appears and select any font on your system. You type the actual text message in the Text area. Clicking in a viewport places the Text *string* (a line of text) in the scene.

Weird and wonderful shapes

The last two spline options located in this Command Panel, Helix and Section, are not really 2D shapes at all — they are imaginary constructs that inhabit 3D space (insert spooky sci-fi movie music here). All the other splines visited in this chapter inhabit 2D space, where they lie around on a flat 2D plane and show no depth at all. Not these two beauties, however.

Helix

The Helix is a conical spring shape, or you may even liken it to a tornado. When selected, its parameters are displayed in the Command Panel, where they can be adjusted.

Radius 1 and Radius 2 set the radii that start and end the Helix. If both are equal, the resulting Helix is cylindrical. If one is much smaller than the other, the resulting Helix is conical. The Height value determines the total height of the Helix, from starting radius to ending radius. Setting a Turns value determines how many windings the Helix has.

Bias, which determines the spread of the Helical windings, can range from -1 to 1 (the default is 0, which produces a totally unbiased helix). Setting Bias to -1 will push most of the windings toward the radius 1 point; setting Bias at +1 will force the Helical windings toward the Radius 2 point. CW sets the windings to be clockwise; CCW forces a counterclockwise result. By adjusting some or all of these values, you can create interesting variations. As a rule, work in the Top Viewport when you create a Helix. Click-and-drag movements do the job; you can make any adjustments later in the Command Panel parameters. Figures 5-9 and 5-10 tell the (winding) tale of the Helix.

Figure 5-9:
A Helix with a Bias of -1 on the left, 0 in the center, and +1 on the right create some interesting variations.

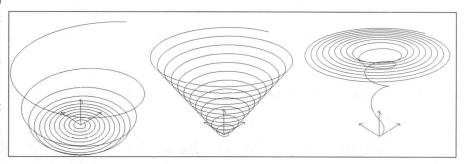

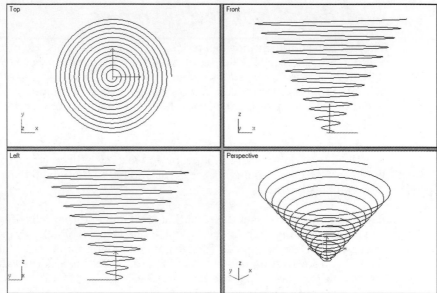

Figure 5-10:
Create the
Helix in
the Top
Viewport.

Section

Although a Section is a flat 2D shape, it owes its existence to a 3D object. A Section is a visual slice (like a CAT scan) of the 3D model. To explore the creation of a Section, follow these steps:

1. **Place a Standard or Extended Primitive in a scene.**

   I have used a Sphere as an example in the illustration.

2. **Choose Create⇨Splines in the Command Panel, and click Section.**

3. **Choose any Non-Perspective Viewport.**

4. **Left-click and drag from one point (vertex) on the model to an opposite edge, and then right-click.**

5. **In the Section's Command Panel controls, click Create Shape.**

   The Section appears in the viewports, as shown in Figure 5-11.

Open and closed shapes

It's pretty obvious that the Circle, Ellipse, Rectangle, and other 2D splines (shapes) are closed. A closed shape has a continuous border around it, so it has an *inside* and an *outside*. But what if you're creating a sharp-cornered or smooth-cornered Line, and you want it to become a closed shape? No problem; here's the drill:

1. **Choose the Line option from the Splines Command Panel.**

2. **Choose the viewport you want to work in, and start creating an interesting shape by click-and-drag movements.**

3. **To close the shape, move the mouse so the pointer is above the first point you created. Then click once.**

   A window appears, asking whether you want to close the shape.

4. **Click Yes if you want to close the shape, as shown in Figure 5-12.**

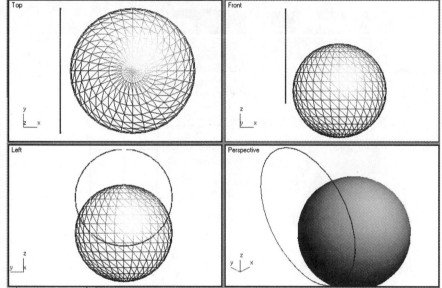

Figure 5-11: I used a Sphere as the Sectioning target, so the Section is a circular slice.

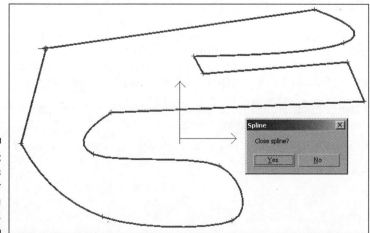

Figure 5-12: Clicking Yes closes your freeform shape.

Adding Color to Your Shape

2D shapes are not always easy to see in a viewport. You see a small color swatch at the right of the Name and Color area in the Create⇨Splines Command Panel. Click in the color area to bring up the System Color Palette, and select another color, preferably a darker one, for your 2D option, as shown in Figure 5-13.

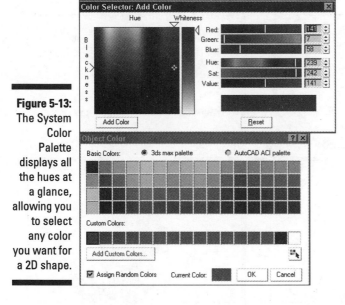

Figure 5-13: The System Color Palette displays all the hues at a glance, allowing you to select any color you want for a 2D shape.

Transforming Shapes into Objects

When placed in a 3D scene, 2D shapes don't look the way they were created; they merely act as skeletons from which 3D objects can be created (see Chapter 9). You have two alternatives for transforming an open or closed 2D shape into an actual object that can be displayed in a scene:

- **Using the Render options:** This method works for displaying open or closed 2D shapes in a 3D scene.

- **Converting a closed shape to a mesh:** This method works only for closed 2D shapes.

2D Shape Render options

Until you take specific actions, 2D shapes are just imaginary and invisible in a rendered 3D scene in 3ds max. This first action works on either open or closed 2D shapes (remember they are also called *splines*) to add some visible flesh to their invisible bones. Follow these steps:

1. **Create any 2D shape you like, open or closed, in a viewport.**

2. **Click the Rendering button in the Command Panel for the 2D shape to open the shape's render options.**

3. **Click the radio button next to Viewport or Renderer (you'll use Viewport here).**

4. **Click in the box next to Renderable to place a check mark in it.**

5. **Change the value in the Thickness input box to 3.0 from its default value.**

6. **Create the selected 2D shape in a viewport. Look in the viewports to see the results.**

   Note that your frail 2D shape has now become a substantial object (Cool!), as Figure 5-14 shows.

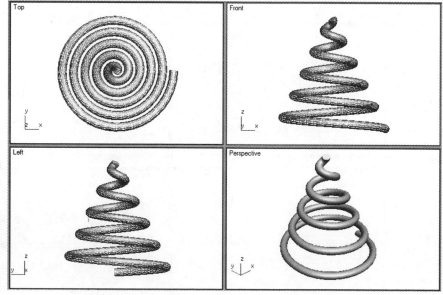

Figure 5-14: The Hydra shape has been transformed into a wiry spring.

Mesh translation

Hey! What's a *Mesh* anyway? A Mesh is a collection of polygons that define a surface. All 3D objects (well, *most*) are created from a mesh of polygons. A 2D closed shape has a perimeter, but it is not defined by a polygonal Mesh. You can modify the closed 2D shape into a Mesh in many ways. Here is one way:

1. **Create any closed 2D shape.**

   I have selected a Rectangle shape to illustrate this example, but you may select (or create) a different closed 2D shape.

2. **Click the Modeling tab in the Tab Panel, and then click the Surface Modifier icon.**

3. **Click the Surface Modifier, which is icon number 11 from the left.**

   A small label appears, telling you this is the right icon. Instantly, the shape is surfaced with triangular faces. It is now an object that has length and width, but no thickness, as shown in Figure 5-15.

Don't bother using the Surface Modifier process on the Helix. Nothing will explode if you do, but it won't work.

See Chapter 10 for information on how to use 2D splines (shapes) in the creation of 3D models.

Figure 5-15:
The closed 2D shape is transformed into a true mesh that can be used anywhere in a 3D scene. Notice that the surface is now filled with polygons.

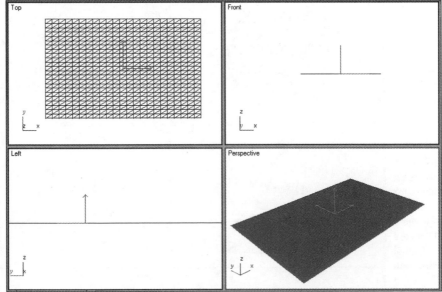

Chapter 6

Compound Interest

*T*his chapter walks you through the creation of Compound objects in 3ds max. Compound Objects are the result of performing operations on multiple objects. After working with Primitive objects, Compound Objects are the next natural step in the modeling process. Compound objects reward you with much more complex 3D model designs, because they too can be used as basic elements in the construction of ever more complex forms — Scatter, Connect, Conform, Boolean, and Loft. You can access Compound Objects from the Compounds Tab on the Tab Panel, but it's handier to use the Command Panel for access. To display the Compound Object options, choose Create⇨ Geometry⇨Compound Objects in the Command Panel, as shown in Figure 6-1.

Figure 6-1: The Command Panel display for Compound Objects appears only if and when you have created some 3D or 2D content in a scene.

Scatter to the Winds: Creating Two-Object Compound Scatters

Scattering is the process of making an object (or multiple copies of an object) conform to the surface of another target object, and it can result in some pretty complex and fantastic 3D models. Scattering allows you to use one object as the base upon which other objects are duplicated and placed, in much the way boulders are placed on terrain.

To create a Compound Scatter Object, follow these steps:

1. **Create or import two objects into a 3ds max scene.**

   For example, I placed a larger Sphere Standard Primitive and a smaller Cone Standard Primitive in a scene. Use any viewport.

2. **Choose Create⇨Geometry⇨Compound Objects in the Command Panel.**

   For the example, make sure the Cone is selected; make the cone tall and pointed.

3. **Click Scatter in the Compound Objects list.**

4. **In the parameter options that appear in the Command Panel, click Pick Distribution Object.**

   The Distribution Object serves as the base upon which the duplicates of another object are scattered.

5. **Click the Distribution Object (the Sphere) in any viewport.**

6. **Set the Segment value in the Command Panel.**

   In this case; set the Sphere's Segment value to 16. You have now attached the Cone to a Distribution Object (the Sphere).

7. **Check your Perspective Viewport.**

   For this example, it should display an image similar to Figure 6-2.

8. **In the Command Panel, choose the list of options under the heading Distribute Using.**

9. **Click the All Edge Midpoints radio button.**

   You have now placed a large number of cones on the surface of the Sphere, one at every center point of every edge of every polygon on the surface of the Sphere. This operation creates a spiky ball, shown in Figure 6-3.

You can tweak the other values in the Command Panel to see what you get.

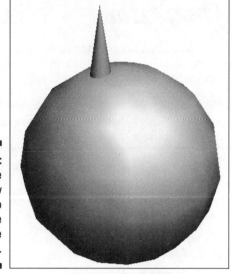

Figure 6-2:
The Cone
is now
attached to
the surface
of the
Sphere.

Figure 6-3:
This is not a
ball you
want to play
catch with.

Using the Connect Operation

The Connect operation binds any two objects together so 3ds max treats them as a single object. If you build a tower of diverse Primitives, for example, you can use the Connect operation as many times as needed to bind every object to the others as part of the tower.

The original object being connected to another object (the Operand) substitutes its texture over that of the other object.

When you plan to use the Connect option, remember that you don't have to place connected objects near each other. Connect works its magic across space, connecting selected objects into one object.

Creating a single object from two objects using Connect

The Connect operation builds a bridge between two selected objects. The result is a single object with a connecting 3D form. To use Connect on two objects, follow these steps:

1. **Create any two objects/models and place them in a 3ds max scene.**

   The objects can overlap, just touch, or remain at a distance from each other.

2. **With one of the objects selected, choose Create⇨Geometry⇨ Compound Objects in the Command Panel.**

   Click the Pick Operand command in the Command Panel.

   Doing so activates the Connect operation.

3. **Click the other object (the target object) to which you want to connect your original object (the source object).**

   The target object turns the same color as the source object, telling you that the operation has taken place. Try to move what was one of the objects, and you'll see that they both move; they are now connected.

Building a connected object

The Connect option can glue more than two objects together. If you build a tower of diverse Standard and Extended Primitives, for example, you can use the Connect option to cement all the parts in place as one model. When you click Pick Operand in the Command Panel, it stays active while you select as many objects in the scene as you like. All are cemented to each other as one model, as shown in Figure 6-4.

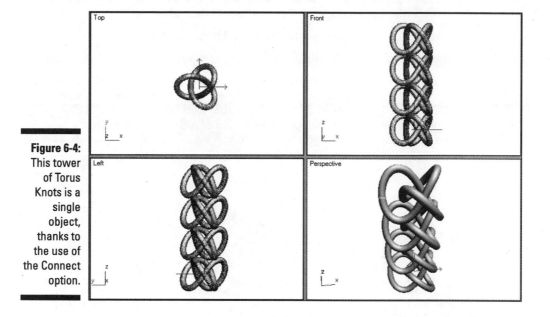

Figure 6-4:
This tower of Torus Knots is a single object, thanks to the use of the Connect option.

Performing the Basic Conform Action

Conforming is a term that usually makes rugged individualists leap and twitch, but using the Conform operation in 3ds max is actually pretty creative. The Conform operation attempts to force-fit a selected object into another object's skin, so the original object's form is altered as a result. Sometimes the result is subtle — and sometimes quite bizarre.

As an example of a Conform operation, I use the two Standard Object Primitives most often thought of as 3D opposites . . . the cube and the sphere. When you have mastered this example, you can use the Conform operation on any Primitives or imported models. Follow these steps:

1. **Place a Standard Primitive cube and sphere in a 3ds max scene. Use any viewport.**

2. **Move the sphere so it is half-embedded in the cube.**

3. **With the sphere selected, choose Create⇨Geometry⇨Compound Objects in the Command Panel.**

4. **Select the Conform option. Click the Wrap To Object button in the Command Panel, and click the cube in any viewport.**

5. **Click to put a check next to the text in the Command Panel that reads Hide Wrap-To Object.**

6. **Move the original cube out of the way so you can see how the sphere attempted to change its form to that of the cube.**

   In this case, you see a sphere with a flattened hemisphere, as shown in Figure 6-5.

Do not take one example of this process as the definitive be-all end-all of your observations. Literally dozens of variations are possible for any two objects. Distance, overlap, what each object's form is, and other Command Panel parameter alterations all affect the outcome of a Conform operation. Experiment each time till you get a good working sense of what factors create the specific results you're after.

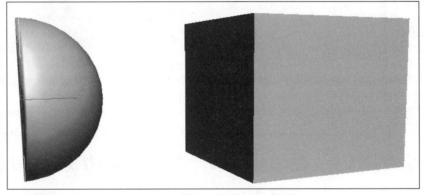

Figure 6-5:
The sphere is flattened on one side where it tried to emulate the cube.

Booley-Booley: Creating Objects with the Boolean Operations

Boolean operations are among the most common modeling options in professional 3D programs. A Boolean operation makes changes in 3D models mathematically, in much the same way that numbers can be combined to create other numbers. The on-screen results from the following three operations look like magic:

- **Boolean Add:** Adding objects together results in a single object with one overall surface.

- **Boolean Subtract:** Subtracting one object from another produces a hole or depression in one object that conforms to the dimensions of the subtracted object.

✔ **Boolean Intersection:** When two objects intersect, this operation leaves only the intersecting parts of each surface.

Although the following examples use a sphere and a cylinder, you can apply a Boolean operation to any Primitive, imported model, or created model.

Adding 'em up

Boolean Addition combines two objects into a single object with one surface. To explore Boolean Addition, follow these steps:

1. **Place two intersecting objects in a 3ds max scene.**

   I used a Standard Primitive Sphere and a Standard Primitive Cylinder in this example, as shown in Figure 6-6.

2. **Select the larger of the two objects.**

3. **Choose Create⇨Geometry⇨Compound Objects⇨Boolean in the Command Panel.**

4. **Under Operation, click Union.**

5. **Click the Pick Operand B button.**

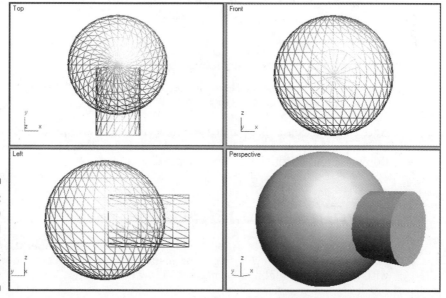

Figure 6-6: Place two intersecting objects in a 3ds max scene.

6. **Click the other object in any viewport.**

Your two objects have been added together, married till a transform does them part (the Move, Rotate, and Scale transforms can be applied to either through an editing operation in the Modify Command Panel). All modifications now will address both previously singular forms as one. (Should there be organ music here?)

Boolean Subtraction

Of all Boolean options, Boolean Subtraction is the one most called upon. Cutting holes in objects is necessary when you want to create many complex forms, and this operation performs that feat easily. Boolean Subtraction cuts holes and depressions in objects. If you really like making holes in things, follow these steps:

1. **Place two intersecting objects in a 3ds max scene.**

2. **Choose Create⇨Geometry⇨Compound Objects⇨Boolean in the Command Panel.**

3. **Select the larger object.**

This object is now referred to as Object A (or *Operand A*).

4. **Choose Subtraction (A–B) in the Command Panel.**

5. **Click Pick Operand B.**

6. **Choose any viewport.**

7. **Click the smaller intersecting object.**

Instantly you see a hole or depression in Operand A (Object A) that matches the shape of Operand B.

Note that the Command Panel also allows a B-minus-A operation, but this is by far the less common of the two Boolean Subtraction options. Explore Boolean Subtraction with more complex objects.

The difference leftover

The Boolean Intersect operation is the least-used Boolean operation, but it can be quite handy; trying to get the resulting form would be quite difficult with any other modeling alternative. Follow these steps:

1. **Place two intersecting objects in a 3ds max scene.**

2. **Choose Create⇨Geometry⇨Compound Objects⇨Boolean in the Command Panel.**

3. **Click your larger object to select it.**

4. **In the Command Panel, click Intersect.**

   All that remains of the two objects is the surface area of their intersection, as shown in Figure 6-7.

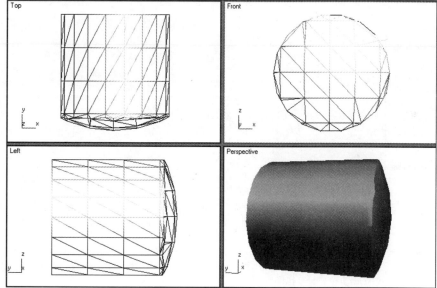

Figure 6-7:
Boolean
Intersection
of a sphere
with a
cylinder,
resulting in
a shorter
cylinder
with a
rounded top.

Using the Boolean Cut Operation

3ds max offers you another Boolean option not found in other 3D software: *Cut*. Cut is at one and the same time similar to Subtract and Intersect, as well as being something else. Using Cut, you can perform interactions between a 2D shape and a 3D object, which is often necessary to create some special 3D forms. Follow these steps:

1. **Create a donut shape in the Top Viewport.**

2. **Create a Standard Primitive Sphere that overlaps one side of the donut shape.**

3. **Select the donut shape, and choose Create⇨Geometry⇨Boolean⇨Cut in the Command Panel.**

4. **Select the sphere as the operand.**

   The sphere cuts a spherical bite out of the shape. The shape is also fully polygonized in the process, as shown in Figure 6-8.

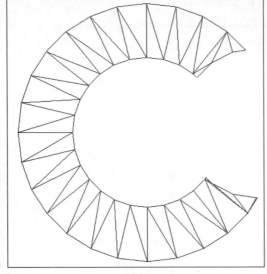

Figure 6-8:
This was
originally a
2D donut
shape, and
now it's a
flat 2D
object.

Be sure to explore other 2D shapes and 3D object interactions as well to get a better idea of just what the Boolean Cut operation can do.

Selecting Boolean with any 2D shape selected instantly turns the shape into a true 3D object by creating polygons inside the shape. This technique also works for text shapes, but not for the helix.

ShapeMerge

ShapeMerge is the quickest way to transform a 2D shape into a 2D object. The difference between the two is that a 2D shape is seldom rendered in a scene; a 2D object renders as a 3D object does. This is especially helpful when you want to use a text object (meaning a line of text) in an animation, or perhaps even as a flat sign in the scene. Follow these steps:

1. **Choose Create⇨Shapes⇨Text, and input the text message you want to use.**

2. **Click once in any viewport to write the 2D Text Shape to the scene.**

3. **Click the 2D text object to select it.**

4. **Choose Create⇨Geometry⇨Compound Objects.**

5. **Click ShapeMerge.**

   The 2D text shape now becomes a 2D object with all polygons in place, as shown in Figure 6-9.

Figure 6-9:
Top: 2D
Text Shape
before
activating
Shape
Merge.
Bottom: fully
polygonized
2D Text
object after
Shape
Merge.

Figure 6-9: Top: 2D Text Shape before activating Shape Merge. Bottom: fully polygonized 2D Text object after Shape Merge.

Up in the Loft: Creating and Editing Lofted Objects

Creating 3D models by lofting is an essential modeling option for 3D artists and animators, and 3ds max has some of the finest lofting controls around.

The lofting process requires that you have two 2D shapes placed in a scene. One of the 2D shapes acts as a *path*; the other 2D shape is defined as a *cross-section*. The cross-section is basically pulled along the path to form a 3D object or model. If you can't quite visualize this action, perhaps this analogy helps. Suppose that someone asked you to model a sausage (it could be a tofu sausage for all you non-meat-eaters). A sausage is sort of like a cylinder, except it usually has a slight curve along its length. A cross-section of the sausage, literally a slice at some point along its length, is a circle. A curved line segment — the path — could represent the whole length of the sausage. If you had a method of pulling the circular cross-section along a slightly curved Path, a 3D sausage model would be the result. Here are a few different loft ideas for you to explore. Each uses different paths and cross-sections.

Lofty ideas

A *penta-tube* is my term for a 3D form that is tubular with five equidistant bends, like a garden hose that bends back on itself. Here's how to create a penta-tube loft. Follow these steps:

1. **Choose Create⇨Shapes⇨NGon, and create a pentagon in the Top Viewport.**

2. **While Create⇨Shapes is still in effect, choose Circle and create a cir-cular 2D shape.**

   Make the pentagon about ¹⁄₁₂ the scale of the Circular 2D shape, as shown in Figure 6-10.

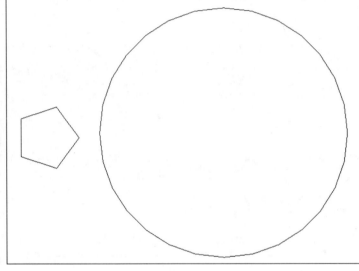

Figure 6-10:
Your Front
Viewport
should look
like this,
containing
both a circle
and
pentagon.

3. **Choose Create⇨Geometry⇨Compound Objects.**

4. **Choose the Circle and click Loft.**

5. **Click Get Shape in the Loft Command Panel, and then click the penta-gon in the Top Viewport.**

   You have generated a lofted object, as shown in Figure 6-11.

To explore another loft operation, return to the screen that shows just the two 2D shapes: choose Edit⇨Undo twice. Here's the second operation:

1. **Select the pentagon.**

2. **Choose Create⇨Geometry⇨Compound Objects⇨Loft.**

3. **Click the Get Shape button.**

4. **Click the circle in any viewport.**

   The pentagon acts as your path, with the circle as the cross-section. This creates a different lofted 3D model than before, as Figure 6-12 shows.

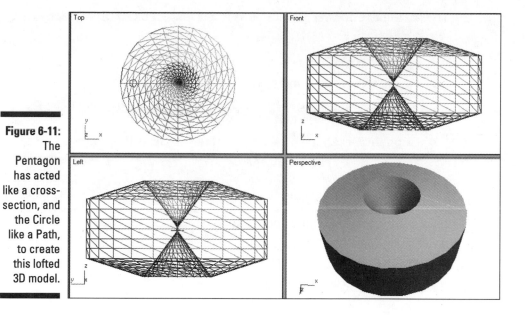

Figure 6-11:
The Pentagon has acted like a cross-section, and the Circle like a Path, to create this lofted 3D model.

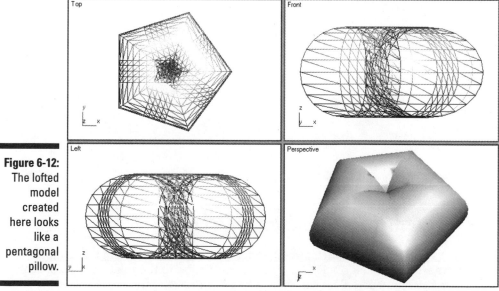

Figure 6-12:
The lofted model created here looks like a pentagonal pillow.

The path shape doesn't have to be a closed shape. Follow these steps to get an open shape:

1. **Choose Create⇨Shapes.**

2. **Create a curvy line and a circle in the Top Viewport.**

3. **Select the curvy line shape, and then choose Create⇨Geometry⇨ Compound Objects⇨Loft.**

4. **Using the Get Shape process, select the circle as the shape.**

    Figures 6-13 and 6-14 show the results.

One of the coolest 2D shapes to use as a loft path is the hydra — a coiled path through 3D space. Figure 6-15 shows a 2D star shape as a cross-section for a hydra path in a lofting operation.

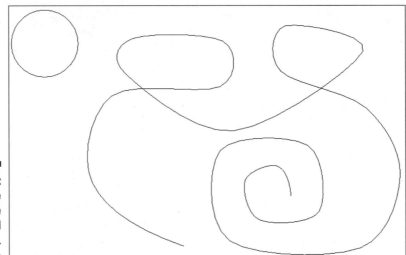

Figure 6-13: Here is the 2D shape you started with.

Tweaking the cross-sections

As you have probably noticed from the lofting operations in this chapter, the 3ds max Loft operation pays little attention to the relative sizes of cross-section and path. You can, however, edit the size of the cross-section. If you plan to create a lot of lofted objects, you're in luck: You can edit them all from within the Loft Command Panel.

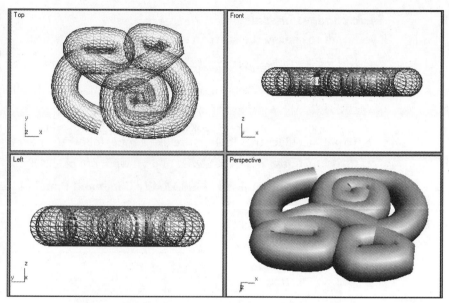

Figure 6-14:
This is a result of lofting the circular cross-section to the curvy path. Is it a discarded hose? A hastily squeezed volume of toothpaste?

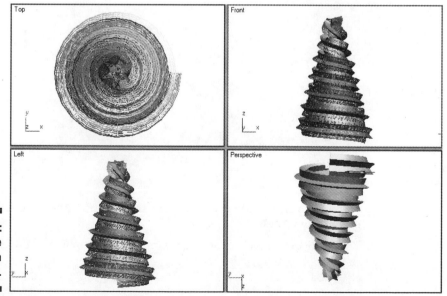

Figure 6-15:
A star shape lofted to a hydra path.

Basic changes in scale

If you want to change the size of a lofted object, here's the drill:

1. **Create some lofted scene content.**

   For this example, create a random curved path — and then loft a circular cross-section to it, as shown in Figure 6-16.

   The model in Figure 6-16 looks bloated, as if it soaked in water too long. To get an object that looks more like a rope, follow the next few steps.

2. **Click the lofted object selected in a viewport to select it.**

3. **Choose the Loft options in the Modify Command Panel — in particular, Deformations.**

   The Deformation controls open.

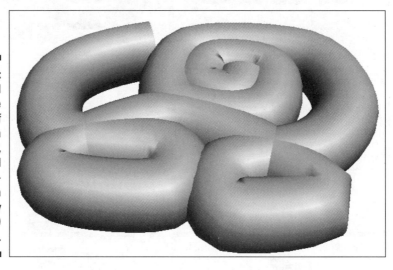

Figure 6-16:
This lofted object is the result of lofting a circular, 2D, shaped cross-section to a randomly curved 2D path.

4. **To edit the size of the cross-sections that contribute to the lofted object, click Scale.**

   The Scale Deformation Panel appears, as shown in Figure 6-17.

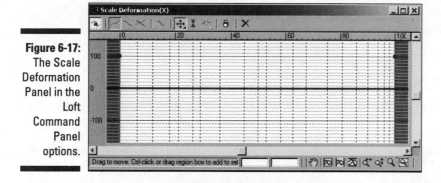

Figure 6-17:
The Scale
Deformation
Panel in the
Loft
Command
Panel
options.

The Scale Deformation Panel gives you some choices to make:

- **Scaling down to zero:** A bold horizontal line at the zero point represents a scale of zero (in effect, an object too small to see). Values above the zero point increase the size of a cross-section; values below the zero point shrink the cross-section.

- **Scaling up to 100%:** Above the graph, a crosshair icon is selected by default; a red line shows at the 100% point. At each end of the red line is a black circular control point. Placing your mouse pointer over either dot enables you to move this control point up or down — toward or away from a scale of 100% (which is, in effect, a "full-size" object).

- **Choosing your starting and ending points for the path:** The dot at the left represents the size of the cross-section at the start of its path; the dot on the right represents the size of the cross-section of the lofted object at the end of its path.

5. **Click and drag both control points to a value of about 20 on the graph.**

6. **Close the Scale Deformation Panel.**

   You can now see the lofted object in any viewport.

Changing the scale for specific parts of an object

If you scale the starting point small and the end point large, you get the object shown in Figure 6-18.

Figure 6-18:
Here's the
result of a
small-scale
value for the
cross-
section's
start point,
and a large
value for the
end point.
This could
be the start
of a 3D
model of a
snake.

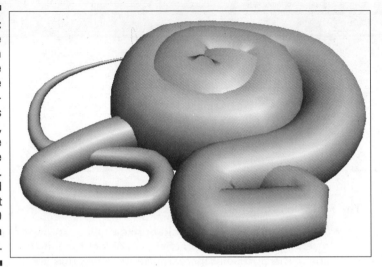

But if you want to get fancy with the process of deforming objects, how about altering the cross-section sizes at several points along the length of the path? Can you do that? Yep. Click and hold down the mouse button over the Scale Deformation menu; then select an icon from the list that appears. The Insert Corner Point icon creates sharp corner points whereas the Insert Bezier Point icon adds smooth curves to the scaling path. For now, select the Insert Bezier Point icon.

When one of these control icons is active, you can click the scaling line to add a curve point. Add as many as you like. After they're added, you can move them up and down to adjust the scale of the cross-section at that point on the path, as shown in Figures 6-19 and 6-20.

In addition to the Scale option in the Deformations options of the Loft Command Panel, another four items are available: Twist, Teeter, Bevel, and Fit. With a bit of practice, you'll have little trouble customizing lofted objects with these deformations as well.

Although you access lofting by choosing Create⇨Geometry⇨Compound Objects, it could just as well be considered a way of modifying an object — especially when you're using the Deformation options. That's right handy for this book — because the next chapter gets into 3ds max modification options.

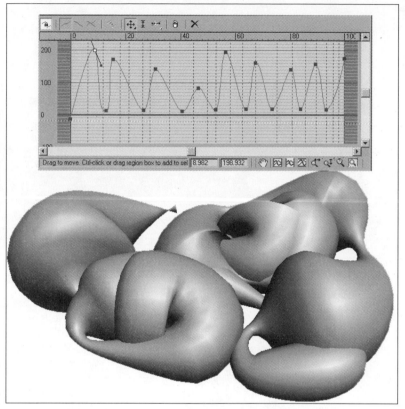

Figure 6-19:
Top: The Scale Deformation curve after several curve points are added and moved. Bottom: The resulting cross-section scaled object (T. Rex intestines? Yuck!).

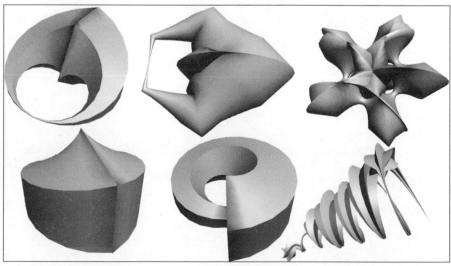

Figure 6-20:
Using the Loft Scale Deformation process, you can create an infinitely varied number of lofted objects.

Part III
Applying Modifier Alchemy

The 5th Wave — By Rich Tennant

"Look into my Web site, Ms. Carruthers. Look deep into its rotating, nicely animated spiral, spinning, spinning, pulling you in, deeper... deeper..."

In this part . . .

1 find it very dangerous to go into hardware stores. Wandering the aisles looking for the one item that brought me in brings me into contact with a million wrenches, hammers, saws, routers, and other tools I have never seen before but know I must have. There is a suspicion I think we all have that if we can just get our hands on that one special all-purpose mega Swiss Army knife, we will be able to fix anything that comes along.

In some ways, that's the same feeling you get when you discover how to use the Modifiers in 3ds max, that is, that you are getting your hands on 3D wrenches and screwdrivers and chisels that can solve any modeling challenge . . . and that's true. Unlike the everyday world, where the existence of all-purpose tools remain permanently out of reach, the Modifiers in 3ds max really do allow you to push, pull, and tweak your models until they are transformed from the ordinary into the spectacular. This part of the book is devoted to the use and mastery of a wide range of max Modifiers.

Chapter 7

Working with Modifiers

This chapter is an introduction to Modifiers, 3ds max tools and processes helpful for both restructuring models and for creating animated movement targets (although animation itself is covered in Part VI of the book). Modifiers act to reshape any model into a new form, either subtly or radically, depending on what you require.

Finding the Right Modifier

As with many other 3ds max features, Modifiers can be accessed in a number of different ways. Most 3D users select the way that is most comfortable for their work habits, though some projects you do may commence more smoothly if you choose to work with select Modifiers in a specific location.

You can access Modifiers in three ways: on the menu bar, on the Tab Panel, and on the Command Panel. In the following sections, I cover the benefits and details of using each.

The menu bar

You can access the Modifiers from the Modifier menu if you want to narrow your search to a specific modification parameters, like Mesh Editing, Free Form Deformations, or any of the other Modifier categories. The other two Modifier location alternatives aren't as orderly and purposeful as the Modification menu in their display of modification topics.

Modifiers have their own drop-down menu on the top menu bar (shown in Figure 7-1). Twelve submenus list the 3ds max Modifiers you can access from the menu bar. Each group of Modifiers has its own specific tasks to address, whether it be for modeling, animation, texture modification, or other purposes. You can open the submenus by simply putting your mouse pointer over their right-pointing arrows, and then selecting an item from the list.

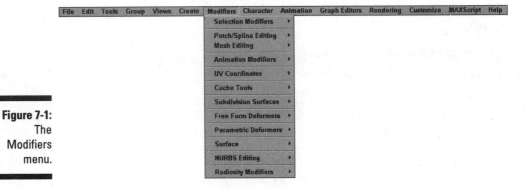

Figure 7-1:
The
Modifiers
menu.

The Tab Panel

If you are a visual person who tends to be attracted to pictures rather than words, you may find yourself accessing the Modifiers from the Tab Panel instead of using the other alternatives. Using the Modifier icons from the Tab Panel is also the quickest way by far to apply them. One click activates the selected Modifier.

If you click the Modifiers tab in the Tab Panel, the modifiers are listed as icons. Passing your mouse pointer over any icon reveals its label, as shown in Figure 7-2.

Figure 7-2:
The
Modifier
icons in the
Tab Panel.

The icons displayed for various Modifiers under the Modifier tab in the Tab Panel are grouped horizontally according to Modifier Type. Selecting any Modifier option here (or by the Modifier menu method) also reveals that

Modifier in the Command Panel (more on that next). The icons are designed to be as easy as possible to recognize, though some may look a little mysterious until you get the hang of using them.

The Command Panel

Always use the Modifier display in the Command Panel when you want to apply parameter changes from any selected Modifier. The Modifier itself may be selected from the Modify menu, from the Modify tab in the Tab Panel, or directly from the Modify list in the Modify section of the Command Panel.

On the right of the Create arrow icon in the Command Panel is the Modify icon. It looks like a bent cylinder. If you go to Modify without selecting content in a viewport, nothing shows up in the Modify Command Panel. When something is selected in a scene, the Modify display in the Command Panel lists all the modification options, as shown in Figure 7-3.

Figure 7-3: Left: An empty Modify display in the Command Panel. Right: With a sphere in the scene selected, the sphere's initial modification parameters are displayed.

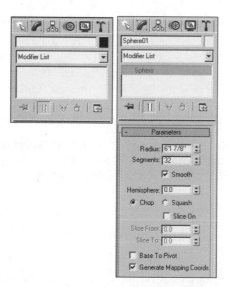

Anything selected in the scene immediately has all its parameters displayed in the Command Panel. You can access other Modifiers (whether listed in the Modifiers menu or accessible from the Modifiers tab in the Tab Panel) in the Command Panel; just click the downward-pointing arrow at the right of the Modifiers List box. Clicking the arrow opens the Modifiers list shown in Figure 7-4.

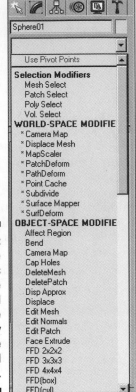

Figure 7-4:
The
Modifiers
list can be
opened
from the
Modify
option in the
Command
Panel.

As you can see in Figure 7-4, the Modifiers are placed in categories just as they are when accessing them from the Modify menu bar. Selecting any Modifier places all the Modifier's parameters in the Command Panel, as shown in Figure 7-5.

After you alter any Modifier parameters in the Command Panel, simply press Enter on your keyboard to apply those changes to the selected item in the viewport.

When you create an object Primitive or import a 3D model, that data on the object/model is displayed in the Create➪Geometry or Create➪Shapes Command Panel. You probably also know that clicking anywhere outside the item in a viewport causes the parameter display in the Command Panel to annoyingly vanish.

You can regain access to that data easily. Simply select the item in any viewport and go to the Modify display in the Command Panel. You can select or deselect any item in any viewport and its data appears in the Modify Command Panel. Always and forever, any selected item in your 3D scene is shown, along with its list of Modifiers, in the Modify Command Panel.

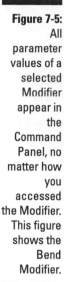

Figure 7-5: All parameter values of a selected Modifier appear in the Command Panel, no matter how you accessed the Modifier. This figure shows the Bend Modifier.

Accessing Modifiers the mysterious fourth way

A fourth way to access Modification parameters does exist — although this method works best if you've been twiddling with 3ds max regularly for about a year or so, long enough to use some of its features more than others. This access is supplied by what are called *keyboard hot-keys*. Hot-keys are user-configured multiple keyboard keys that instantly apply a process or command to a selected item in the 3D scene. Everything in 3ds max can respond to a hot-key stroke, but most users use a limited number of hot-keys because they are a strain to remember unless you use them all the time. Using hot-keys is also known as working in *professional mode* (to intimidate you), though to be honest, I know of no professionals who work with hot-keys alone with no menus or toolbars displayed. As shown in Figure 7-6, you can click any empty area in the Tab Panel or Main toolbar, and select Customize from the pop-up list. This opens the Customize User Interface window. Then click the Keyboard tab to configure hot-key combinations for any selected item on the 3ds max GUI. Click the Assign button when you're done.

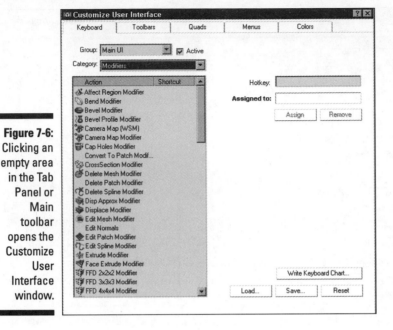

Figure 7-6:
Clicking an
empty area
in the Tab
Panel or
Main
toolbar
opens the
Customize
User
Interface
window.

Where Did 1 Put That Spheroid? Locating Lost Objects for Modification

If you have just a few items in your 3D scene, you won't have a problem selecting any one you want to work on or transform. But most interesting 3ds max scenes can be complex, and they may contain many dozens of diverse objects, some of which may be hiding behind other objects or even out of view (as shown in Figure 7-7). When this happens and you target a single object for modification or transformation, you have to know how to navigate to the right tools to help you do the job.

Labels

Your first option for locating any item in a scene is a simple one. Move your mouse pointer over the scene, and stop its movement (without clicking) where you thing your needed object may be. A small label appears, showing the name of the object your mouse pointer is over. If the label that appears is the item you are looking for, click to select the item at that point. This works in any viewport.

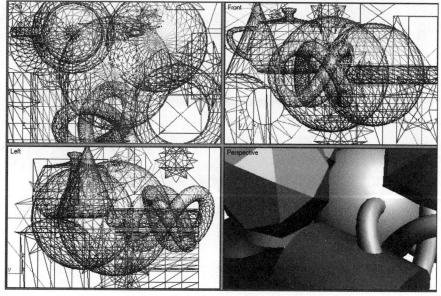

Figure 7-7:
Here's a nightmare of a scene. Not only do many objects intersect, some hide from view in any viewport.

Finding and selecting anything, anytime

Although you create content for any 3ds max scene, everything you add to the scene is posted in a list. You can access this list in one of two ways: by choosing Edit⇨Select By⇨Name, or by pressing the H key on your keyboard.

Sorry, you can't access the list by pressing Shift+H or capitalizing the H. Either of these actions brings up the Select Objects panel.

Absolutely every item in your scene — all models, lights, cameras, particle systems, and so on — is listed in this panel. You can sort the list alphabetically, by type, color, or size. You can uncheck any items in the *List Types* area to hide those items in the list. Items in the list are selected by a click. If you hold down the Shift key and select one item in the list and a following item, all the in-between items are selected as well. For non-contiguous selections, just hold down the Control key and click the multiple items you want to select. When you're finished, just click the Select button to select the item(s) in all viewports. Note that all similar items are numbered in the list.

Playing hide-and-seek

Sometimes just locating and selecting one item from the multitude is still not enough. When you want to modify that object's geometry, for instance (a process that may require a number of in-viewport mouse actions), other objects may still be blocking your view, and you may continuously be selecting them by mistake with the mouse pointer as the modification process commences. When that happens, it's time to play a little hide-and-seek. Here's how:

1. **Select the object by its Label, or through the Select Objects panel (shown in Figure 7-8).**

2. **Click the Display icon at the top of the Command Panel.**

   The icon looks like a TV screen, four icons to the right of the Create icon. The selected item's Display properties open.

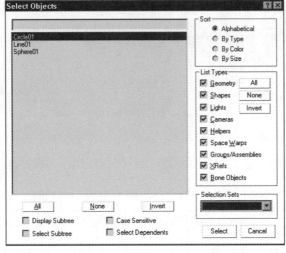

Figure 7-8:
The selected item's Display properties look like this when they open.

3. **Click the Hide button to reveal some options.**

4. **Click Hide Unselected to make everything in all viewports invisible except for your selected item.**

   Now you can work on that item by itself, with no fear of selecting another item.

5. **When you are finished working on your chosen item, return to the Display options in the Command Panel and click Unhide All.**

   Everything in all viewports becomes visible again.

6. **Repeat this process as needed to work on other items in the scene.**

Subsequent chapters in this part of the book investigate how powerful Modifiers can be in the creation of unique 3D models. You can use dozens of Modifiers in 3ds max, with dozens more available as plug-in add-ons from other developers. If you get familiar with the Modifiers covered in this book, you'll have no problem taking on any new ones that interest you, and mastering their use quickly.

Chapter 8

Creating Duplicated Objects

*B*y now, most people are familiar with the term *cloning*. Images of sheep and goats come to mind readily. Cloning a life form means to create a genetic copy that's virtually identical to the original. *Higher* life forms (as we humans confidently call ourselves) present more complications if we want to clone exact duplicates.

Fortunately, cloning 3D objects in 3ds max is far less complicated than (say) cloning Elvis in a laboratory. Cloning is a technique common to all 3D software, though each piece of software has different ways of going about it. (The cloning operations in 3ds max are extremely user-friendly.) But why use cloning anyway?

Well, cloning saves time that would best be used in other creative pursuits. Suppose that you wanted to create a flock of birds, perhaps 20 of them. You could model one, set it aside, model another, and so on. That would work, but it would also drain your energy and become pretty boring after about the second one. Wouldn't it be far easier to create the original, and then simply clone the other 19? Definitely.

Cloning Your Own Sheep

3ds max offers you several different ways to clone a selected object, each with its own purpose. In the strictest sense, you aren't really modifying an object when you clone it — you're just modifying the space that the object occupies in a scene. (Hmmm. Wonder what Einstein would say about that.)

Keyboard entry creations

I call this the *look-Ma-no-hands* cloning method. That's because you don't have to do any manual operations in a viewport to pull it off. This is a quick way to duplicate objects while maintaining some control over their position and geometry in space at the same time. This method is also a precursor to *arrays*, which are covered later in this chapter, and is more of a duplication rather than a cloning process. I am going to use the Standard Primitives Teapot as an example. Here's how it's done:

1. **Make sure the Top Viewport is active so objects are created from this orientation.**

2. **Choose Create⇨Geometry⇨Standard Primitives⇨Teapot.**

   Don't create anything manually in any viewport.

3. **Under the Parameters heading in the Command Panel, click Spout and Lid to uncheck them.**

   Doing so ensures that you create a cup instead of a teapot.

4. **Click the Keyboard Entry bar to open the Keyboard Entry parameters.**

   The Keyboard Entry parameters (data similar to what you see in Figure 8-1) appear in a panel on-screen.

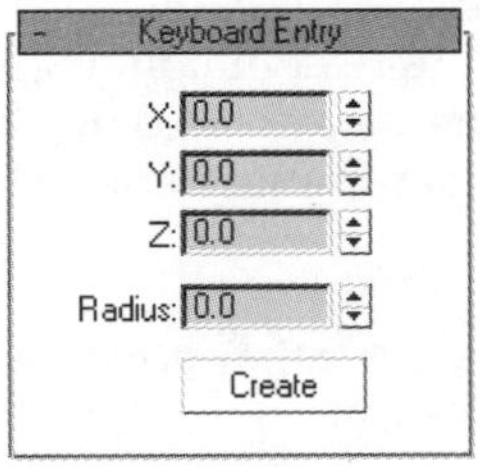

Figure 8-1:
The Keyboard Entry panel.

Keyboard Entry
X: 0.0
Y: 0.0
Z: 0.0
Radius: 0.0
Create

5. **Delete the data in the Radius area and input the value 12.**

   Doing so determines the size of the teapot object. The XYZ values determine the object's position in 3D space.

6. **Click the Create button to place your object in the scene at XYZ position 0-0-0.**

   A cup appears, as shown in Figure 8-2.

What if you are throwing a tea party, and you invite a group of folks of different sizes. Wouldn't it be interesting if you could provide each guest with a cup scaled to fit his or her size? Maybe not, but pretend.

7. **Back in the Command Panel, change the Radius value under Keyboard Entry to 8 to create a cup for that special smaller friend. Enter 20 in the X position value, so your new cup isn't created inside the first one. Click Create.**

   Now your scene has two different-size cups, as shown in Figure 8-3.

Figure 8-3:
Two cups
appear in
the scene.

8. **To add a teapot to this scene, first click in a viewport to make sure the present objects remain as they are.**

9. **With the Teapot Primitive still selected, check the Spout and Lid items again.**

10. **Use the Create function in Keyboard Entry to create the teapot.**

    Make sure you alter the X and Y position values so the teapot does not overlap the other objects (if it does, you can move it). Figure 8-4 shows the teapot safely added with nary a spill.

Figure 8-4:
The teapot
is added to
the scene.

Your mission, should you choose to accept it, is to repeat similar operations on other Standard and Extended Primitives, creating multiple object scenes.

Copy cloning

Ahhh — now we get to do some real cloning. 3ds max makes cloning so easy, you won't even have to memorize the selected object's genetic code.

1. **Select any object in your scene in any viewport.**
2. **Click the Select and Move tool in the Main Toolbar.**
3. **Hold the Shift key down while you click and drag over the object.**

   The Clone Options panel appears.
4. **Click OK to accept the defaults.**

   A perfect clone of your object appears in the scene.

If you want to create an army of clones in a hurry, the Number of Copies parameter in the Clone Options Panel is the slickest way to do it. By default, this is set to 1, which creates (yep) one cloned copy of the selected object. As you might guess, setting this value to any other positive whole number gives you that many clones. The neat thing is, the cloned objects all maintain the same distance from each other as the distance between the original object and its first clone.

Using instancing

Oh, no! Not another term to remember! Breathe deep and relax. This won't hurt at all. The term *instancing* denotes a special type of cloning, different from Copy cloning, though both use the same process. So what is instancing?

Think of it this way. Suppose that someone creates a clone of you, but the clone really doesn't have complete control over its own actions. Instead, the clone follows your every action and modification. If you cut your finger, a cut appears on the clone's finger. If you suddenly develop a pointy head, your clone's head does the same thing. If your clone develops a pointy head, your head goes through the same process. Instancing ties the cloned objects to the original object.

Referencing is a separate type of instancing. With Reference switched on in the Clone Options panel instead of Instancing, the relationship between the original object and its clones is a bit more complex. Whatever happens to the original object in terms of modifications happens to all the clones as well. But each of the clones also keeps a kind of independence. Any modifications applied to a referenced clone can affect only that clone, and no other object, not even the original. See Figure 8-5.

Figure 8-5:
Instancing
and
Referencing
are set in
the Clone
Options
panel under
Object.

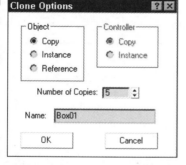

 Because the purpose of cloning is to create multiple objects quickly, 3ds max makes it easy to do. Whether via the Copy, Instance, or Reference processes, cloning works with any of the three Transformation tools: Move, Rotate, and Scale. You can Move Clone, Rotate Clone, and Scale Clone to create multiple objects.

Lord of the Ring Arrays: Creating and Controlling Arrays

An *array* is commonly defined as two or more similar objects arranged in 3D space. When you create a cloned line of objects, you are in essence creating an array. But cloning has its limitations. For instance (no pun intended), cloning an object is not the right approach if you're in a hurry to create identical objects in all three spatial directions at the same time. Cloning is also not suitable if you want to create rotated duplicates in different sizes or positions as the sequence of objects progresses. For these and similar modeling needs, you need another process: creating a 3D array.

Place a sphere in the scene and choose Tools➪Array in the menu bar. This brings up the Array panel, as shown in Figure 8-6.

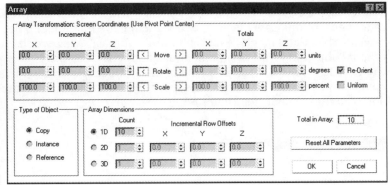

The following sections describe each parameter option.

Incremental/Totals

The Incremental and Totals values are interchangeable. You can alter either row of values under either heading. To see what the Incremental values look like as Totals, just click the right-pointing arrow between them. To enter values under Totals, just click the left-pointing arrow between them to see what the Incremental values look like.

- **Move:** This value represents the XYZ distance that each clone moves, compared to the first clone's distance from the original object.

- **Rotate:** This value determines how each clone will rotate, compared to its neighbor in the chain of clones.

- **Scale:** This value determines how much larger or smaller each clone is in comparison to its neighbor in the cloned chain, on any XYZ axis combination.

Type of Object

The Type of Object can be a Copy, Instance, or Reference, the same three types used to define an ordinary cloned object.

Array Dimensions

Count and Incremental Row Offsets values are listed under the Array Dimensions. A 1D array is basically the same as a cloned line of objects. It takes its position, degree of rotation, and relative scale from the Incremental/ Totals input values — and the number of objects equaling the 1D Count value. A 2D array multiplies the number of 1D arrays by its Count value. A 3D array multiplies the 1D × 2D × 3D Counts together. As you can imagine, this process can get complex.

Array functions in other 3D software tend to be easier to understand than they are in 3ds max. Although the Array function in 3ds max is not at all intuitive, it becomes somewhat easier to understand after you mess around with the values for a while. In practical terms, not-playing-with-the-program is "not an option." To get the hang of how the Array values create object clones, you absolutely have to spend some time playing with different objects and different Array values.

Take a look at Figures 8-7 through 8-10. They include both some values in the Array panel, and how those values act on an object (a teapot in this case) to create an Array.

Figure 8-7: To make five teapots appear along the X-axis, you need only an X incremental value, a 1D array dimension, and an object count of 5.

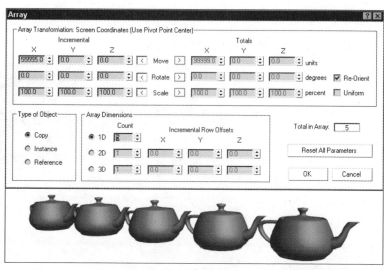

Figure 8-8:
Changing
the Array
values to 2D
with an
offset in the
Z-axis with
a count of
5 for 2D
creates
$1D \times 2D$
objects —
25 teapots in
5 rows and
5 columns.

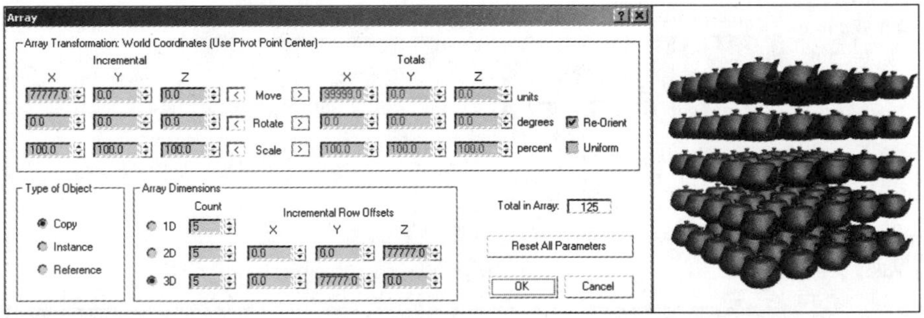

Figure 8-9:
Checking
the 3D array
with a value
of 5 creates
$1D \times 2D \times$
3D objects,
or $5 \times$
$5 \times 5 = 125$
teapots.
Using a Y
value in the
3D array
row makes
the total
array three-
dimensional,
like a
Rubik's
Cube made
of teapots.

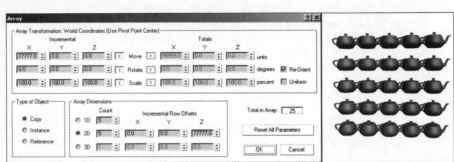

Remember to try the Array function with different values and objects to get a better idea of what it can help you create.

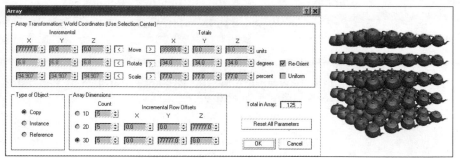

Figure 8-10:
Adding
Scale and
Rotation
values
to the
Incremental
or Totals
parameter
creates
a less
mechanical
array.

Cloning Arrays

Each cloned object in an array is a separate object. To perform a cloning operation on the entire array forces you to transform the separate objects in the array into a single object first. One way to do that is by Boolean Union (described in Chapter 6). Try this:

1. **Place a sphere in a scene from the Top Viewport with a radius of 20.**

2. **Create an array with the values displayed in Figure 8-11.**

   Take a look at your viewports. You should have an array of four spheres, descending in size.

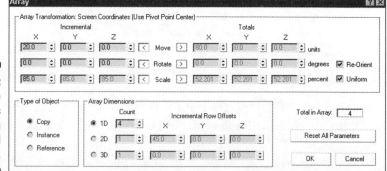

Figure 8-11:
The
parameters
for setting
up the initial
array.

3. **Select the first sphere and then choose Create⇨Geometry⇨Compound Objects.**

   Make sure that Union is your Operator.

4. **Click Pick Operand B, and then click the second sphere in a viewport.**

   You have created one object from the two spheres.

5. **Click an empty space in the viewport, and then click your two-sphere object.**

   A new, third sphere appears where you clicked.

6. **Link the new sphere to your two-sphere object by repeating the Boolean Union procedure.**

   This time make the third sphere your choice for Operand B.

7. **Click the Modify Command Panel icon; click the Create Command Panel icon; then repeat Steps 5 and 6.**

   Doing so creates a fourth sphere and joins it to the single object. Now the four spheres are a single object, no longer an array of separate objects. If you use Move, Rotate, or Scale on this object, you see the mass of spheres change, but not the individual spheres.

8. **Choose Hierarchy⇨Affect Pivot Point Only, and move the Pivot Point to the edge of the largest sphere in the Front Viewport.**

   Figure 8-12 shows the result.

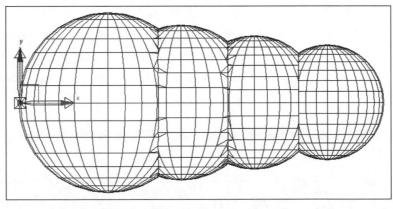

Figure 8-12:
Move the
Pivot Point
to this
position in
the Front
Viewport.

9. **Select the Top Viewport. Deselect Affect Pivot Point by clicking it.**

10. **With the object still selected, hold down the Shift key and use the Rotate tool over the Pivot Point.**

11. **Rotate the object on its Z-axis to what appears to be 90 degrees, or a perpendicular axis to the original form.**

The Z Value box just below the viewports indicates when you've reached the 90-degree value. When you've completed the rotation, the Clone Options panel appears.

12. **In the Clone Options panel, input a value of 3 clones.**

You create an object like the one shown in Figure 8-13.

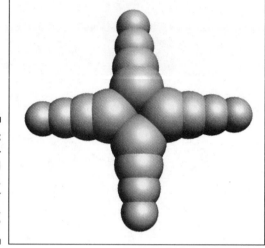

Figure 8-13:
At last —
the cloned
object.
Rubber
starfish,
anyone?

Be sure to set aside a fairly substantial amount of 3ds max playtime to try out these same methods on various objects.

Chapter 9

Making Mirrored Objects

M irrors are one way the real world mimics the world of fantasy. As in Lewis Carroll's *Alice Through the Looking Glass,* the mirror image of an object exactly reverses the visible features of the object — right is left and left is right. Take, for instance, your head — two nearly symmetrical eyes, two nearly symmetrical ears, and two nearly symmetrical nostrils. In each pair of features, the parts are about the same distance from an imaginary vertical dividing line at the horizontal center of your head. Normally, when you look in a mirror, your features are reversed (your left eye appears to be where your right eye should be, and so on) — no surprise there. But if you set the edge of a small, rectangular mirror on a full-face snapshot and turn the mirror perpendicular to the photo (so it divides the face vertically), what you see is a perfectly symmetrical face. Making a mirrored object in 3ds max produces a similar result — but it's really another cloning operation.

Such *mirror cloning* works because many real-world objects — dinner plates, bass fiddles, airplanes — are symmetrical (or nearly so) from front to back and when viewed from below or above. Using such an object's symmetrical features, you can sculpt half the model and then use mirror cloning to get the other half — a real timesaver.

Adjusting the Pivot Point

Mirroring uses an object's *Pivot Point* (an imaginary point at the object's vertical and horizontal center) as a reference. The Pivot Point is the center of gravity around which all actions take place. To change the view of any 3D object in 3ds max, you can adjust (move and/or rotate) the object's Pivot Point. A quick review of this process (for more details, see Chapter 4) is a good way to get into mirror cloning.

If you look at any object as it appears in any viewport, the Pivot Point of the object is not visible (well, of course not — it's imaginary). To make the Pivot Point visible — yes, you can do that — select the object and click the Hierarchy tab in the Command Panel. The rollout that appears includes the Affect Pivot Only command. Clicking that option makes the Pivot Point appear in the viewports. Clicking this same command again makes the Pivot Point invisible again, as shown in Figure 9-1.

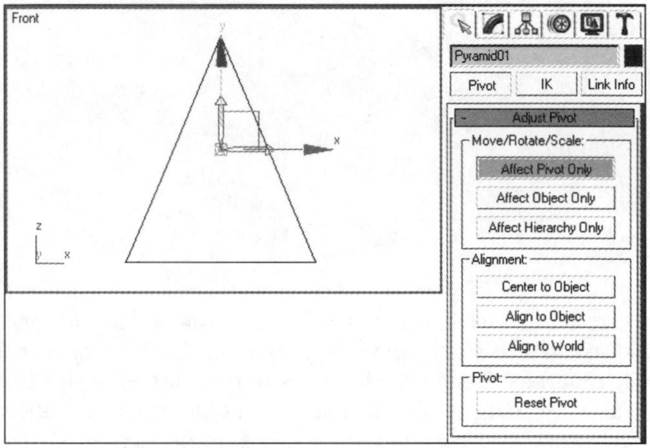

Figure 9-1:
Clicking
Affect Pivot
Only makes
the selected
object's
Pivot Point
visible in the
viewports.

By default, an object's Pivot Point is located at the center of the object's 3D volume. When it is visible however, you can use the Transform/Move or Rotate tools to reposition and/or rotate it, as shown in Figure 9-2.

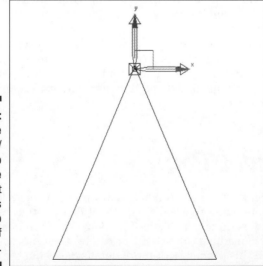

Figure 9-2:
Using the
Transform/
Move tool to
move the
Pivot Point
of this
pyramid to
the apex of
the object.

Before you engage in any mirroring operation, make sure that the selected object's Pivot Point is where you want it to be.

Mirroring without Cloning

When Alice transits through the looking glass, she becomes her reflection — her entire body *switches its axial symmetry,* making her left foot her right foot and so on. Sometimes you may want a selected 3D object to switch its axial symmetry in the same way (for example, if you want to create an identical model of a car with the steering wheel on the opposite side). If this happens, you'll need to employ a mirroring operation.

Activating mirroring

Mirroring an object either flips the object in reverse on a selected axis, or performs the same operation on a duplicate (clone) of the object. The mirroring operation is activated from choices you make in the Mirror: Screen Coordinates panel. You can get to this panel from either of two places: the Tools⇨Mirror selection in the menu bar or the Mirror tool in the Main Toolbar.

 Either alternative brings up the Mirror: Screen Coordinates panel shown in Figure 9-3.

If you want to mirror a single object without cloning it, you simply leave the No Clone option selected.

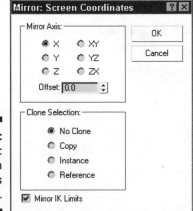

Figure 9-3:
The Mirror:
Screen
Coordinates
panel.

Determining axis and offset variance

The area under Mirror Axis in the panel shown in Figure 9-3 contains options for you to determine the *axis variance* — the selected axis on which the mirroring takes place. Offset variance is determined by the value in the box next to Offset. This value is in viewport units, so you always have to experiment a little to set the correct amount. The neat thing is that your settings are immediately reflected in the viewports, so you can make adjustments before clicking OK.

Axis variance

You can use any object/model you prefer, primitive or imported, to explore mirroring operations. In this case, I have selected the Standard Primitives Pyramid. I left the pyramid's Pivot Point at its default. In this case, the only way to illustrate the mirroring without doing any cloning is to set mirroring to the Z (vertical) axis. For working on objects without cloning, you can leave the Offset value set to 0, as shown in Figure 9-4.

Offset variances for non-cloned mirrored objects

Using Offset Values other than the default of 0 when no cloning is involved is a waste of time in most cases; all it does is move the object by that amount in relation to the position of the source object. It's better to move the object after mirroring by using the Move tool.

Figure 9-4:
Flipping the pyramid upside down after mirroring on the Z-axis. At left: The original orientation. At right: the mirrored result.

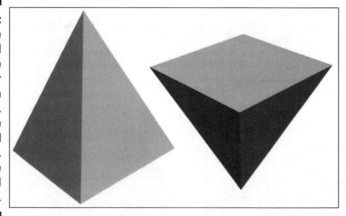

Finding Your Twin

Although you can perform mirroring on non-cloned objects, it's far more common to do when cloned objects are involved. Why? Because the mirroring operation was designed to solve the problem of creating opposite symmetries.

Mirrored cloning options

Three options affect how a mirrored clone relates to the source object: the position and rotation of the source object's Pivot Point, what Mirror Axis is selected, and what the Offset Value is. By themselves and in combination, adjusting these three options leads to differing results.

Pivot Point options and mirrored clones

Mirrored cloning uses the placement and angle of the Pivot Point as a reference to create the cloned object. Standard cloning does the same thing, without mirroring the cloned object. Here are a couple of examples.

✔ **Pivot Point Position:** Place one of the Standard or Extended Primitives in a scene. Leave its Pivot Point at its default position (the center of the object). Create a mirrored clone of the object on the X-axis, with Offset set to 25, as shown in Figure 9-5.

Now repeat the previous example — this time moving the Pivot Point about 25 units outside the object first. With the same Offset of 25, the result is quite different, as shown in Figure 9-6. That's because the operation is based on the position of the object's Pivot Point, not on that of the object itself.

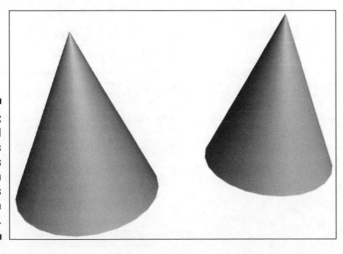

Figure 9-5:
A mirrored clone of this cone was created on the X-axis with an Offset of 25.

Figure 9-6:
Placing a
mirrored
clone
farther from
the source
object
(using the
same values
as in the
previous
example) by
moving the
Pivot Point.

✔ **Pivot Point Rotation:** After placing an object in the scene, use the
Rotation tool to rotate the Pivot Point to a new orientation. Mirror
cloning references the XYZ angle of the Pivot Point in the creation of mirrored clones. On the Main Toolbar, you will see a box with the word *View*
in it. This is the *Reference Coordinate System* selection, which is set to
View as a default. Click this area to bring up a list of options; move down
the list and select Local. The Reference Coordinate System is now set to
Local. Create mirrored clones on the X-axis with alternate Offset values,
and with the Pivot Point set to different rotations, as shown in Figure 9-7.

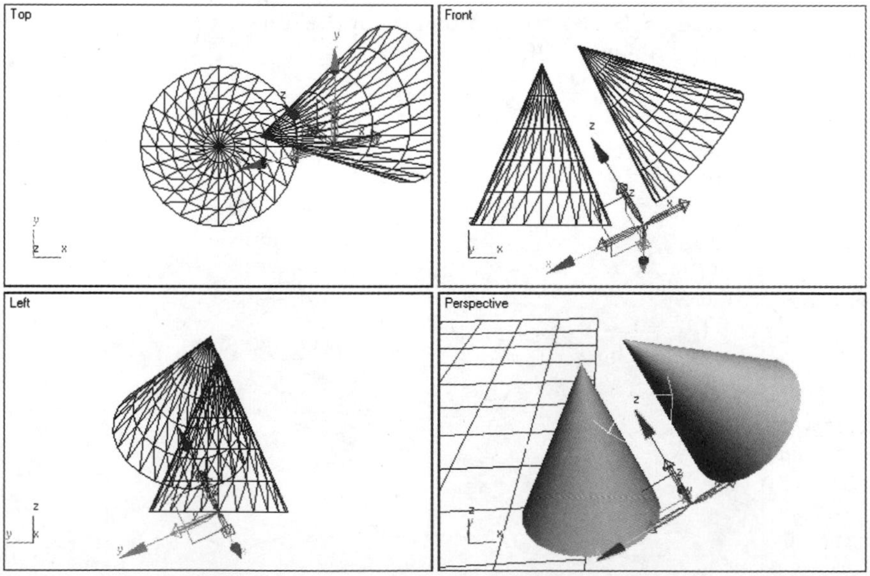

Figure 9-7:
With the
Local
Reference
Coordinate
System set,
the mirrored
clone
references
the new
angle of the
Pivot Point's
axis.

To return the Pivot Point to its default location and rotation, simply click the Reset Pivot command in the Hierarchy Command Panel.

Axis options and clones

When you access the Mirror function, the Mirror: Local Coordinates panel appears. The Axis options are listed under Mirror Axis in this panel, shown in Figure 9-8.

Figure 9-8:
The Mirror
Axis
options.

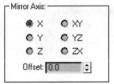

Selecting any one of these options — whether from the singular-axis references on the left or the double-axis references on the right — determines the axis used for the mirrored-clone operation.

Before you settle on a final orientation for the clone, try out some options to get a better idea of exactly how they orient the mirrored clone.

Offset options and clones

The Offset value is entered into Offset area, as displayed in Figure 9-8. This value can be a negative or positive number, and can be a decimal value as well. Greater values (negative or positive) will move the mirrored clone farther away from the source object on the selected axis or axis pair. Lesser values (negative or positive) will move the mirrored object closer to the source object, with a setting of 0.0 forcing the mirrored clone's Pivot Point to be positioned exactly on top of the source object's Pivot Point. You can use an Offset value instead of repositioning a Pivot Point to control the position of the mirrored clone.

Creating wings — whether animal or mechanical — is a common challenge best met with mirroring in 3ds max. I suggest working in the Top Viewport. It's also a good idea to center the Pivot Point of a wing (whether it's for a 747 or a pterodactyl) on the body of the model you're creating. This way, the pair of wings maintains a proper distance relative to the body of the object. Use the model provided, or a wing of your own design, to master the art of creating wings with the Mirror function; Figure 9-9 shows an example.

Figure 9-9:
The Mirror tool makes creating a pair of wings a snap. You can also use the Symmetry Modifier in max when you need to create a mirrored clone of a model that represents half of a character's form.

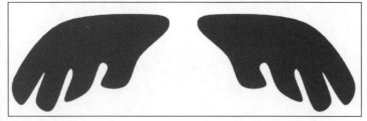

Chapter 10

3D from 2D

● ●

● ●

Chapter 5 details the creation of 2D shapes *(splines)*. A 2D shape is not really an object, though it's part of the way to an object. Without some manipulation, a 2D shape will not render, and it won't accept any textures. This chapter covers three ways that a 2D shape can be modified into a true 3D object, a form that occupies XYZ space, and that can be set to receive textures like any other 3D object in a scene. These three methods are Visibility Rendering, Extrusion, and Lathing.

Making 2D Shapes Visible: The Rendering Method

To turn a spline into a 3D object, you must first make it visible by adjusting some settings in the Command Panel. Choose Create⇨Shapes⇨Splines and select Circle. Before doing anything in a viewport, notice that the parameters of the circle appear in the Command Panel. Click Rendering to bring up the Rendering Command Rollout, as shown in Figure 10-1.

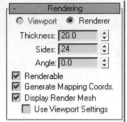

Figure 10-1:
The
Rendering
commands
in the
Command
Panel for all
splines.

Notice that Figure 10-1 shows Renderable, Generate Mapping Coordinates, and Display Render Mesh as checked. Also, the Thickness value adds an observable thickness to the selected spline — and the higher the Sides value, the smoother the object. You can use these values as defaults when transforming a spline into a 3D object. Try different thickness values to create a wide variety of 3D objects based on splines of different shapes. This greatly expands your ability to create unique 3D objects quickly.

The changes you make under the Rendering Commands will remain for all future splined objects until you alter them.

Now you can select any splined object and create it in any viewport. It no longer looks like a linear splined construct, but resembles a true 3D object with an observable polygon mesh. You can alter the Thickness value at any point to create thicker or thinner object meshes.

The Renderable 3D Helical Spline

Sounds like a good title for a fairy tale, doesn't it? ("Once upon a time there was a small village of splines that wanted to be rendered. . . .") The Helix is a unique spline in 3ds max because it exists in 3D rather than 2D space. Rendering a helical spline with a suitable thickness value (a value best for you to explore) is one of the best ways to create springlike 3D objects, as shown in Figure 10-2.

To explore the creation of diverse helical springs, use different values for the number of turns, try out different Renderable Thicknesses, and imagine how big the pogo stick would have to be for each one (well, okay, that last one's optional).

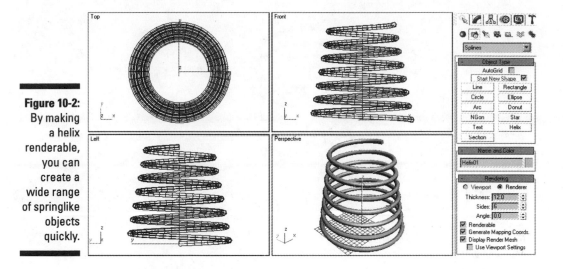

Figure 10-2:
By making a helix renderable, you can create a wide range of springlike objects quickly.

Cloning Splines

Any spline can be cloned, regardless of whether it is renderable. The same cloning rules apply to a 2D spline as to a 3D object. A spline has a Pivot Point that can be moved and/or rotated as a reference for the cloning process. Shift/moving a selected spline will initiate the cloning operation, just as with a 3D object, by bringing up the familiar Clone Options or Mirror: World Coordinates panels. Figure 10-3 shows one example.

In Figure 10-3 the Pivot Point was moved to the very top end of the coils; then a mirrored clone was created on the XY axis. Notice how the two helical springs mirror each other; the coils twist in opposite directions.

Although you may want to clone some nonrenderable splines in a scene as you create a series of 2D shapes, you're likely to have more fun tinkering up complex 3D objects by cloning renderable splines. The basic secret of this technique is to pay attention to the position and rotation of the Pivot Point *first*.

Figure 10-3:
Here is an
interesting
object that
began as a
renderable
helix.

Extruding 2D Shapes

In 3ds max, *extrusion* — in effect, pulling one shape out of another — is one of the three most common ways to create a 3D object from a 2D shape or spline. (Another is lathing, which I cover in the next section.) Extrusion involves dragging a 2D shape along a line perpendicular to the plane of the 2D shape. Imagine a circle. Now envision a line of a fixed length, starting at the center of the circle and perpendicular to the plane of the circle. Extruding the circle along that line would create a cylinder. In effect, a cylinder is an extruded circle; in this case, the perpendicular line is the *axis of extrusion*. (In some cases it's called a path, but that's another story.)

Most extrusions take place with the Pivot Point of the shape left at its default position. The Extrude operation is activated by selecting either Modifiers⇨ Mesh Editing⇨Extrude from the Main Menu, or by clicking the Extrude tool in the *Extrude* Modifier under the Modeling tab on the Tab Panel.

 Using either method will trigger the Extrude Parameters rollout in the Modify Command Panel, as shown in Figure 10-4.

The most important choices in this rollout are the Amount value, and whether Cap Start/Cap End are checked. The Amount value determines the height of the extruded object. Checking Cap Start or Cap End determines whether the object has a capped surface on either or both ends. The rest of the parameters can be left at their defaults until you get comfortable with these options.

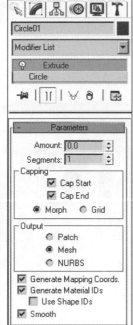

Figure 10-4:
The Extrude
Parameters
rollout in the
Modify
Command
Panel.

If you extrude a renderable spline, extrusion removes the rendered thickness. This also holds true if you Lathe a spline that has been set to renderable.

Extruding open shapes

Extruded open shapes can be used as walls or ribbons in a 3D scene. Do the following to explore the creation of an open 2D shape or spline:

1. **Choose Create⇨Shapes⇨Splines⇨Line in the Command Panel.**

2. **Create a wavy line in the Top Viewport. Do not close the shape.**

3. **Click the Extrude tool in the Modeling Tab of the Tab Panel.**

   The Extrusion Parameters appear in the Modifiers section of the Command Panel.

4. **In the Command Panel, input a value of 25 for the Amount.**

   The Cap Start and Cap End choices aren't available for open shapes. You should immediately see a ribbonlike 3D object appear in your viewports.

To get a good working sense of this operation, create a variety of open spline shapes and extrude them with different Amount values, as shown in Figure 10-5.

Figure 10-5:
A variety of
open-spline
extruded
shapes.

Extruding closed shapes

Most of the 2D splines you will transform into 3D objects by extrusion will be closed shapes. Extruding a closed spline creates a 3D object that appears to have volume. You can also create capped ends on a closed extruded spline. Try the following:

1. **Choose Create⇨Shapes⇨Splines⇨Circle and create a circle in the Top Viewport.**

   Make sure Renderable is switched off.

2. **Click the Extrude Modifier in the Modeling Tab Panel.**

3. **Set the Amount of the Extrusion to 75 in the Command Panel.**

4. **Check Patch instead of Mesh to generate a different polygon arrangement.**

   Try this operation with Cap Start and Cap End on and off; you can see the results in the Perspective Viewport, as shown in Figure 10-6.

Repeat the previous set of steps, this time with 2D text. Extrusion creates awesome 3D text objects. Create a variety of 2D shapes and extrude then to create different objects.

Extruding helical ribbons

Extruding the helix shape creates a spiraling ribbonlike object. Cap Start/Cap End settings make no difference to the helix; it's an open shape. The Amount value determines the thickness of the ribbon, as shown in Figure 10-7.

Figure 10-6:
Left: Cap Start/Cap End are both switched on. Center: Cap End is switched off. Right: Cap Start and Cap End are both switched off.

Figure 10-7:
Compare this extruded helix object with the renderable helix object shown in Figure 10-2.

Spinning 'til You're Dizzy

If you've ever visited a woodworker's shop, you've seen a lathe — the machine that spins a piece of wood so it can be smoothed and symmetrically carved while spinning. 3ds max provides a virtual equivalent: the Lathe function.

Lathing a 2D spline (whether open or closed) creates 3D objects known as *objects of revolution* (and no, it has nothing to do with radical politics). The three most important parameters in the creation of a lathed object are the placement of the 2D spline's Pivot Point, the reference axis, and the degrees of revolution value. The Lathe function can be accessed from the Main menu (choose Modifiers⇨Patch/Spline Editing⇨Lathe) or by clicking the Lathe icon in the Tabs Panel under the Modeling tab.

 Accessing the Lathe function reveals its settings in the Modify Command Panel, as shown in Figure 10-8.

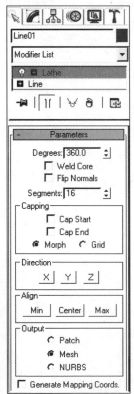

Figure 10-8:
The Lathe settings in the Modify Command Panel.

Lathing open shapes

This is how to proceed when using the lathing operation to create a 3D object from an open shape:

1. **Choose Create⇨Shapes⇨Splines, and select the Line tool.**

2. **Create an open shape in the Front Viewport.**

3. **Move the Pivot Point to the last point clicked on the shape.**

   Figure 10-9 shows an example. Note that the upward-pointing axis on the Pivot Point is the Y-axis when you work in the Top, Left, or Front Viewport while using the VIEW coordinate system. This will be the axis of rotation.

4. **With the shape still selected, access the Lathe operator.**

   The lathe settings appear in the Command Panel.

5. **Enter the following values: Degrees = 360, Segments = 32, and a Direction of Y (which sets the axis of revolution as the Y-axis).**

   A 3D object appears in your viewport — a lathed form that uses your line source as its axis.

One of the most common lathed objects that all beginning 3D artists create is a wineglass. To create the initial spline shape for a lathed wineglass, create the form displayed in Figure 10-10, paying attention to the position of the Pivot Point.

When lathed, the 3D wineglass is shown in Figure 10-11.

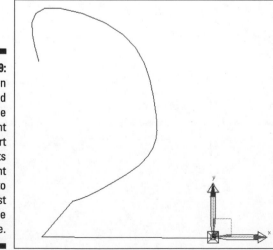

Figure 10-9:
An open splined shape in the Front Viewport with its Pivot Point moved to the last point of the shape.

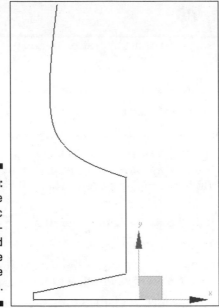

Figure 10-10:
This is the
basic
wineglass-
shaped
open spline
that will be
lathed.

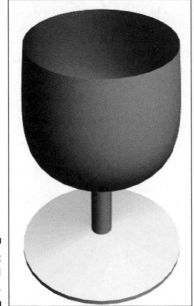

Figure 10-11:
The lathed
wineglass.

This wine glass, however, has a problem: its sides have a width of 0 (based on the spline used to create the lathed object). A better solution to the wine-glass lathe is shown in Figure 10-12.

Figure 10-12:
A more useful wineglass-lathing spline is displayed on the left, with the resulting 3D object on the right.

Lathing closed shapes

In the creation of 3D objects of revolution, open spline shapes are more commonly subjected to lathing than are closed shapes. That's because lathed objects created from closed shapes take up more memory when stored. But what the heck. Try lathing some closed shapes anyway; lathing produces interesting results.

Lathed cut-aways

If you cut a slice of bread from a new loaf, the end of the bread will show a cross-section of the loaf. Another more common name for this cross-section is a *cut-away*. If you set the Degrees to less than 360 in the Lathe Command Panel, you will wind up creating a cut-away view of the lathed 3D object. The most common cut-away degree value is 180; in effect, that value cuts the 3D object in half, exposing its insides.

Compound lathes

You can even lathe more than one shape at a time without even breaking a sweat. First, select all the objects you've created with the Select-and-Move tool (just click and drag a marquee around them). When they're all selected, adjust the position of the Pivot Point so it lies outside all the objects (that is, to the left or right of them); then Lathe. This process creates a series of concentric rings, as shown in Figure 10-13.

Lathing serves to create a wide range of 3D objects. Be sure to put the 3ds max lathing feature through its paces whenever you have some time.

Figure 10-13:
This object was created in one step by lathing a number of closed shapes at the same time.

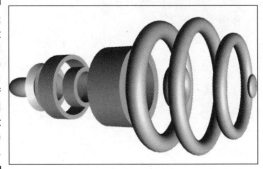

Chapter 11

Getting Hitched: Grouping Objects

• •

In This Chapter

▶ Creating Grouped objects

▶ Linking objects

▶ Generating Attached objects

• •

*I*f you are a member of a group (an organization, an ensemble, a tribe, a family), you realize that certain circumstances demand that you surrender a degree of your freedom and individuality for the sake of the whole. As Mr. Spock said in one of the *Star Trek* movies, "the needs of the many outweigh the needs of the one." Certain actions of the group pull you along with it. On the other hand, there are some types of groups that allow you to maintain your own personality, to a lesser or greater degree. In 3ds max, selected objects can participate in several grouping alternatives — each defined by the freedom (or lack of it) given to single members of the group.

In Chapter 6, I detail the method of combining multiple objects into a single object through Boolean Union. Several other ways exist for reinforcing a bond between objects in a 3ds max scene. Knowing which process to use plays a big part in creating objects that do what you want them to do.

Using Grouping and Ungrouping

The Group function in 3ds max attaches all selected members so they form one unit — in effect, one object. When you gather objects together by using the Group function, they lose the freedom to be treated as individual objects. This situation may seem undemocratic, but in this case, there's an advantage: The numerous selected items within the group can be gathered into one unified object — functioning like one model with multicolored parts. All grouping options are contained and accessed in the Group menu on the menu bar. The options include: Group/Ungroup, Open/Close, Attach/Detach, and Explode. (Group is the only option available before a Group is actually created.) To create a group, follow these steps:

1. **In any viewport, use the Select/Move tool to click and drag a marquee around all items you want in the group.**

   Release the mouse button when all items are selected. If you missed an item, simply hold down the Shift key while you click it.

2. **Click the Group menu and choose Group.**

   The Group Panel appears.

3. **Type a name your new group, click OK, and then press H.**

   The Select Objects panel appears, listing your newly named group.

Grouping options

After you create a group, the other group options become available to you in the Group menu: Ungroup, Open/Close, Attach/Detach, and Explode. Because singular items in a group have lost the freedom to be treated as individual components, the options are used when you need to go into the named Group to manipulate separate items. I describe your options in the following sections.

Ungroup

If you select Ungroup while a group is selected, the group immediately reverts to its separate components. Ungroup is like an immediate divorce, giving each component of the group its original individuality again. Sometimes, for example, you may want to create a temporary group to move items *en masse* to another position or orientation in a scene, and then ungroup them after they get there so you can again manipulate them individually.

Open/Close

Using the Open/Close options, you can temporarily ungroup the connected items so you can select them and manipulate them individually. As you may imagine, Open is the command that opens the group so you can tweak its members; Close makes separate manipulation impossible again. This is like a tribe allowing one or more of its members to go through some needed transformations without having to disband the tribe to do it.

Attach/Detach

Using the Attach option is like adopting an object into a group: You select an item in the scene that is not connected to any group, choose Attach, and click the group. *Voilà* — the previously singular item is now in the group. To detach the new member of the group from the whole, the group has to be opened first, and the adopted item selected. Then you choose Detach to cast that item out into the cold. After that, you select an item in the Opened Group and then the Close option to return the group to its original membership.

Explode

The Explode option immediately destroys the Grouping function of all selected groups (though it leaves the formerly grouped objects intact). You can use it on one group or any selected number of groups in a scene, even nested groups.

Grouping rules

Here are a number of things to keep in mind when working with groups:

- No single member of a group may be made a member of another group unless or until it is removed from the original group first.

- You can connect two or more groups to create a higher group. To ungroup this higher group, you select the higher group and then ungroup, which gives you back the original groups. If you have to take this process further, you can use ungroup a second time to dismantle those groups into the individual items that make them up.

- Nesting allows one object to be a member of more than one group.

- You can use Edit➪UNDO to reverse an Ungroup or Explode action.

- A group has a single Pivot Point that you can move and rotate just as if the group were a single object.

- All modifications and transformations applied to the group use the group's single Pivot Point as their reference point.

Linked Hierarchies

Linking is a way of grouping objects so they form a hierarchical chain of *parent* and *child* members. Each member of the hierarchy has the freedom to move, rotate, and be scaled — but if you transform the chain that a member is linked to, you also transform the member's movement, rotation, and scaling. The linkage works much like that of the human arm. You can regard your arm as a whole unit or as a series of linked parts: Your shoulder is linked to your torso; your upper arm is linked to your shoulder. Your forearm is linked to your upper arm; each hand is linked to each forearm. The digits of your fingers are linked in a chain, and each of the finger chains is linked to your hand. You can move any one of your fingers without moving your hand, but when your hand moves, it takes your fingers along with it. Your hand is the parent of your fingers, and your fingers are the children of your hand. Thus, in 3ds max terms, your upper arm is the parent of your forearm, which is the parent of your hand.

In 3D character models, the central parent of a body is its mid-section, with all the other parts linked in a hierarchical chain of parent and child elements. To use an astronomical analogy, the sun is the parent of the earth, which is a child of the sun. The earth's moon is a child of the earth, and the earth is the parent of her moon. Sounds sort of mystical, doesn't it? But in 3ds max, it's sheer practicality: All members in a linked chain have separate degrees of freedom; they are (at the same time) controlled by their parent elements in the chain. Everything in a hierarchical, linked chain works together in harmony — even though the separate elements in the chain are *articulated* (given their own specific parameters of action).

Linking and unlinking objects

To activate the Link/Unlink functions, you select their icons in the Main Toolbar. If you click an object or group in any viewport, and then click the Link icon, you can then designate a parent for the object you've selected by clicking another object or group in the scene. You always Link to a parent, not to a child. Linked objects don't have to be next to each other — or within any specified distance — as long as they're in the same scene.

The most important thing to do before you create a hierarchical chain of linked elements is to move the Pivot Points of all the separate elements to where you want them! To avoid teeth-gnashing and miscellaneous woe, move the Pivot Points *before* you link the selected objects.

Think about that linked chain of shoulder-arm-hand again, and imagine you've created an on-screen model of a human being. If you want a realistic effect from the whole when you link the parts, they all have to rotate from the correct Pivot Point position. Thus the form of the object puts some restrictions on where you put the Pivot Point:

- ✔ The Pivot Point of the shoulder would be closer to the torso than to the elbow. The Pivot Points of the upper and lower arm would be at the top-center of each of these objects.

- ✔ The Pivot Point of the hand would be at the top-center of the hand.

- ✔ The finger joints would be treated accordingly, with the Pivot Point of each segment moved into position.

To unlink any member of the linked chain, click it to select it and then click the Unlink icon. This divorces the object from its parent object, though it does not separate the selected object's children objects from it.

You can use this process as a basis for creating the arm of a character or a mechanical contrivance. Do the following:

1. **Use Boolean Union to cement a sphere and a cylinder together in the Front Viewport, as shown in Figure 11-1.**

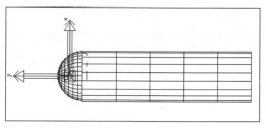

Move the Pivot Point to the position displayed. The resulting object serves as the upper arm.

2. **Copy Clone this object to create the lower arm, and then place it as indicated in Figure 11-2.**

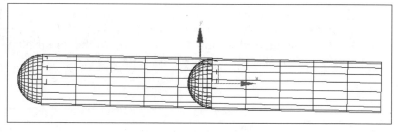

3. **Use cloning and scaling to create the hand, which is constructed from seven cloned and scaled parts, as displayed in Figure 11-3.**

4. **Move the hand and its fingers into position relative to the lower arm, as shown in Figure 11-4.**

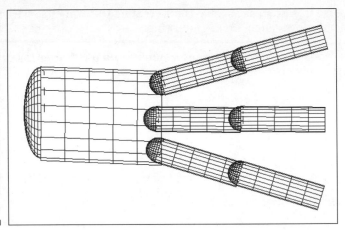

Figure 11-3:
Construct
the hand
from seven
separate
cloned and
scaled
parts, as
displayed
here.

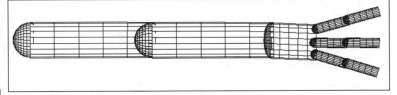

Figure 11-4:
Move the
hand and
fingers into
position.

5. Create the Links among the appropriate objects.

To do so, you select the tip of the finger, and link to the next finger segment. Repeat this for all three fingers. Link each of the three upper finger segments to the hand. Link the hand to the forearm and the forearm to the upper arm, as shown in Figure 11-5.

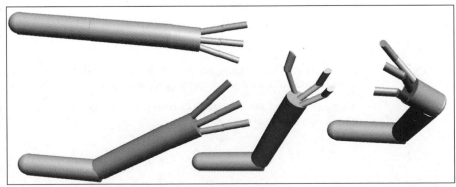

Figure 11-5:
When the
objects are
completely
linked, you
can rotate
the arm
parts to
create a
linked series
of arm
movements.

Forming Attachments

There is a vintage science fiction book written by Peter Lindsay called *Voyage to Arcturus*. In the story, the hero hugs other characters and completely absorbs them into his own body. In a sense, this is what you do when you perform a Boolean Union on objects, melding them together. There is another process that you can use in 3ds max to blend objects together, and it will allow you to get formally acquainted to a vital object modification alternative: the *Edit Mesh Modifier*.

The Edit Mesh Modifier

Okay, formal introductions first: "Edit Mesh Modifier, this is (insert your name here)." The Edit Mesh Modifier allows you to get down to the polygon level of a model to create modified forms. The quickest way to locate the Edit Mesh Modifier is to find its icon on the Tab Panel.

 Selecting this modification tool after selecting an object in any viewport will bring up the Edit Mesh Modifier Command Panel rollout. See Figure 11-6.

In this chapter, I cover just one of the options in the Edit Mesh Modifier. At different parts of the book, I return to other options offered here. Every possible operation in the Edit Mesh Modifier will not be covered in this book, but you will become familiar with many of the options. We are interested in the Attach option. The difference between using Attach in the Edit Mesh Modifier as compared to doing a Boolean Union is that standard Booleans work on entire objects, while functions in the Edit Mesh Modifier allow you to select parts of the object's polygon mesh. Place a sphere in a scene; it serves to illustrate the basic mesh-modification editing commands in the next section.

Mesh Editing Selections

Here's how to select parts of a model's polygon mesh:

1. **Place a model or object in a scene.**

   In this case, use a Standard Sphere Primitive.

2. **On the Main Toolbar, click and hold on the Selection Region option tool; then choose an option to use from the drop-down list.**

   Figure 11-7 shows what to look for.

Figure 11-6:
The
Command
Panel for
the Edit
Mesh
Modifier.

3. **With the object still selected, click the Edit Mesh Modifier icon in the Tab Panel under the Modeling Tab.**

4. **In the Command Panel for the Edit Mesh Modifier, select the quadrangular polygon icon under Selection to highlight it.**

Figure 11-8 shows what happens.

Figure 11-7:
Choose one
of the
Selection
Region
options. The
default
is the
Rectangular
option.

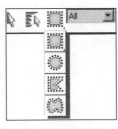

Figure 11-8:
Select the quadran-gular polygon icon under Selection in the Command Panel.

5. **Select part of the polygon mesh by clicking and dragging over your object in any viewport.**

   The selected polygons change color.

6. **Just to prove that you have selected just a part of the sphere's polygon mesh, click the Hide button in the Command Panel.**

   Your selected polygons vanish from view. You now have the power to select a defined part of the polygon mesh. Check your results against Figure 11-9, and allow yourself a mad-scientist laugh.

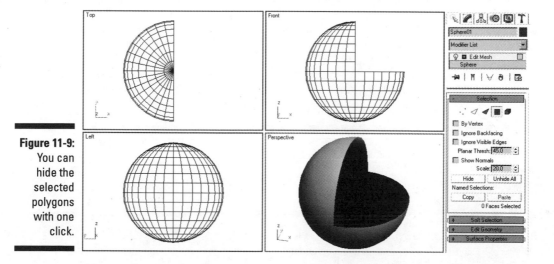

Figure 11-9:
You can hide the selected polygons with one click.

Using the Attach command

When you're comfortable using Edit Mesh Selection to select just those polygons you want to modify, the Attach operation makes a lot more sense. The Attach command does somewhat the same thing as a Boolean Add does, but the attached objects can no longer be addressed as separate forms. To take a crack at attaching an object, follow these steps:

1. **Create a new scene with two overlapping Standard Primitive Spheres in it.**

   Work in any viewport you like.

2. **Select one of the spheres, and activate the Edit Mesh Modifier.**

3. **Make sure you are in the Polygon sub-object mode. Use the quadrangular selection option, and click and drag a marquee with the Select and Move tool so that the marquee encompasses the entire sphere.**

4. **Under Edit Geometry in the Edit Mesh Modifier's Command Panel, click Attach.**

5. **Click the other sphere in any viewport.**

6. **Right-click Edit Mesh at the top of the Command Panel.**

   A menu of choices appears.

7. **Choose Collapse All.**

   A warning panel appears.

8. **Click Yes to set the object as completed.**

Congratulations! You have successfully created a single object from the two spheres. Note that the Pivot Point of this new unified object remains at the center of your initial mesh object; you may have to move it. Pat yourself on the back with both hands and shout, "Horatio! I have reached land!" (Amaze your friends. . . .)

Chapter 12

Vital Modifier Magic

• •

• •

*T*his chapter covers the uses of a series of important Modifiers. Although it would take several books to cover all the Modifiers contained in 3ds max (not to mention those you can add from external developers), this chapter guides you through the application of a series of the most common Modifiers. When you discover the principles involved in selecting and applying these Modifiers, you can figure out any of the additional Modifiers you may run across quickly.

Nothing bores a viewer more than knowing exactly what options were used to create a model; this instant recognition robs the graphic or animation of its believability. By using a Modifier to contort and distort the object's geometry, whether grossly or subtly, you add a certain amount of mystery to your model. Nothing compliments a 3D artist/animator more than a simple question: "How did you *do* that?"

Uncovering Modifiers

Although Modifiers can be used to customize the geometry of any object or model, they are especially useful when you build a model from Standard or Extended Primitives. Primitive objects have some degree of variability through the manipulation of their parameters in the Command Panel, some more than others. Even with that possibility, however, the basic Primitive forms remain pretty much the same, and are easily identifiable.

You can access the Modifiers in three ways.

✔ **Choosing Modifiers from the menu bar.** The benefit of using the menu bar is that Modifiers are grouped in different categories. Most of the Modifiers I talk about in this chapter are included under parametric deformers, as shown in Figure 12-1.

✔ **Clicking the Modifiers icon in the Tab Panel on the Modifiers tab.**

✔ **Selecting it from the Modifiers list in the Command Panel under the Modify icon.** This method is convenient when you want to add more than one Modifier in a Modifier stack (see Figure 12-2).

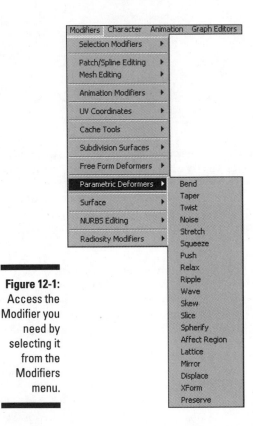

Figure 12-1:
Access the
Modifier you
need by
selecting it
from the
Modifiers
menu.

Managing the stack

You need to remember two important things when working with Modifiers:

✔ You can use as many Modifiers as needed on the same object. This includes multiple instances of the same Modifier.

✔ The order in which you use multiple Modifiers can change the resulting modeling effect.

Figure 12-2:
Access
Modifiers
from the
Modifier List
in the
Command
Panel.

As you add Modifiers, they appear in a list in the Command Panel (called the Modifier List or Modifier Stack). See Figure 12-3.

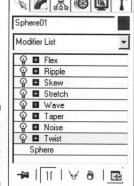

Figure 12-3:
The
Modifier List
or Stack.

At any time, you can select any Modifier in the Stack to highlight it. When you've selected a Modifier, you can change its parameters in the Command Panel. You can also click and drag any Modifier to a new position in the Stack. If you do this and then look at the targeted object, you may find that although it uses the same Modifiers as before, the effects make the object appear quite differently. That's because the lowest Modifier in the Stack gets applied first, and the others get applied in succession after that.

You can also selectively switch off any Modifier in the stack by clicking the symbol at the far left of the Modifier's name. Clicking again switches it on.

As you apply the required Modifier(s) to customize the geometry of your selected object, eventually everything appears just the way you want it (honest!). At that point, you may want to collapse the stack, so your object maintains its customized personality when you save it. When that happens, simply right-click any Modifier in the stack and choose Collapse All. Click Yes when the scary warning flag appears.

The Modifiers Command Panel

Directly under the Modifiers Stack are the parameter buttons and fields in the Command Panel. These parameters differ from one Modifier to the next. Some have more controls, and some less. All Modifiers have some parameter adjustments in common, with the main ones being a value that indicates the strength of the Modifier being applied, and the axis on which the effect is to be addressed. Remember that you can apply the same Modifier several times, so you can apply it at the same (or different) strength to the X-axis, then the Y-axis, and then the Z-axis. All this makes more sense after you explore using Modifiers yourself. I promise.

Applying Modifier Presets

Modifiers remain ghosted out and unselectable until you have an object or model targeted in a scene. You'll probably find that you gravitate towards one of the three Modifier selection methods more than the other two. I enjoy using the Modifier icons in the Tab Panel most. Most Modifiers can be applied to any of the following:

- Any object/model that has a polygonal mesh or *Patch* surface (a Patch surface is defined by three-sided polygons).
- Multiple-selected objects with polygonal surface attributes.

- Grouped objects. Please remember that Modifiers reference the Pivot Point of singular, multiple, or Grouped objects.

- Any Instanced Clone source object. The Modifier effect is applied to all Instanced Clones in the chain if either the source or any clone is modified.

- Any Referenced clone in a cloned chain, without being applied to any other clone in the chain or to the source object.

A gaggle of Modifiers

These are the most common Modifiers applied to entire polygon meshes and patch objects, either in whole or in part (the next chapter looks at Modifier effects for just part of the mesh, or *sub-selections*). Using combinations of these Modifiers is a quick way to model complex forms.

Bend

Although you can bend any selected object with this Modifier, it works best when the targeted object is elongated and thin. Make sure that the object has a fairly heavy polygon count to get a smooth-looking bend. A cylinder, for instance, should have at least 15 height segments. After you select the Bend Modifier with an object selected, its Command Panel appears. See Figure 12-4.

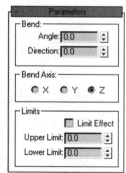

Figure 12-4: The Command Panel for the Bend Modifier.

The basic commands are pretty self-explanatory. Bend Angle and Direction can be any values you like. A 360-degree Bend Angle, for instance, attempts to bend the object into a circle. Pivot Point position makes all the difference. You can select the Bend Axis in real time, watching a viewport to see the results. You also have to make sure that the object has a dense enough polygon mesh to create a smooth bend. Don't tamper with limits until you get some experience with what the other values do. Figure 12-5 provides an example.

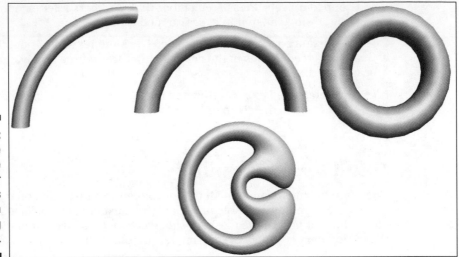

The cylinder in Figure 12-5 has 15 Height Segments for a smoother bend, and was created in the Top Viewport. Left to right at the top, the Bend Angle was set to 90, 180, and 360 degrees. The Z-axis was used in all cases. The bottom figure uses the same cylinder with a 360-degree angle on the Z-axis, but the Bend Modifier was used twice with the same settings to create this complex object.

Taper

The Taper Modifier makes one end of an object's axis smaller or larger than the other end. An example would be a Cone, which is simply a tapered cylinder.

Amount of the Taper ranges from -10 to 10. The Curve value (also -10 to 10) alters the way the Taper is applied. Taper Axis has a Primary option and an additional Effect axis. Combining the two varies the result. Choosing Symmetry forces a symmetrical parameter on the object.

Skew

Skew creates the effect witnessed by a stack of books leaning towards one side.

The two most important values in this panel are Amount and Skew Axis. The Amount can be a negative or positive value, setting the "leaning" one way or the other, while the selected axis takes on the skew.

Twist

The Twist Modifier does exactly what you'd expect it to do. It twists the object on any selected axis. Angle and Axis are the two core parameters set in the Twist Modifier's Command Panel. As with most of the other Modifiers, a denser polygon mesh allows for the creation of smoother Twist effects. See Figure 12-6.

Stretch

The Stretch Modifier does not perform the same action as basic scaling on an axis. Instead, Stretch pinches the object as well. The Twist Modifier stretches the object in two directions from its center. Stretch Amount, Axis, and Amplify are the main parameter controls. Amplify sets the extent of the pinching effect. See Figure 12-7.

Noise

Noise creates irregular surface bumps on a targeted object, roughening it up (see Figure 12-8). In this way, a sphere can be modified to look like a planetoid with an irregular surface. Noise works best when the mesh is dense; it rearranges the object's surface geometry. You can set the roughness of the noise, as well as its strength, on the X-, Y-, and Z-axis.

Figure 12-6:
Left, a Torus twisted at 180 degrees on the Y-axis. Center, a Torus twisted at 540 degrees on the Y-axis. Right, a Torus twisted three times at 180 degrees, once on each of the X-, Y-, and Z-axis.

Figure 12-7: This object started as a sphere. The Stretch Modifier was applied to the Z-axis at a strength of 1.5, with Amplify values set to -45, 2, and 45, respectively.

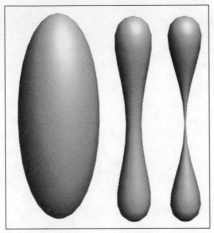

Figure 12-8: This object started out as a dense sphere, with 128 segments. A Noise Modifier was applied with a Scale of 335, Roughness set to 1, and a strength of 11 on the X, Y, and Z-axis. Could it be a scoop of ice cream with nuts?

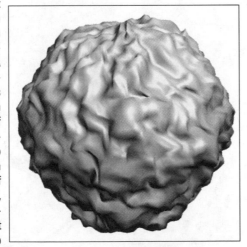

Wave

The Wave Modifier creates a linear wave from the vertical axis onto the X-axis of the object. You can control the Amplitude (strength) and the Wavelength in the Command Panel. See Figure 12-9.

Figure 12-9: Here, the Wave Modifier was used on a cube, with an Amplitude setting of 25/5 and a Wavelength of 25.

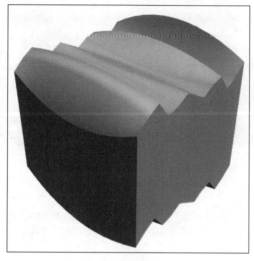

Melt

Melt is normally an animation Modifier; it can cause any selected object to melt into a puddle over a specified time. You can also use it to create interesting object modifications if you choose Collapse All afterward. You can control the Amount (strength) of the melt, the Percentage of the melt (0 to 100), the axis of the effect, and whether your object melts like Ice, Glass, Jelly, Plastic, or a custom material. Figure 12-10 illustrates some possibilities.

Figure 12-10: A Melt targeted to a sphere, with Amount set to 85 and a Percentage of 100, melting just like (left to right) Ice, Glass, Jelly, and Plastic.

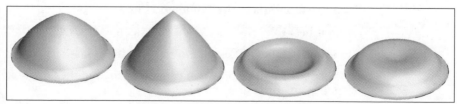

Spherify

The Spherify Modifier forces the selected object to become spherical, as much as possible. It has one setting: Percentage (0 to 100). Figure 12-11 shows several degrees of this setting.

Figure 12-11: Spherify targeted to a cylinder at 25%, 50%, 75%, and 100%, respectively.

Ripple

Using the Ripple Modifier causes the same effect as watching a pond after a rock is thrown in. You control Amplitude and Wavelength in the Command Panel.

FFD (Free-Form Deformation)

FFD modification is like working with clay to form objects. Free-Form Deformation is a bit more complex to work with than most of the other Modifiers. The following general steps illustrate a typical instance:

1. **Choose either Box FFD or Cylinder FFD for the targeted object.**

   FFD creates a cage made up of a lattice of points around your object. The cage can remain box-like or cylindrical, or it can be forced to conform exactly to the shape of your object.

2. **To shape the cage to your object, click Conform to Shape in the FFD Command Panel.**

3. **Set the number of XYZ control points in the FFD lattice by clicking Set Number of Points in the Command Panel.**

   I find it best to use at least eight points on each axis.

4. **Double-click the FFD option in the Modifiers List.**

   FFD becomes active. Now you can move any number of points in the FFD lattice in any direction.

5. Use the Select and Move tool to move lattice points.

The object responds by smoothly assuming a new, curved shape.

You can use FFD to create all manner of unique forms, including organic models like heads and other body parts, but it takes practice. See Figure 12-12.

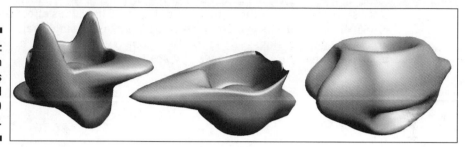

Figure 12-12:
A selection of spheres transformed with the FFD Modifier.

Lattice

As you work more with Modifiers, you'll have favorites. Lattice is one of mine. Other 3D software might call this Modifier *Sticks-and-Balls*. The "sticks" are called *Struts* in the Lattice Modifier; they refer to the polygonal edges of the target object. The "balls" are called *Joints,* and correspond to the vertices of the polygons. You can control the number of sides and the size of the Struts, and the type (Tetrahedron, Octahedron, or Icosahedron) and size of the Joints. The result is a skeletal version of your model that looks like something under construction. Figure 12-13 shows some nifty examples.

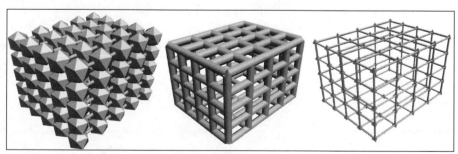

Figure 12-13:
A variety of boxes targeted by the Lattice Modifier with different Strut and Joint parameters.

Optimize

You just can't get along without *Optimize*. Optimization alters the polygon count of an object. It's especially vital when you are creating models for games, where the polygon count has to be kept low, while at the same time keeping the general form of the targeted object. The main control in the Optimize Modifier's Command Panel is Face Threshold. Lower settings (0 being the lowest) affect the number of polygons least, while higher settings start to decrease the number of polygons. The values affect the targeted object according to its geometry, so you can't use any single value for all objects. Higher settings can deform the geometry of the object severely, so use with care. Figure 12-14 shows a typically Optimized result.

Figure 12-14:
The original polygon count of a sphere with 32 segments is on the left. The second figure shows an optimization with the threshold set to 7, while the right-hand image displays what happens when the Optimize threshold is set to 12.

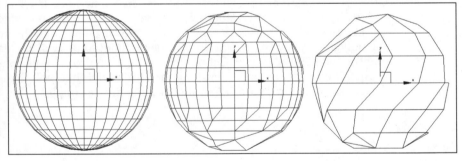

Where have all the polys gone?

Most Modifiers work better when their polygonal mesh is denser. When the polygonal mesh has been optimized too severely (that is, when the number of polygons in the mesh has been reduced to a small number), there may not be enough polygons involved to create the smooth Modifier effect you need. Modifiers applied over and over emphasize — and eventually exaggerate — the effect they create.

Creating Models with Modifiers

Believe it or not, the purpose of using Modifiers (beside having great belly-laughing fun, of course) is to create 3D models.

1. **Create an object (for example, place a Primitive in a viewport).**
2. **Apply a Modifier with settings that do what you want done to the object.**
3. **Rotate the resulting form as needed.**
4. **Move the Pivot Point as needed.**
5. **Apply other Modifiers as desired.**
6. **Clone to create an army of objects or Mirror Clone to create a symmetrical second half for your existing object.**
7. **Repeat this process to your heart's content.**

A couple of examples show how easy the process can be, even for a fairly complex model.

Horns

If you've always wanted your own virtual Viking helmet, here's how to create some great 3D horns.

1. **Place a Cone Primitive in the Top Viewport.**
2. **Apply a Bend Modifier on the Z-axis at 90 degrees.**
3. **Rotate the resulting form so its base is vertical instead of horizontal.**

4. **With the Pivot Point at the center, twist the form 90 degrees on its X axis.**

5. **Mirror Clone to create the other horn.**

Spaceship

Thousands of ways exist to develop ultracool 3D spacecraft models. Here's a really basic but sleek one.

1. **Copy-Clone four Primitive Capsule objects, and place them in a square arrangement in the Top Viewport.**

2. **Place an elongated cylinder at the center, also from the Top Viewport.**

3. **Group all, and use a Taper Modifier to narrow the top of the group. Set the Amount to -9.**

4. **Add four Tube Primitives for exhaust nozzles, select all, and Group again.**

5. **Create a wing from a flattened Pyramid Primitive in the Left Viewport. Bend it on the Z-axis at 45/90.**

6. **Mirror-Copy the wing in the Front Viewport to create the other wing.**

7. **Place everything in position and Group all.**

   Figure 12-15 shows the completed ship.

Figure 12-15: Rev up the warp drive, cap'n!

To paraphrase an old Beatles song . . . "*the 3D models you take are equal to the 3D models you make.*" Spend some time exploring how to use Modifiers on various primitives to create your own unique 3D models.

Chapter 13

Modifying Sub-Objects

· ·

In This Chapter

▶ Selecting vertices

▶ Selecting polygonal edges

▶ Selecting polygons

▶ Using the editable Mesh commands

▶ Using the editable Polygon modifications

▶ Using editable Patch modifications

▶ Cloning sub-object selections

▶ Using standard Modifiers on sub-object selections

· ·

*S*ub-objects are nothing more than parts of an object's polygon mesh (or patch, or parts of a NURBS model, which I detail in Chapter 14). To put it simply, sub-objects are the polygons that make up the objects and the polygon parts (face, edge, and/or vertex). Your nose can be considered a sub-object of your head, so the next time your nose itches, tell people you need to scratch your sub-object and watch their expressions! I talk about sub-objects in detail in Chapter 13. In this chapter, I cover how to select sub-objects for modification and what happens when you apply specific Modifiers to them.

The Mesh Select Modifier

 The Mesh Select Modifier has everything you need to select sub-objects on any targeted mesh. The easiest way to activate the Mesh Select Modifier is by clicking its icon in the Tab Panel. You must already have a targeted object in the scene to use this Modifier, otherwise it will be grayed out. When selected, the Mesh Select Command Panel opens, as shown in Figure 13-1.

Figure 13-1:
The
Command
Panel for
the Mesh
Select
Modifier.

The row across the top of the Mesh Select Modifier's Command Panel displays five icons. Hovering your mouse pointer over them reveals them —
(from left to right) Vertex, Edge, Face, Polygon, and Element. These five sub-object types determine what your sub-object will be composed of. I describe them in detail in the following sections.

Vertex points

Vertex Points are the points where two polygon edges meet. When you click Vertex Points, your entire object's vertex points are displayed. To select specific points from the matrix, either click them with the Control key held down, or click and drag a marquee over them. The selected Vertex Points will change color so you can see which ones are SubSelected. When any Vertex Points are SubSelected, you can apply any Modifier — but only to those points.

Living on the edge

Polygonal Edges (the edges or lines that create the polygon boundary) are SubSelected the same way that Vertex Points are. The SubSelected Edges are displayed in a separate color in all viewports, and are ready to have a Modifier applied, as shown in Figure 13-2.

Figure 13-2:
On the left is a sphere before Edge sub-object, and on the right is the same sphere after Edge sub-object.

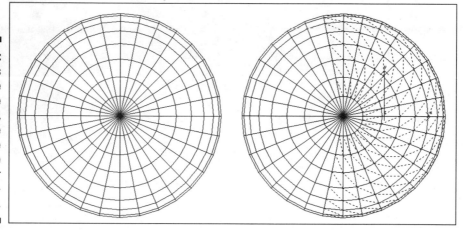

Abouuuuut face!

A Face is a three-sided polygon in 3ds max. If your model is composed of Faces, they can be SubSelected by using this type, either by a marquee or by holding down the Control key and selecting them individually.

Where has poly-gon this time?

Polygons are usually defined as quadrangular, and they can be SubSelected with the quadrangular option chosen as the determining factor. Left-Control-clicking or surrounding with a marquee both work, as shown in Figure 13-3.

Elementally, my dear Watson

If you choose the Element option in the Mesh Select Modifier's Command Panel, any object you click will have all its polygons SubSelected, or all of them visible from the view you're in if Ignore Backfaces is checked.

Figure 13-3:
On the left, a series of noncontig-uous poly-gons has been Sub-Selected using the left-Control-click method. On the right, a contiguous number of polygons has been Sub-Selected using the marquee method.

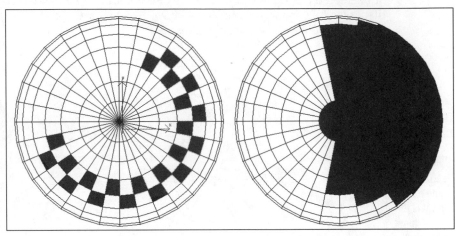

Choosing any one of these options and clicking and dragging a marquee over your selected object will select the SubSelected items enclosed. You can leave all other parameter settings in the Command Panel at their defaults.

When you SubSelect items in any viewport, you select those elements on the side of the object that you see and on the opposite side as well. Placing a check (left-clicking in the box) next to Ignore Backfaces enables you to SubSelect only the items facing your view.

Editable Mesh Modifications

Why is the Editable Mesh Command Panel so important? Because it contains both sub-object options and a bunch of its own Modifiers to work on the SubSelected geometry.

1. **Place any object on the screen.**

   I used a 12 x 12 segmented Plane in Figure 13-4.

2. **Right-click the object in any viewport.**

   A menu appears.

3. **Choose Convert To⇨Convert To Editable Mesh.**

The Editable Mesh Command Panel appears, shown in Figure 13-5, the top portion looking similar to the Mesh Select Command Panel.

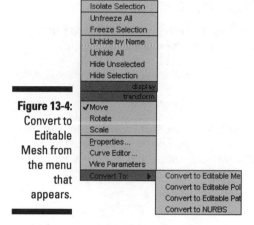

Figure 13-4: Convert to Editable Mesh from the menu that appears.

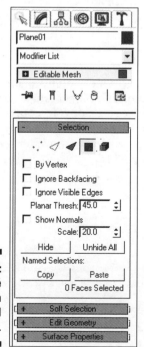

Figure 13-5: The Editable Mesh Command Panel.

4. Click the Edit Geometry button.

Edit Geometry commands and parameters appear.

Important Edit Geometry Modifiers

The Edit Geometry Modifiers and commands can be a useful way to quickly modify selected objects to create your own unique models. The Edit Geometry Modifiers are used on selected sub-object parts of the targeted object or model.

Create

Left-click Create to activate it. Create enables you to add new vertices on your model, so that three connected vertices form a new polygonal face. Adding faces to build modeled parts is rather tedious, but at times being able to add faces here and there to fill a gap in the model can be important.

Delete

Delete is a useful modeling tool. Selecting Sub-Object components (vertices, edges, faces, or polygons) and left-clicking the Delete command enables you to remove all the selected sub-objects. This is a great way to cut holes in selected object meshes.

Attach/Detach

Although I cover Attach in Chapter 11, it's worth mentioning again here. Attach enables you to select another object or sub-object and attach it to your source object. After selecting a sub-object area of your source object, Detach (just click it) creates a separate object made up of the sub-object selection(s), as shown in Figure 13-6.

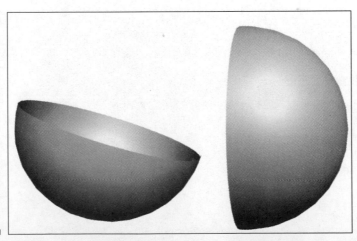

Figure 13-6:
Half of this sphere was selected as a sub-object; using the Detach command made the selected part into a new object.

Divide

Divide serves to separate polygons into triangular polys by left-clicking a polygon edge. This is a useful way to create more detailed geometry on any selected polys in a model. This process is new to version 5, replacing the older Break command.

Extrude

This is one of the most useful commands in the Edit Geometry rollout. Selected sub-objects are extruded manually or mathematically along their Normals. The Normals can be set to Group, which basically sets all Normals as one, or to Local, which sets the Normals for each sub-object polygon, as shown in Figure 13-7.

Figure 13-7:
Left: A sphere showing the sub-object selection. Center: Extrusion takes place with Normals set to Group. Right: Normals set to Local.

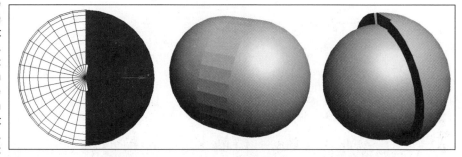

Bevel

This commands adds a defined Bevel to the selected sub-object polygons. Bevel can either be applied manually, by clicking and dragging over the sub-object surface, or mathematically in the Command Panel.

Weld

Weld is targeted to selected vertices. It causes the selected vertices within a threshold distance to collapse into a single vertex.

Tessellate

Tessellation is a process that splits quadrangular sub-object polygons into triangular polys. Applying Tessellate multiple times will keep subdividing the polygons. This is good for finely detailed editing — but not so good for storing the object mesh later: The more polys in the object, the more storage memory is required. Aside from tessellating small areas of the object that need smoother editing (and so require more polygons), use this command sparingly.

Editable Polygon Modifications

If you right-click a model in any viewport and choose Convert To⇨Convert to Editable Poly, another collection of geometry Modifiers appears in the Command Panel. Check out these Modifiers.

The three jewels

Many Modifiers are available in the Editable Polygon Command Panel. They all do their work after you have selected sub-object data from your targeted object in a viewport. Many of these Modifiers are the same ones listed previously for Editable Mesh modification — but three stand out as uniquely useful modeling tools: Flip, Collapse, and Make Planar.

✔ **Flip:** This command works on the Normals of the sub-object selections you choose. As detailed in Chapter 2, every polygon has a Normal — an imaginary line perpendicular to the center of its surface. Triangular Polygons have a Normal that cannot be twisted out of the plane of the polygon. When the Normals face outward from the object, those polygons are visible. When a polygon's Normals are reversed so they face inward, the polygons are not visible. The Flip command reverses the selected sub-object polygons on an object, as shown in Figure 13-8.

Although you can use the Flip command to create some interesting modeling effects, its more dedicated use is to fix the polygons on imported models, which often load into 3ds max with their Normals flipped.

✔ **Collapse:** This command in Editable Polygon mode does the same thing that the Weld command does in Editable Mesh mode. It gathers all the selected vertices in the sub-object selection into a single vertex.

✔ **Make Planar:** This command flattens the selected sub-objects into a flat planar surface. The Planar surface is perpendicular to the viewport you are working in.

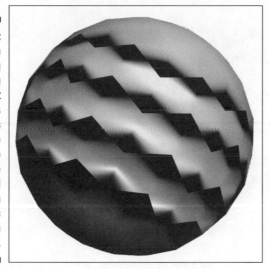

Figure 13-8:
An interesting banding effect appears on this GeoSphere Primitive after the banded polygon Normals have been flipped.

Editable Patch Modifiers

A Patch object is made up of triangular polygons. If you right-click a model or object and choose Convert To⇨Convert To Editable Patch, the object is transformed into a Patch object. Editing a Patch object leads to somewhat smoother results than you'd get if the same object were an Editable Mesh or an Editable Polygon type. The Editable Patch Command Panel offers much the same command options as the Editable Mesh or Editable Polygon types, so getting handy with any one of these three environments prepares you for working in the other two.

Cloning Sub-Object Selections

If you engage in a Shift-Move operation on the sub-object selection of an Editable Patch, the cloned copy of the sub-object selection will be a *Surface Patch* (see Figure 13-9). Patch Surfaces are often created from larger objects and then attached together to form other models. The cloned surface will remain connected to the main object, unless and until you sub-object-select the main object and delete it.

If you engage in a shift-move operation on the sub-objects of an Editable Polygon, the cloned copy is either *Cloned to Object* or *Cloned to Element* — options that you choose in a separate window that appears. If Cloned to Object, the cloned surface remains connected to the object. If Cloned to Element, it becomes a separate object on its own. The same is true for any Editable Mesh object and sub-object selections you may have cloned.

Figure 13-9:
A sub-object selection, when cloned from a Patch Object, forms a separate Surface Patch.

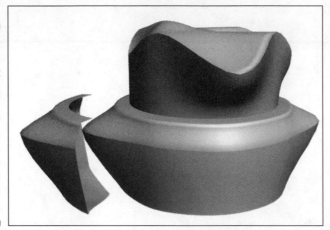

Using Standard Modifiers on Sub-Object Selections

You can use any of the Modifiers detailed in Chapter 12 on sub-object selections, as well as on entire objects. Three factors determine the results you get: the Modifier you select, the geometry of the sub-object selection, and the geometry of the original target object. To use a Modifier on a sub-object, follow these general steps:

1. **Create or select an object.**
2. **Convert the object to an editable form.**
3. **Sub-object-select the part of the object you want to fine-tune.**
4. **Select a Modifier to use on the part you've selected.**
5. **Tweak the Modifier's settings to suit.**
6. **Apply the Modifier to the sub-object.**

Here are some examples:

✔ To get the column shown in Figure 13-10, you'd start by creating a tall Cylinder Primitive in the Top Viewport. Then all you have to do is convert to an Editable Mesh, sub-object-select the top part of the Cylinder, and Tessellate once to create a denser poly mesh. To finish up, you'd apply a Taper Modifier with Amount = 3, Symmetry on, and a Taper Axis of Z/XY.

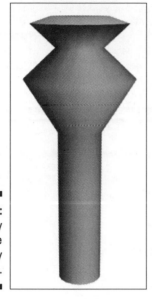

Figure 13-10:
A quick way
to create
a fancy
column.

✔ To create the ring shown in Figure 13-11, you'd start by creating a Torus Primitive (in the Top Viewport) with 48 Segments and 48 Sides. Because it starts out as a dense polygonal mesh, you'd convert it to an Editable Poly, and then sub-object-select the polys on the right side of the Torus (as seen in the Top Viewport). Then you'd simply apply a Spherical Modifier set to 100%.

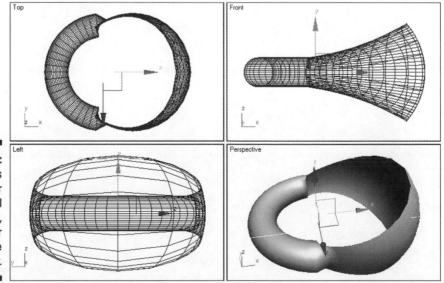

Figure 13-11:
The ring is
ready for
a virtual
finger, nose,
or major
movie
poster.

✔ To get the wire fence shown in Figure 13-12, you'd start by placing a Torus Knot Primitive in the scene from the Top Viewport. After converting the object to an Editable Mesh, you'd sub-object-select the top half of the object's polygons (in the Front Viewport). Then you'd use the Select and Move tool to pull the sub-object selection up by about 200%, and select the entire object in the Top Viewport. A quick use of the Select and Scale tool would squash the mesh along its Y-axis, flattening it out about 90% (which would give you one strand of the wire). Then you'd Shift-Clone to create the rest of the fence.

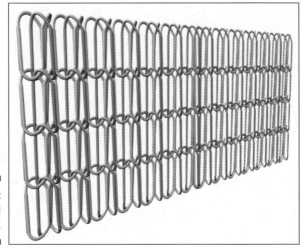

Figure 13-12:
The finished
wire fence.

Chapter 14

Invasion of the NURBS

. . . .

In This Chapter

▶ Creating and modifying NURBS curves

▶ Transforming polygonal objects to NURBS models

▶ Working with NURBS surfaces

▶ Using Modifiers on NURBS

. . . .

*T*his chapter introduces NURBS modeling. What are NURBS anyway, besides something with a strange name? If you answered Non-Uniform Rational B-Splines (as a guess), you get the prize. Working with NURBS is truly like working with clay to build models. Be warned however; 3D artists either love NURBS or hate them. You should at least know about them and how they can be used. Working with NURBS requires a different thought process and a bit more manual dexterity than working with polygons. Many 3D artists prefer NURBS as a modeling method for creating organic-looking characters; the models tend to display smooth curved surfaces.

In this chapter, I give you the framework to start working with NURBS. Beyond that, you can research the topic on your own as deeply as you want (and I'd suggest picking the brains of experienced NURBS modelers for advice) if you want to master NURBS creative pursuits.

Creating NURBS Curves

Creating a NURBS Curve is usually the first step in creating a NURBS object. Choose Create⇨Shapes⇨NURBS Curves. The NURBS Curves Command Panel appears, as shown in Figure 14-1.

As you can see in Figure 14-1, you can create a NURBS Curve in two ways:

✔ **Point Curve:** This is a spline that passes through the points placed down.

✔ **CV (Control Vertex) Curve:** This control curve is meant to alter the geometry of the NURBS object it relates to. CV points can have the capability of affecting the associated NURBS object.

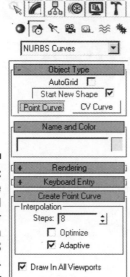

Figure 14-1:
The
Command
Panel for
creating a
NURBS
curve.

Checking AutoGrid

By checking AutoGrid, you can draw a NURBS Curve that adheres to the surface of any selected 3D object. This can be useful for creating patches that follow the curve of another object's surface (for example, a mask that fits a 3D head perfectly).

Drawing a curve by Draw in All Viewports

Draw in All Viewports is a special 3ds max command that can be activated for all splines. Checking it enables you to switch amongst viewports to create your splined data in 3D. In this way, whether you make the spline renderable or make it a path for a Loft operation, you can create real 3D components.

Follow these steps to create a NURB Curve:

1. **Choose Create⊏⇨Shapes⊏⇨NURBS Curves⊏⇨Point Curve.**

2. **Make sure Draw in All Viewports is checked in the Command Panel rollout under Create Point Curve.**

3. **Using the left mouse button, click and drag to create NURBS Point Curve sections.**

   Switch among the Left, Top, and Front Viewports after every click.

4. **Right-click to finish the NURBS Point Curve.**

5. **In the Command Panel, under Rendering, make sure Renderable is checked and that Viewport is selected. Use a Thickness of 12.**

   Figure 14-2 shows the result.

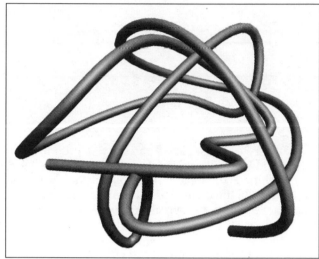

Figure 14-2:
A
Renderable
3D NURBS
Point Curve.

There are hundreds of finer points to mastering the creation of NURBS components in 3ds max. This book doesn't have room for all of them, but the next section of this chapter looks at a few that can accelerate your NURBS learning curve (pun intended).

Turning a NURBS Point Curve into a 3D Object

NURBS Point Curves are basic to the creation of 3D objects, because by adjusting the points, you shape new curves. Access NURBS Point Curves in the Modify Command Panel under Create Surfaces.

Create surfaces

After you create a 2D or 3D NURBS Point Curve, you may want to use it as a basis for creating a NURBS 3D object. Doing that requires some specific tools. With your Point Curve object selected, open the Modify Command Panel, and move down to the Create Surfaces options. As you can see in Figure 14-3, some familiar modification options are listed.

Figure 14-3:
The NURBS
Point Curve
Create
Surfaces
options
in the
Command
Panel.

Create Surfaces	
CV Surf	Point Surf
Dependent Surfaces	
Transform	Blend
Offset	Mirror
Extrude	Lathe
Ruled	Cap
U Loft	UV Loft
1-Rail	2-Rail
N Blend	Multi-Trim
Fillet	

Of all the Create Surface options, please pay special attention to two old friends — Extrude and Lathe. If you're asking, "Why not use the standard Extrude and Lathe Modifiers instead?" (and *some* of you were asking), the answer is practical: Using the commands in the Create Surfaces Command Panel keeps the resulting object as a NURBS model. Using the standard Modifiers would translate the model instantly into a polygonal model.

When you use the Create Surfaces version of Extrude or Lathe, you simply click the NURBS Point Curve in any viewport to create the NURBS model. You can select an alternate extrusion or lathing axis in the Command Panel. In Figure 14-4, for example, the bottom row shows Lathe and Extrude applied to the same NURBS Point Curve on the X-, Y-, and Z-axes.

Figure 14-4:
Using a 3D
NURBS
Point Curve
with Lathe
(top row)
and Extrude
(bottom
row) to
create
three
NURBS
objects,
alternating
the X-, Y-,
and Z-axes.

Adjusting points on a NURBS curve

After you create a NURBS Curve, you can edit the position of the points that control the curve. To do so, right-click the curve in any viewport. When the menu selections appear, choose Sub-Objects⇨Point. All the points become active and visible; you can move them with the Select and Move tool. Pressing Delete while a NURBS Curve Point is selected deletes that point and reshapes the NURBS Curve. Right-clicking the NURBS Curve displays what you can do to it.

If you create a CV Curve and want to modify it, you find CV points outside of the curves that can be moved to reshape the curve.

Transforming a Primitive to a NURBS Model

In my humble opinion, NURBS modeling is best used to modify an object that starts out as a polygonal mesh. Polygonal objects are easier to create initially to get the basic form. You can then use NURBS CV editing to add smoother details to the object. Follow these steps:

1. **Choose Create⇨Geometry⇨Standard Primitives, and create a sphere in the Top Viewport.**

2. **With the sphere still selected, choose the Modify Command panel.**

3. **Right-click the sphere at the top of the Modify Command Panel.**

4. **Choose Convert to NURBS from the menu that appears.**

   Your sphere is now a NURBS model, and it no longer shows any polygons, but just a few surrounding splines, as shown in Figure 14-5.

5. **Left-click the NURBS Surface name in the Modifier list.**

   It changes from gray to yellow, and a whole new list of options opens in the Command Panel. Look at the viewports to see the NURBS sphere with its CV points displayed, as shown in Figure 14-6.

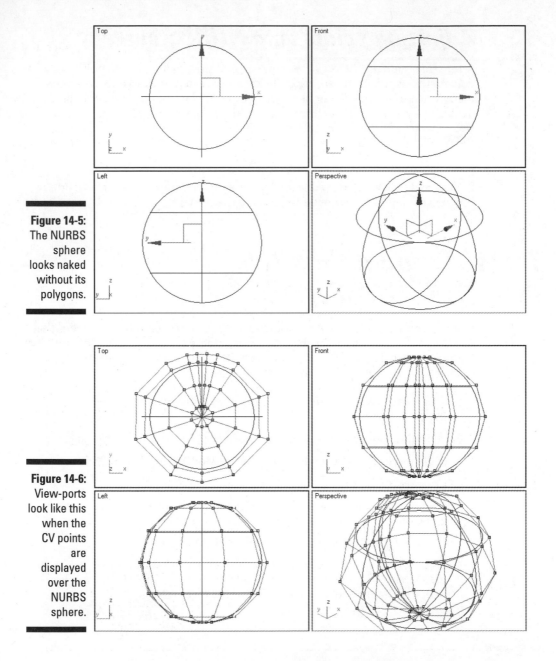

Figure 14-5: The NURBS sphere looks naked without its polygons.

Figure 14-6: View-ports look like this when the CV points are displayed over the NURBS sphere.

6. **Using the Select and Move tool, draw a rectangular marquee around the CVs on the right of the NURBS control lattice in the Front Viewport.**

Pull the lattice upward, or in any direction you like. The stretched and contorted NURBS model stays smooth, no matter how it is manipulated by its Control Vertices.

You can move other CV vertices to get a feel for how smooth NURBS modification is. Watch the viewports for what happens to your sphere in the process.

7. **When you're satisfied, right-click the NURBS modified sphere in any viewport, and choose Convert To⇨Convert To Editable Mesh.**

   The polygon mesh becomes denser to replicate the smoothness of the corresponding NURBS model, as shown in Figure 14-7.

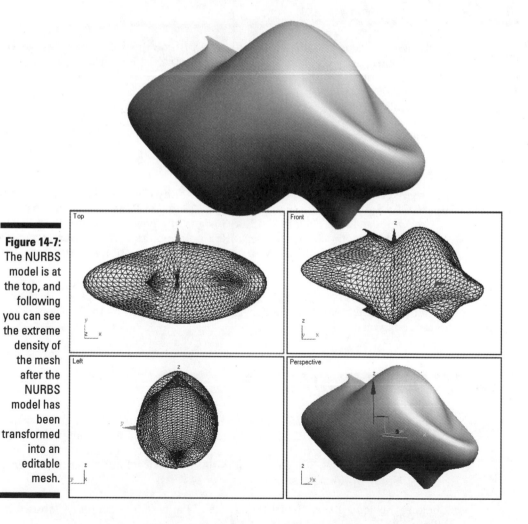

Figure 14-7: The NURBS model is at the top, and following you can see the extreme density of the mesh after the NURBS model has been transformed into an editable mesh.

But why bother with translating a NURBS model to a mesh anyway? After all, a NURBS model is smoother and takes far less memory to store. The reason has to do with what you are going to do with the model after it is created. If you plan to use it outside 3ds max, few 3D software programs can accept the importation of a NURBS model, even if they readily accept polygon-mesh models created in 3ds max. If you plan to work in max alone, then you don't have to translate NURBS to meshes.

Sadly, trying to Copy-Clone CV vertices doesn't get you anywhere. You can, however, Copy-Clone NURBS models.

NURBS Surfaces

A NURBS Surface is initially a gridded plane with no thickness. You can create a NURBS Surface by choosing Create⇨Geometry⇨NURBS Surfaces. Then choose either Point Surface or CV Surface.

You can alter a NURBS Surface after creating it by applying any of the standard Modifiers. (Applying a Spherify Modifier, for example, transforms the rectangular surface into a circular surface.) Before you apply standard Modifiers to a NURBS Surface, right-click the surface and choose Sub-Objects⇨Top Level from the menu that appears.

After you create a NURBS Surface, open the Modify Command Panel and click the NURBS Surface title to highlight it. The Command Panel modifications options appear. Right-click the NURBS Surface in any viewport and then choose Sub-Objects⇨Point. All the NURBS points on the Surface object are revealed. You can use the Select and Move tool to reposition any surface points, which in turn reshapes the surface itself.

Don't move NURBS points or Control Vertices so they overlap other vertices, or unpredictable results will occur. Think of this warning as the Do-Not-Remove tag on a mattress.

The NURBS Toolbox Panel

When you create a NURBS Surface and then move to the Modify Panel (without highlighting the NURBS Surface heading), the Command Panel Rollout displays a small button that resembles a grid. This is the on/off toggle for the NURBS Toolbox Panel. You can find it under the General heading, to the right of the Display Options, as shown in Figure 14-8.

Clicking this icon places the NURBS Toolbox Panel on the screen, as shown in Figure 14-9.

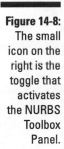

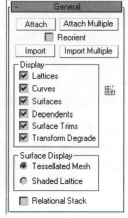

Figure 14-8:
The small icon on the right is the toggle that activates the NURBS Toolbox Panel.

Figure 14-9:
The NURBS Toolbox Panel.

If you plan to do a lot of NURBS modeling in 3ds max, you'll find the tools in this panel absolutely essential. You can apply most NURBS modifications from here. All the tools contained in this toolbox are dedicated to modifying the presently selected NURBS Surface or NURBS 3D model. The three groups of tools represented in this panel are grouped according to *Points, Curves,* and *Surfaces.* I cover them in detail in the following sections.

The Point tools

The six Point tools used to help you create and move points are as follows: Create Point, Create Offset Point, Create Curve, Create Curve-Curve Point, Create Surface Point, and Create Surface Curve Point.

Create Point

Place (left-click) independent points anywhere in the scene, and they will still be connected to the targeted NURBS Surface or model. Use these points to control the NURBS Surface or model from anywhere in the scene. The points also serve as points on a Fit Curve, a spline that connects selected points. Create points first, and then connect them with a Fit Curve.

Create Offset Point

An Offset Point is tied to another selected point that already exists, on or off the NURBS Surface or model. It starts coincident with the selected point, and then is Offset in any XYZ direction by adjusting the values in the Command Panel. Clicking Replace Base Point causes the new point to replace the original point.

Create Curve Point

Curve Points are placed on an existing curve, or made relative to that curve (by Tangent, Offset, or Normal options in the Command Panel). Checking Trim Curve deletes the selected Curve from the present Curve Point to the end of the curve. Flip Trim selects the opposite range of the curve.

Create Curve-Curve Point

Curve to Curve Point creates a point on each of two selected independent curves, bonding them together. It's a lot like a Weld operation.

Create Surface Point

A Surface Point can be placed anywhere on the targeted NURBS Surface. It can also serve as one point on a newly created Curve. *Offset, Tangent,* or *Normal* serves to move it away from the targeted surface, though it remains tied to it.

Create Surface Curve Point

This option creates a point where a Curve intersects the Surface.

Altering points in the Command Panel

In the Command Panel, you can click any of the options in the *Selection Display* to choose a Single Point, Row or Column of Points, Row and Column of Points, or All Points. Placing a marquee around the point or points you want to alter allows them to be repositioned or otherwise adjusted.

- **Extend:** Click and drag an existing point to create new curve segments.
- **Fuse:** Click one point and then a *target* point to Fuse the points together, creating a new closed curve. This is similar to a polygonal vertex Weld operation.

✔ **Delete:** Click any point (or select a row or column of points), and then click the Delete command to remove the targeted points completely.

✔ **Refine:** Prepare for finely detailed sculpting of a NURBS Surface by adding points to Curves, Rows, Columns, or Rows and Columns.

The Curve tools

You guessed it — the Curve tools in 3ds max allow you to draw, resize, move, join, or otherwise change curves.

You get 18 Curve tools in the NURBS Toolbox Panel:

✔ **CV:** Draws a freehand CV Curve by clicking and dragging.

✔ **Point:** Creates a Point Curve, either or both on and off of the NURBS Surface.

✔ **Fit:** Connects freestanding points into a new curve; use it by selecting the first point and then the target point.

✔ **Transform:** Clones any Curve already existing on the NURBS Surface.

✔ **Blend:** Creates a spline *bridge* that connects selected Curves.

✔ **Offset:** Clones an existing Curve and resizes it at the same time. The new Curve remains on the same Surface plane as the source Curve (similar to the Scale Transform operation for a polygonal mesh).

✔ **Mirror:** Creates a cloned Curve that mirrors the source Curve on any selected axis, by simply clicking in any viewport with this option active.

✔ **Chamfer:** Creates a separate curve between two points on other coplanar curves.

✔ **Fillet:** Creates a smooth curve between two other coplanar curves with the Fillet tool.

✔ **Surface to Surface Intersection:** Creates a NURBS Surface initially, and another intersecting Surface when you are in the Modify Command Panel. Then apply this tool, and Trim either or both NURBS Surfaces according to the Curve that represents their Intersection. (This option can be difficult to master without some dedicated practice.)

✔ **U Iso/V Iso:** Creates a U Iso (longitudinal) or a V Iso (latitudinal) curve or line on a NURBS Surface. On a NURBS sphere (for instance), you can trim away slices of the form. Seen in a Front or Left/Right viewport, U Iso Curves run horizontally and V Iso Curves run vertically.

✔ **Normal Projected:** Uses a selected, separate Curve as a cutter to trim a selected NURBS Surface. Just select the cutter curve and then the Surface it applies to.

✔ **Vector Projected:** Offers an alternative way to trim a NURBS Surface.

✔ **CV Curve on Surface/Point Curve on Surface:** Creates CV or Point Curves that can only be generated on the NURBS Surface.

✔ **Surface Offset:** Clones a Curve already positioned on a NURBS Surface, and offsets its position in 3D space by an input value.

✔ **Edge:** Selects the Edges you want deleted or moved.

The Surface tools

Points serve as the building blocks for Curves, and Curves serve as the building blocks for Surfaces. You get 16 Surface options in the NURBS Toolbox Panel.

✔ **CV and Point:** Creates a CV or Point Surface at any angle, and automatically connects the new surface to the existing NURBS Surface(s).

✔ **Transform:** Works similarly to the Shift-Transform Cloning operation for polygonal meshes, except you don't have to hold down the Shift key.

✔ **Blend:** Creates a smooth surface that joins two other selected Surfaces (or a Surface and a Curve). For instance, you can Blend two rectangular Surfaces spaced apart and parallel to create a book cover whose spine is automatically rounded.

✔ **Offset:** Clones a pre-existing NURBS Surface (using the original Surface's Normals), and places the new object in the same plane as the original.

✔ **Mirror:** Alters the axis of symmetry after the Mirrored Surface is created, just as Mirroring is used on polygonal meshes.

✔ **Extrude/Lathe:** Performs these two processes (examined earlier in the chapter).

✔ **Ruled:** Generates a new NURBS Surface between two pre-existing Surfaces, using them as edge references.

✔ **Cap:** Adds a capped Surface over the open end of an extruded NURBS Surface.

✔ **U Loft:** Lofts a standard splined element without requiring the selection of a Path and a Shape (cross-section) beforehand. You simply create the NURBS Point or CV Curves, activate the U Loft Tool, select the points and curves you want lofted, and watch. The tool automatically creates a NURBS Surface object from the lofted points and curves.

✔ **1-Rail Sweep:** Creates a new NURBS Surface based on a Sweep Path Curve and two *Cross-section* Curves.

✔ **2-Rail Sweep:** Creates a new NURBS Surface based on two Curve Paths and two or more Cross-section NURBS Curves.

✔ **Multisided Blend:** Creates a new NURBS Surface based on three or four open or closed NURBS Curves that enclose an area.

  Multisided Blend is also good for creating a transition surface to span the gap between other surfaces.

✔ **MultiCurve Trimmed:** This tool requires multiple NURBS Curves that have already been joined into a loop, and then trims the targeted NURBS Surfaces. (The trimming is similar to what the Normal and Vector Projected Curves do.) Tricky to use — be prepared for lots of practice!

✔ **Fillet:** Adds a separate, smooth NURBS Surface transition from one selected existing Surface to another. You use this Tool by selecting it and then clicking (one at a time) the surfaces between which you want to make the transition.

Y'know, I could probably write an encyclopedia on NURBS modeling alone (though not right now). Even if some 3D artists and animators lead successful and rewarding lives without it, NURBS modeling is a powerful technique to know.

Part IV
Trees of Fur and Fish of Wood

The 5th Wave   By Rich Tennant

"Evidently he died of natural causes following a marathon session animating everything on his personal Web site. And no, Morganstern—the irony isn't lost on me."

In this part . . .

Although computer graphics software developers spend a lot of time trying to blur the edge between the virtual and real world, making it difficult for you to tell where one leaves off and the other begins, the process also opens up doors to the impossible. Objects that seem real enough at first glance reveal irrational aspects upon closer inspection, when the artist wants them to. Trees can sprout hair in front of your eyes, and fish of wood and stone swim in the ponds. In the world of our everyday experience, the form and substance of things is seldom mutable, that is, objects remain glued to the form they were shaped to be, and their surfaces give us comfortable cues about what they are made of. No such permanence exists in dreams, or in the worlds created by computer graphics.

In mythology, only King Midas could turn something to gold by merely touching it. In the worlds 3ds max is able to bring into existence, everyone has the power to do much more than King Midas ever lusted for. Through the manipulation of materials and textures, you can control whether an object appears to have the surface properties of metals, stone, reptilian scales, clouds, and a million indescribable never-before-seen materials.

Chapter 15

Living in the Material World

You are sitting on a chair in a dimly lit room. Besides you and the chair, the only other objects in the room are a table and a sphere sitting on the table. You can make out the silhouette of the sphere, but not much else. Your curiosity starts to annoy you, so you get up to investigate the sphere, to touch it, perhaps to pick it up. When we can't see what an object is made of, our next impulse is to touch it, to move it in some way. We depend a lot on our eyes for information about the world, so when the circumstances are such that our vision is inadequate, we shift to other senses. Back to the sphere. Just as you are about to try to budge it so you can get some sense of what it is made of, the bright lights come on. You notice how the lights are reflecting off of the surface of the sphere, and your mind immediately identifies the sphere as being made of metal. It's probably too heavy to pick up.

In the everyday world, we get a lot of information about the objects around us by both their identifiable form and from the material it appears they are made of. It would probably seem a bit odd to you if the cat preening itself on a neighbor's window sill appeared to be made out of wood or glass. You would recognize the 3D form of the cat as something your mind would identify as "cat", but the wood or glass material would throw you off, sending your everyday perception into a confused spin. In computer graphics, we have the tools to make the unbelievable believable by altering the substance or material objects seem to be made of in an instant, amazing our friends and distracting our enemies.

In this chapter, I explore some of the ways that you can create interesting materials for your 3ds max objects.

Creating Interesting Textures for Objects

A *preset material* is to a texture what a Primitive is to a 3D model in 3ds max. Just as a Primitive can be used as a jumping off place to create more complex models, or as a model all on its own, a preset material can be used either as the foundation for creating a more complex texture or as it is. Using a preset material is the simplest way to create a texture for your 3ds max objects.

Navigating the Material Editor

The easiest way to access the Material Editor is by clicking its icon under the Rendering tab in the Tab Panel. (It's the fifth icon from the right, the one that looks like four spheres in a rectangular array.)

Clicking the Material Editor icon after you have placed a model (which could be a Primitive) in your scene brings up the Material Editor Panel, shown in Figure 15-1.

The six spheres you see at the top of the panel are all gray by default. Each represents a possible material that can be applied to your selected object. The panel is filled with options, many of which are for advanced 3ds max users. I don't cover every option in this book, but by the time you finish this chapter, you'll be able to create a wide range of interesting materials.

The first thing to do is to decide what type of Shader you want to create. Under the Shader Basic Properties area of this panel, you see a Shader Type area that by default reads BLINN. This is one Shader Type. To access the other Shader Types, left-click and hold the downward-pointing arrow next to BLINN. When the list appears, select the PHONG Shader Type, one of the most common. After you have selected the PHONG Shader Type, the PHONG Basic Parameters appear at the bottom of the panel, as shown in Figure 15-2.

Under Phong Basic Parameters, at the upper left, you will see the three basic parameters that you can change to create a basic Phong Material: Ambient, Diffuse, and Specular. Click the lock icon to the right to switch it off, and click the staple-like icons to the left to switch them off. A bit later, you will realize that Ambient, Diffuse, and Specular components are also grouped under what are known as Channels for a material or texture. Ambient, Diffuse, and Specular each display a rectangular area of color to their right. Disregard the smaller square boxes at the right. These larger rectangular areas are *Color Swatches*. Left-clicking a Color Swatch always brings up the Color Selector, allowing you to choose a new hue for that Color Swatch. Do that now. Select a new hue for the Ambient, Diffuse, and Specular basic Phong Parameters. Note that the preview image (the sphere) at the top of the panel displays your new choices.

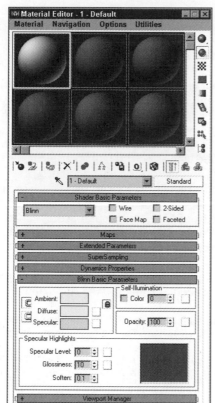

Figure 15-1:
The
Material
Editor Panel.

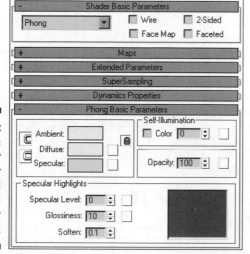

Figure 15-2:
The Basic
Parameter
settings for
the PHONG
Basic
Shader
Type.

What are the Ambient, Diffuse, and Specular components anyway, and how do they differ? The easiest one to understand is the Diffuse component. Diffuse represents the color or texture of a material as seen in the daylight. When you say an apple is red, you could also say, "That apple has a Diffuse color component that displays a red hue." (Try that the next time you go shopping with a friend.) The Ambient component is a bit more complex. You might think of it as the color or texture that an object displays when the lights are off, or in pitch darkness. Normally, this is set to a medium gray, because we lose most of our color sense in the dark. If it were set to a ruby red however, the object that has a Diffuse yellow value in the light would be seen as bright red in the dark. Specular is easy to describe when you think of an apple again. If you take an apple and shine it vigorously and place it on a well lit surface, you will see that the apple has reflective spots of light on its surface. These areas are known as *hot spots* by the computer graphics artist. Because different materials affect light differently, these Hot Spots, or Specular areas, can emit different colors (and even textures). In the Phong Specular Color Swatch, you can set the Specular Hot Spot (also called a *Highlight*) to its own hue.

You set the size and brightness of the Specular Hot Spot by changing the values for three settings under Specular Highlights in the panel:

- ✔ **Softness (a value that ranges from 0 to 1):** This setting affects the edge of the hot spot, whether it is to be soft and fuzzy or sharp.

- ✔ **Specular Level (0 to 999):** This setting affects the brightness of the hot spot, with larger values increasing the brightness.

- ✔ **Glossiness (0 to 100):** This setting affects the size of the hot spot, with increased values reducing the size.

Your mission, should you decide to accept it, is to create multiple objects and explore different value combinations — to seek out new names for the objects and to boldly create a series of different Shaders.

For example, you can create an object Phong Shader for each of the first six Material preview spheres you see at the top of the panel. Explore different value combinations. Type in a different name for each one in the label area provided. When you are finished, click and drag one at a time to your Perspective Viewport, dropping each Shader on whatever object you placed in the scene. This particular process creates Shaders differentiated by their Ambient, Diffuse, and Specular values.

Using preset materials in the Material Editor

The Material Editor enables you to tap into a wide variety of preset materials — which you can either apply directly to an object (by the drag-and-drop method discussed earlier), or customize first.

Accessing the Material Map Browser

The standard 3ds max material presets are found in the Material Map Browser. To access the Material Map Browser, open the Material Editor Panel, and left-click one of the preview spheres to activate it. Then, left-click the rectangular Standard button. This opens the Material Map Browser. Once in the Browser, select Mtl Library under Browse From, as shown in Figure 15-3.

By clicking the icons at the top of the Material Map Browser, you can display the presets as a list or as icons.

Selecting a preset material

Click any preset from the Browser to see it displayed in the preview area at the upper left of the Browser. Then click OK to make that preset appear in the Material Editor in the material slot you selected beforehand. When that's done, the material is ready to be dragged and dropped onto any 3D object in your scene.

Accessing new preset materials folders

At the bottom-left of the Material Map Browser you can see a list of File Commands. *Open* will allow you to search for previously saved preset materials anywhere in your computer. *Merge* will allow you to blend more than one Material Library together. To save your unique material creations as presets for further use, you can use the normal procedures: Save and Save As.

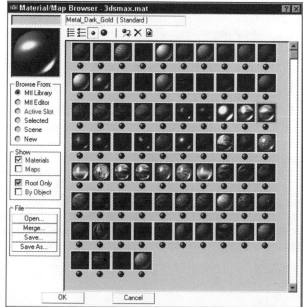

Figure 15-3:
The
Material
Map
Browser.

Applying preset materials to objects

To apply a preset material to any 3D object in your scene, simply use the left mouse button to drag and drop the material onto the object as displayed in any viewport. If you have a scene loaded with multiple objects, you see a label appear with the name of the particular object before you release the mouse button.

Saving your sanity: Go to Parent

3ds max has a materials capability that's the envy of the industry, but this capability comes at a price: the time you spend getting comfortable exploring its controls. My aim is to get you up and running with materials and textures, not to tell you everything there is to know about how to customize everything (which is impossible anyway). You may sometimes forget what you're doing and get hypnotized by the different controls in the Material Editor. Suddenly you may find yourself lost and unable to return to a place in the Material Editor that you recognize. If that happens (it's pretty much a guarantee, so I should say *when* it happens) one magic button in the Material Editor can save your sanity, returning you to a recognizable place — the Go To Parent. You can access Go To Parent by clicking the second-from-the-last icon on the right of the Material Editor. (It's a lot like running home to Mom for sanctuary when the neighborhood dog is chasing you.)

Go To Parent moves you toward the surface of the Material Editor Panel when you find yourself buried somewhere at the depths. Click it as many times as necessary, until your surroundings in the panel look recognizable.

Using Your Own Textures

Although the terms are used somewhat interchangeably, *materials* and *textures* also refer to two different ways of creating a "look" for your 3ds max objects. Materials can be composed of different kinds of components, some generated from mathematical formulas (called *procedurals*) and some based upon bitmapped images or pictures, the types of images you find on a CD collection or the ones you take with a digital still camera. The bitmapped images are what we normally call *textures* (or in 3ds max, *maps*) — image data based on photographic or digitally painted information. Many material presets have both procedural and textural information embedded in them.

Applying Ambient, Diffuse, and Specular texture and other preset content

Follow these steps to explore a preset operation:

1. **Place an object in your scene and open the Material Editor.**

2. **Select a Phong Material type, and go down to the settings under *Phong Basic Parameters*.**

   In the boxed area that contains the Ambient, Diffuse, and Specular color swatches, each of these components also shows a smaller square button to the right. This button serves to tell 3ds max that you want to base the Ambient, Diffuse, or Specular material components on something other than color.

3. **Click the button next to the Diffuse color swatch.**

   The Material/Map Browser opens.

Note that by default, NEW is selected under Browse From, and All is selected under Show. All swatches you see displayed are Maps. As you can see, there's a lot here to explore, including maps for marble, wood, water, and other textures. For a more dramatic effect, however, access one of your personal images stored somewhere on your computer's disk drives. To do this, simply click the first swatch in the display, which appears solid black. It's labeled Bitmap; clicking it opens a standard Windows path window. You can then navigate to the exact file on your computer that contains the image you want to use as an object texture, and it will appear in the slot you selected, previewed to the sphere in the Material Editor (as shown in Figure 15-4).

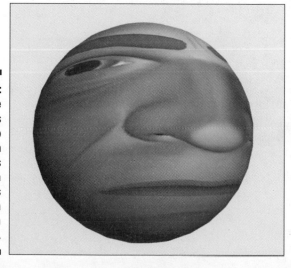

Figure 15-4:
Using the methods described to access an image, this picture of a face was used as a texture for a sphere.

Tweaking the Image Texture's Placement

When you select a bitmap to use as a texture for your material its *Coordinates* parameters appear in the Material Editor Panel. You may have to scroll down to see them, as shown in Figure 15-5.

Figure 15-5: The Coordinates settings for your bitmap texture.

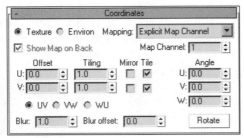

It's common to leave everything at its default here except for two possible values: U and V Tiling. By default, these are each set to 1.0, meaning that only one copy of your bitmap texture is mapped to the selected 3D object. Changing either or both of these values to a higher number (usually a whole number) maps multiple copies of your image-based texture to the object, as shown in Figure 15-6.

Figure 15-6: By changing both the U and V Tiling values to 4, my sphere now displays multiple copies of the image-based texture.

Channeling Your Thoughts

Computer graphics people look at the world differently than other folks, especially when it comes to textures. Where the normal person might describe the apple's texture as simply red and smooth, the computer graphics person needs other data as well to create a replica of the apple's texture on the computer. All this separate information is collected into individual parts called *channels*. Each channel holds specific information concerning the textural/material components of any object. The channels that describe an object's texture can be separated into the following channel types in 3ds max: Ambient, Diffuse, Specular, Glossiness, Self-Illumination, Opacity, Filter, Bump, Reflection, Refraction, and Displacement. In other 3D software, the exact name and quantity of the channels may differ somewhat, but generally these are industry standard channel type terms.

Filling channels with texture content

Just as the Ambient, Diffuse, and Specular channels can take on a bitmap texture (and even a procedural texture), you can also apply a texture to any other channel type in 3ds max. (You better watch out: Such activities can lead to unusual materials and other outbreaks of rampant creativity.) The channel-mapping controls are located in the Material Editor in the Maps Rollout.

When accessing the Maps Rollout, here are some things to remember:

✔ To access the Maps Rollout to use the channel mapping controls, scroll down to the Maps button in the Material Editor, and click it if it is not already open. The separate channel maps for a material appear.

✔ To use a bitmap or procedural texture to any channel in the Maps Rollout, simply click the Map bar next to that channel's name. (All the Map bars are set to None by default.) The numerical value areas in the channels indicate the strength that the selected texture will be applied at. Clicking any Map bar will bring up the Materials/Map Browser, allowing you to select any of the Map presets or to open any image in storage anywhere on your computer.

✔ If selecting content for the Ambient Color channel (selecting a Map for the Ambient channel will create a material that shows the contents of that map wherever the 3D object is lit from), remember that the Ambient and Diffuse channels are usually locked together, but they don't have to be.

- The Diffuse Color channel is the channel most commonly used for a texture map. In graphics-speak, saying that an object is made of cloth (for instance) means that the pattern of the cloth is what forms the Diffuse Color channel's content.

- If you place a texture map in the Specular channel of an object, whenever a hot spot appears on the object, it displays that texture.

- Placing a texture map in the Glossiness channel creates a lacquer-like finish over the targeted 3D object.

- You can set the Specular level by using a texture map instead of a numerical value. The parts of the image that are darker will influence the Specular level less than those areas that are lighter.

- Self-Illumination (also called Glow in other 3D software) is influenced by the lightness and darkness of areas of a texture map, disposing of color. Because you usually want an object to glow evenly across its surface, a solid grayscale texture map serves to control the illumination.

- The Opacity channel of an object's texture controls how opaque/transparent the object will be. As with the Self-Illumination settings, it refers to a texture map's degree of brightness or darkness, not color. Solid black becomes 100% invisible and solid white becomes 100% visible. Grayscale values in between the two extremes become partially visible.

- Setting a Filter Color pattern filters out the textures colors from the targeted object's perceived hues.

- The Bump channel is one of the most common channels to place a texture map in. The colors of the texture map are discarded, and only the lightness/darkness used. The darker areas of the texture map will look like depressions on the surface of the object, while the lighter areas of the texture map will create what appears to be elevated areas. The Bump channel is the only one whose level can be set as high as 999. This technique is called *bump mapping*.

Determining Reflection/Refraction channel content

Placing a texture map in these channels creates a "fake" reflection or refraction. What I mean by that is the contents of the reflection/refraction aren't really present in the environment of the object, but it just seems that they are. If you have a 3D teapot object, for instance, and texture map its reflection channel with an image of a sunset, the surface of the teapot will look as if it is reflecting a real sunset.

Creating a true reflective object in 3ds max requires a slightly different approach. To do that, select Reflect/Refract/Raytrace when you are in the Material/Map Browser. Your targeted 3D object then truly reflects other objects in its environment, as shown in Figure 15-7.

When you work with texture maps in the Displacement channel of a 3D object's material, it's always a tossup whether to call what you are doing texture mapping or modeling. Displacement mapped content actually deforms the geometry of the targeted object's surface, so it's unlike something like Bump Mapping, which is a fake way to do something similar. For that reason, objects to be Displacement mapped should have a larger polygon count, for the displacement to create a smoother result. Use the Tessellate Modifier to create a denser mesh, as shown in Figure 15-8.

Figure 15-7:
The Reflection channel of a sphere texture-mapped with the Reflect/Refract map from the Materials/Map Browser, allowing its surface to reflect the other spheres in the scene (reflection was set to 50%).

Figure 15-8:
Displace-
ment
mapping
affects the
geometry of
a targeted
object,
causing true
depres-
sions and
elevations
on the
surface.

Chapter 16

Using Composite Textures

*I*t makes sense that the more interesting and unique your computer graphics, the more you'll please your audience — and the more time they'll spend focusing on what you do and singing your praises from the mountaintop. In 3D graphics and animation, the terms "interesting" and "unique" can refer to many aspects of a project. For example, the overall theme and subject matter automatically draws a crowd that enjoys that theme, but that alone isn't enough. Consider a science fiction theme. How many bad sci-fi movies have you seen? There are a lot out there, and most of them are full of computer graphics and animation . . . done badly, and in most cases, copied from someone else. With respect to computer graphics and animation, a good presentation deserves a well-crafted story line, interesting and unique 3D models, dazzling effects, and believable (or fantastically unbelievable) textures. Great models with terrible or run-of-the-mill textures don't enhance a good script the way they should. Human actors have to possess a believable, personable, and unique charisma on the screen, and much of the charisma of a 3D model is its texture and perceivable material. Seldom do the pros apply an out-of-the-box texture to a super 3D model without tweaking it, because it would look like everyone else's texture. The object in computer graphics and animation is to make your work stand out, to give it a unique signature. This chapter looks at some ways that you can accomplish that task.

The Mapping Types

Pretend you have a job in a store's gift-wrapping department. Customers bring you all sorts of items to gift-wrap. As long as you can place the items in a box, the wrapping process is a snap. But what if you run out of boxes, and the paper wrapping has to be applied to the item itself? That can be more of a problem. If the item takes up a cubic space, it'll be easy; it's as with wrapping an item in a box (given that you may have to make allowances for anything that protrudes from the item). Problems arise when the items to be wrapped are not cubic at all. If someone brings you a beach ball, for instance, you have to gather and bunch the wrapping at two of the poles of the ball to wrap it securely. If the item is a cylindrical tin of candy, wrapping the sides is easy enough, but you'll have to account for the two ends. If someone purchases a model of the Great Pyramid of Cheops, a tetrahedral form, then other problems crop up.

When you apply textures to 3D objects in a computer graphics program, the computer has to take into account how the texture *maps to* the 3D surface so any pattern in the texture is not stretched or distorted. There are a number of different *mapping types* that the computer can call upon to make the wrapping calculations easier and faster.

Applying the right mapping type

Time to get a couple of definitions out of the way before I cover Mapping Types. When you apply mapping to a 3D object, it's called *UVW Mapping*. The U is equivalent to the X axis (horizontal axis) of an image, bitmap, or procedural. The V is equivalent to the Y axis (vertical axis) of an image. The W is equivalent to the perpendicular Normal of a 2D image, or its Z axis. To apply a Mapping Type, the first thing you have to do is to place an object in a scene. Any object will do, but for starters, I use a sphere primitive. I'll apply a bitmapped image as a texture in the sphere's Diffuse Channel (see Chapter 15). See Figure 16-1.

As you can see in Figure 16-1, the image consists of a photo of a face inside a gridded backdrop. After the image is selected for the Diffuse Channel of the sphere, we have to activate the UVW Mapping Modifier. You can do so by choosing the UVW Mapping Modifier from the Modifier list. The UVW options appear in the Command Panel.

At the top of the UVW Modifier Command Panel are seven Mapping Type options:

- ✔ Planar
- ✔ Cylindrical (with or without a Cap)
- ✔ Spherical
- ✔ Shrink Wrap
- ✔ Box
- ✔ Face
- ✔ XYZ to UVW

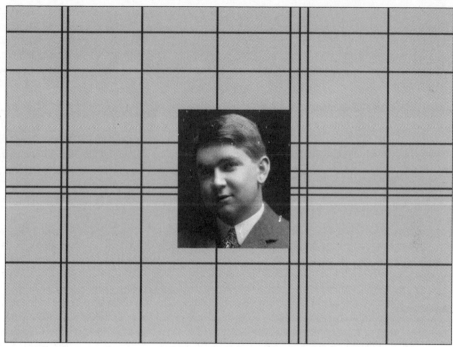

The last selection is best used for 3D procedural textures — textures created from mathematical formulas. The Length/Width/Height values in the center of the Command Panel represent the dimensions of your targeted 3D object. Following that section are the UVW Tiling options, including the capability to Flip the texture on any UVW coordinate.

I get into more detail about the other options a bit later in this chapter. The purpose of having the Mapping Type options is to choose the one that wraps your texture in a way that produces the best mapping of the 3D object you're working with. It's pretty obvious that you would use the Planar option to map a planar 2D or 3D object, a Cylindrical Mapping Type to map a cylinder, and so on. The Shrink Wrap option is used when you are mapping a texture to a complex 3D surface, like the head of a character for instance.

Every rule in a 3D application is meant to be understood, and then at least explored further if not broken. In this case, it means that you should see what happens when you use a Cubic Mapping Type on a sphere, or a Spherical Mapping Type on a Cone, and so on. You may come up with some pretty unique and useful texture mapped objects in the process. At the least, you'll get a better intuitive feel for how the Mapping Types work. See Figure 16-2.

Figure 16-2:
A sphere mapped with various Mapping Types. Clockwise from left top: Planar, Cylindrical without Caps, Cylindrical with Caps, Spherical, Shrink Wrapped, Box, and Face.

Selecting the mapping axis

The lower part of the UVW Map Modifier's Command Panel reveals a number of options listed under Alignment. The X, Y, and Z options represent the axis that you are targeting a specific Mapping Type to. It's usually a good idea to select each one in turn, and to take a look at the Perspective Viewport to see how that particular axis alignment affects the texture you are mapping. In Figure 16-3, Alignment was targeted to the X-, Y-, and Z-axis — and it's pretty clear that aligning to the Z-axis worked best in this case.

Figure 16-3:
The same texture when mapped using the Cylindrical Mapping Type with Caps on.

In the Alignment section at the bottom of the Command Panel, you can see eight alignment commands. Clicking on any one of these options further refines how the texture is mapped to the object, so you should explore each one to see what it does. The Fit command is important here; it attempts to shrink the mapping type to more closely fit the targeted 3D object. View Align can provide an interesting choice. Using View Align, the view you have from any selected viewport serves to determine the angle at which the texture is mapped to the object. The Length, Width, and Height in the UVW Map Modifier are useful when getting a photo of, for example, floor tile to be scaled to real-world units (a bitmap of a 12" floor tile can be mapped using Planar: length=12", width= 12").

Marrying Bitmaps and Procedurals

One more option in the UVW Map Modifiers Command Panel is worth a closer look — the Map Channel number. Think of a Mapping Channel as one item in a sandwich, like a piece of ham or some Swiss cheese. Just as you can add as many ingredients to a sandwich as needed to satisfy your appetite, so you can have as many Mapping Channels as needed to create a composite material.

If you are an Adobe Photoshop user, you can equate a Mapping Channel with a Layer, knowing that image data on separate Layers in Photoshop is what creates a final, composited image.

To give a Mapping Channel a specific identification number, you must first apply a texture (bitmap or procedural) to a 3D object. When you do that, the Coordinates Rollout opens in the Material Editor, as shown in Figure 16-4.

Figure 16-4:
The Coordinates Rollout opens up in the Material Editor.

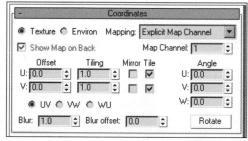

By default, Mapping is set to *Explicit Map Channel*. Next to *Map Channel* is an input area that enables you to number the Map Channel any whole number you desire. When set, this number is stored in the computer, and can be used to set specific types and alignments in the UVW Command Panel.

Making texture sandwiches

In 3ds max, a composited texture works like a texture sandwich whose separate ingredients can include either or both types of texture (bitmap and procedural). Three main types of composited textures are available: Blend, Top/Bottom, and Composite.

Blend

A *Blend* is a combination of two separate textures, at least at first glance. Here's how to create a Texture Blend:

1. **Place an object in a 3ds max scene.**

2. **With the object still selected, open its Material Editor. (Select a preview slot that doesn't contain a Material yet.)**

3. **Click the button that reads *Standard* by default.**

   The Material/Map Browser appears.

4. **Choose Blend from the list, and click OK to accept your choice.**

   A panel appears asking you whether you want to Discard Old Material or Keep Old Material as a Sub-Material.

5. **Choose Discard Old Material.**

   The Blend Basic Parameters rollout appears in the Material Editor (see Figure 16-5.

6. **Choose Material 1 or Material 2 to select a separate material or texture from the Material/Map Browser.**

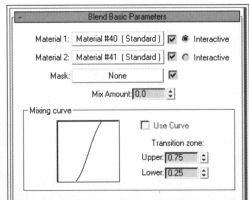

Figure 16-5:
The Blend
Basic
Parameters
rollout.

You can set the Mix Amount as a percentage (50% would give each Material half of its content on the object) or by placing values in the Mixing Curve area.

7. Choose Bitmap for each Material component.

You can create a Material composed of two blended bitmap images, or a mix of Bitmap and Procedural Textures.

Use the UVW Map Modifier to set the Map Type and Alignment options.

Top/Bottom

The Top/Bottom texture sandwich creates a Material that uses one texture (bitmap or procedural) for the top part of an object, and another texture (bitmap or procedural) for the bottom part of the object.

1. Place an object in a 3ds max scene.

2. With the object still selected, open its Material Editor.

Select a preview slot that doesn't contain a Material yet.

3. Choose the button that by default reads Standard.

The Material/Map Browser appears.

4. Choose Top/Bottom from the list, and click OK to accept your choice.

A panel appears, asking whether you want to Discard Old Material or Keep Old Material as a Sub-Material.

5. Choose Discard Old Material.

The Top/Bottom Basic Parameters rollout appears in the Material Editor, as shown in Figure 16-6.

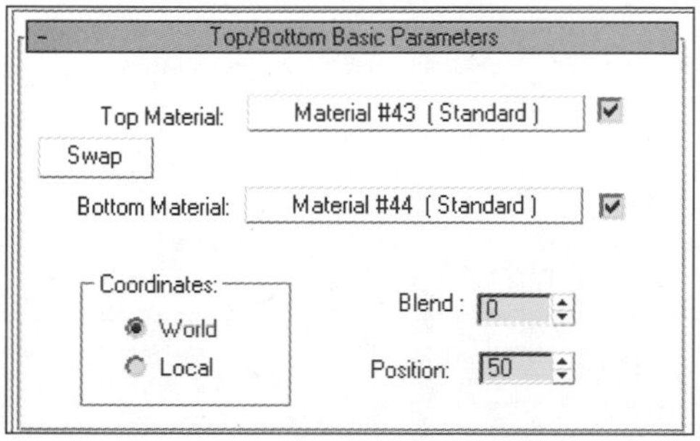

Figure 16-6:
The Top/Bottom Basic Parameters rollout.

6. As before, use the Top Material and Bottom Material buttons to select your textures by way of the Material/Map Browser.

Decide whether the textures should refer to the World or Local axis. The Blend value determines the boundary between the two textures, with 0 being a sharp edge and higher values blending the boundary. The Position value determines the position of the boundary between your two materials, which by default is set to 50.

Composite

When it comes to making texture sandwiches (textures that call upon a multitude of components), this is the mega-Dagwood you've been dreaming about. Here's what to do:

1. **Place an object in a 3ds max scene.**

2. **With the object still selected, open its Material Editor. Select a preview slot that doesn't contain a Material yet.**

3. **Select the button that by default reads Standard, which brings up the Material/Map Browser.**

4. **Choose Composite from the list, and click OK to accept your choice.**

   A panel appears, asking whether you want to Discard Old Material or Keep Old Material as a Sub-Material.

5. **Choose Discard Old Material.**

   The Composite Basic Parameters rollout appears in the Material Editor, as shown in Figure 16-7. The Composite option enables you to mix nine separate materials together; each of them can contain any number of sub-Composite (or any other) materials.

Figure 16-7:
A super texture sandwich, with as many sub-Composites or other materials as look good to you. (Pass the mayo, please.)

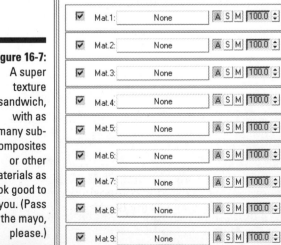

6. **In the Composite Basic Parameters rollout, set the parameters for the Base Material by clicking the Base Material button.**

   You can set the Base Material to use any Channel Map combination you like.

7. **Set the other nine Materials in the stack.**

   Each Material can contain bitmap or procedural textures, and each can also reference a whole new set of Composite or other Material Types. You can composite each layered Material to the others (Composite Type) by choosing A (adding it), S (subtracting it), or M (multiplying it). Setting the percentage values determines the strength of each layer.

The number of variations in creating unique texture-based Materials with the Composite method is really as infinite as you can imagine. Well, okay, maybe not as far as the Hubble Telescope can see, but I'm sure you could cover all the bases in a mere 100 years of exploration.

Using the Maps Rollout

As if your head wasn't already swimming with the possibilities, I need to torture you with one more important way to create multiple texture sandwiches. This method involves using the standard Map Rollout in the Material Editor. If that looks a bit familiar, it's no accident; procedures covered earlier in this chapter applied a bitmap or procedural texture to the Mapping Channels. Choosing the Bitmap option in the Material/Map Browser means you can use any bitmap image on your system as a texture. Dozens of additional options in this Browser are available; as usual, feel free to try them out. One of those options, in particular, is worth a closer look as an alternate way to create texture sandwiches: RGB Multiply, shown in Figure 16-8.

Choosing the RGB Multiply option in the Material/Map Browser brings up the RGB Multiply Parameters rollout in the Material Editor.

At the top of this rollout, you get two separate choices for colors or textures. The rollout won't let you set a percentage, so selecting two colors creates a third color for the texture, just as if you were using paints. Using two textures blends them depending on the Alpha options following. Alpha information depends on the grayscale lightness/darkness of the areas of your images. Try all three Alpha options to see how the textures blend.

You can apply the RGB Multiply option to any Mapping Channel (and even many Channels at the same time) to get interesting composited results, but pay careful attention to four specific Mapping Channels when you use this method: Diffuse, Bump, Opacity, and Displacement.

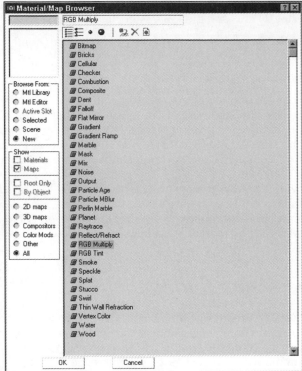

Figure 16-8:
Choose the
RGB
Multiply
option in the
Material/
Map
Browser for
any Map
Channel
you like.

RGB-Multiply-with-Diffusion-Channel sandwiches

Using RGB Multiply in the Diffusion Channel creates some intriguing surface-patterned textures; Figure 16-9 provides a sample.

Figure 16-9:
The RGB
Multiply
method
creates
interesting
surface
textures
when used
in the
Diffusion
Channel.

RGB-Multiply-with-Bump-Channel sandwiches

Used in the Bump Channel, the RGB Multiply result can provide a look that no other process can match, as shown in Figure 16-10.

Figure 16-10:
The dark areas of multiple textures create seeming depressions in a Bump Map; the lighter areas result in an "elevated" look, as seen on this "scratched" sphere.

RGB-Multiply-with-Opacity-Channel sandwiches

When you use the RGB Multiply method in an object's Opacity Channel, the combined grayscales in the textures create visible and invisible areas, as Figure 16-11 demonstrates.

Figure 16-11:
RGB Multiply creates complex areas of opacity and transparency when used in an object's Opacity Channel.

RGB-Multiply-with-Displacement-Channel sandwiches

Remember that Displacement Mapping alters the actual geometry of a 3D object, so take care in applying a low or medium strength of the Displacement Mapping data (usually, an amount of 25% or less is sufficient). Because displaced geometry works best on objects with a higher polygon count, Tessellate the object a couple of times to thicken the 3D mesh. After that, you can try using the RGB Multiplier option in the object's Displacement Channel — which results in an image similar to Figure 16-12.

Figure 16-12:
Using the RGB Multiply option in the Displace-ment Channel warps the actual geometry of the object.

Take some time to test-drive all the options in the Material/Map Browser. Make some notes on any especially interesting texture data you create for your Mapping Channels.

Chapter 17

Backdrops and Backgrounds

• •

In This Chapter

▶ Creating color and material backdrops and backgrounds

▶ Using bitmap image backgrounds

▶ Using a movie file as a background

• •

Sometimes the only actor on your 3ds max stage may be a single 3D model, with no surrounding objects to support its placement. This could happen if the model is a revolving space station or a lone flying bird. If you were to use the singular model in a story sequence without anything else in the environment, the model would look awfully lonely. Even if you did nothing more than use an interesting color against which the model was placed, that would be better than a black or white backdrop. In the case of a space station, you'd probably want to place it against a star populated section of the cosmos. In the case of the bird, it might look more believable if placed against a cloudy sky, or even an aerial view of a landscape. Backdrops and backgrounds can add to or detract from the overall impact of a 3D scene.

Most times, the terms *background* and *backdrop* are used interchangeably. In some 3D software, however, they are distinguished from each other. In that case, the term *background* means an image or animation mapped to a flat plane; *backdrop* means an image or animation always seen flat, no matter how the perspective changes. In this book, unless I say otherwise, I use the terms interchangeably.

Creating a Glorious Backdrop

Your main actor or central 3D model needs some supporting elements against which to perform. If your main actor is a wooden mannequin for instance, it may be appreciated more if placed on a terrain with a sky in the distance, or on a floor in a room that has other artifacts. Sometimes, a simple color or a gradient of hues is enough to tell a part of the story, or perhaps a wallpaper-like pattern. It all depends on the story you're telling — and the scene from that story being presented. Severe close-ups of your main actor may look best if the background is simple; views from farther off may benefit if you can see exactly what other elements exist in the actor's environment. Selecting the right background is vital when you want to tell a visual story.

Using color hues as backgrounds

The simplest background is a single color hue. Color is also perceived as emotion by the human eye — reds indicate a more active sensibility and blues denote a calmer situation. Backgrounds can also consist of multiple *hues,* colors that blend into each other in various ways.

Creating single-color backgrounds

To create a single-color background that displays any color in the spectrum, follow these steps:

1. **Choose the Rendering Tab in the Tab Panel, and then choose the Environment Tab below it.**

   The Environment Panel opens, as shown in Figure 17-1.

2. **At the top of the panel, click the Color swatch under Background.**

   The Color Selector: Background Color panel appears, as shown in Figure 17-2.

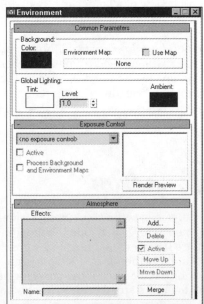

Figure 17-1:
The
Environment
Panel.

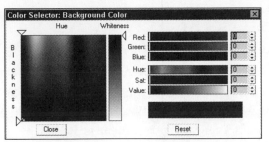

3. **Use the left mouse button to click and drag in the color area until you select the color you like.**

4. **Click Close to apply your chosen color.**

That's it. Your background is now the color you've selected.

Creating multicolor backgrounds

A Gradient Map uses a range of colors to create a smooth gradient. You can create a multicolor background by using a Gradient Map. Here's how it's done:

1. **Open the Material Editor and select a material slot that has no material yet.**

2. **Click the Map button to access the Material/Map Browser, and then choose Browse from⇨New.**

3. **Choose Gradient from the list and click OK to accept your choice.**

   In the Material Editor, the Gradient Parameters rollout opens (see Figure 17-3).

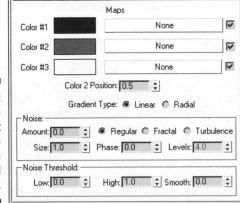

Figure 17-3:
The
Gradient
Parameters
rollout in the
Material
Editor.

4. **Click each of the three color swatches under Maps in the Gradient Parameters rollout.**

   The Color Selector appears.

5. **Choose a color from the Color Selector and set its color value.**

   The value under position determines the blend zone for color #2. You can leave it at its default, or choose another value in the range 0 to 1.0.

6. **Choose the Gradient Type you want, Linear or Radial.**

   For the time being, keep it simple. Other goodies are available for later experimentation. For example, the values under Noise and Noise Threshold are available to explore, though it's best to leave them at their default while you get used to what the main controls do. Some controls under the Coordinates rollout for the Gradient Map allow you to change the direction of the gradient when it maps to a background: the W Angle and the Rotate buttons. Try them out after you get some practice creating Gradient Maps.

7. **Choose Rendering⇨Environments in the Tab Panel.**

   The Environment Panel opens.

8. **Put a check mark next to Use Map, and click the Environment Map button.**

   The Material/Map Browser appears. A dialog box pops up asking if the map should be an *instance* or a *copy*. Choose instance, which will link the map in the material to the environment map so that any changes in the Material Editor will be updated in the environment.

9. **Choose Browse from Mtl Editor.**

   Your new Gradient Map Material shows up in the list.

10. **Choose your new material and click OK.**

    The Gradient Map you designed is now your background image.

Using preset materials as backgrounds

You may think that absolutely any map you create, bitmapped or procedure-based, can be used as a background, and you're right! This means that the same materials you create for using as textures on your 3D objects (Chapter 15) can also be used as backdrops, and vice-versa. Backgrounds, however, require no attention to UVW Map modifications.

Out-of-the-box presets

When you access the materials in the Browse from⇨New section of the Material/Map Browser, you get a number of items in the list that are ready-made for background use. A prominent example is the Gradient option (described earlier), and here's a short list of others to try out: Bitmap, Bricks, Cellular, Checker, Composite, Dent, Marble, Mix, Perlin Marble, Planet, RGB Multiply, Smoke, Speckle, Splat, Stucco, Swirl, Water, and Wood. Figure 17-4 gives you an idea of what to expect from them.

Customizing a material preset for a background

You can customize any preset material you access in the Material/Map Browser if you alter its settings in the Material Editor. The parameter controls that appear for your use will specifically reflect the material you choose. Take, for example, Bricks.

After you choose the Bricks preset in the Material/Map Browser, two associated parameter control rollouts appear in the Material Editor — Coordinates and Standard Controls — as shown in Figure 17-5.

Figure 17-4:
Many presets in the Material/Map Browser are excellent as background textures. Top left to bottom right: Bricks, Cellular, Marble, Noise, Planet, and Wood.

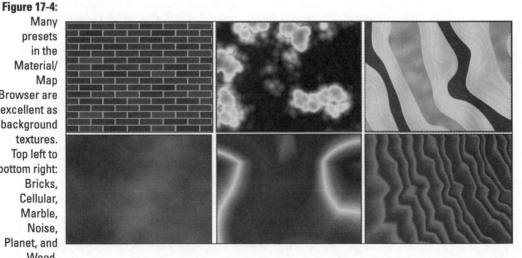

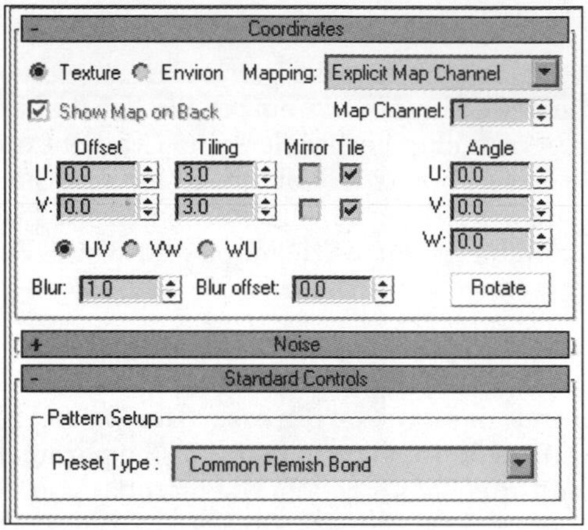

Figure 17-5:
Bricks-
associated
rollouts.

The Coordinates rollout offers a choice between Texture and Environment mapping. If you want to use the Bricks texture for a background instead of a 3D object, choose Environ(ment). When you set the mapping as Environment, you have the choice of several ways to use the map. Screen will stretch the map to fit the rendered image like a flat billboard behind all of your scene objects. Spherical and the other environment settings will wrap the map around a distant sphere, and so on. *Hint:* A noise map with tweaked thresholds will make a 3d starfield background when mapped with spherical mapping. This holds for all texture types when you have this choice presented to you. The higher you raise the U and V Tiling values, the smaller the Bricks and the more of them. Altering the W Angle value rotates the Bricks texture on the background.

The Standard Controls rollout offers some interesting options for the Bricks texture. Here, accessing the available drop-down list, you can choose from a number of Brick types, including Common Flemish Bond and English Bond. This is just one example of how you can customize a preset texture selection using the controls and parameters in the Material Editor's rollouts.

Using Bitmap Images as Backgrounds

When you choose the Bitmap option in the Material/Map Browser, you can access any bitmap photographic or painted image you have on file, and use it as a background image. Using photographic images can lend credibility to a 3ds max scene. For instance, say you just modeled an alien spacecraft. Using an image that displayed the White House as the background would immediately tell a story, and the photographic background would make your 3D-modeled alien ship look all the more believable, as shown in Figure 17-6.

Figure 17-6:
Left: a basic
flying
saucer
model.
Right: the
same
model,
placed
against a
photo-
graphic
image of a
cosmic sky
taken
through a
telescope.

To use any bitmap image as a background, follow these steps:

1. **Open the Material Editor. Open the Environment dialog box. Place them side by side.**

2. **In the Environment dialog box, click the None button.**

3. **Choose Browse from New in the Material/Map Browser.**

4. **Choose Bitmap from the list and click OK.**

5. **Find the bitmap you want to use and click Open.**

6. **Drag the map from the Map button in the Environment dialog box to an unused sample sphere in the Material Editor. Choose Instance when prompted. Note that Mapping in the Material Editor is set to Environment: Screen for you.**

The image you chose is now the background for your scene.

Animated Bitmap Backgrounds

Although Part VI of this book gives you the scoop on animation in 3ds max in detail, I considered it a good idea to cover the use of animated backgrounds here; we are dealing with all sorts of different backgrounds. An animated background is essentially a movie within a movie. In Hollywood, an animated sequence is sometimes used as a backdrop for a live scene. For instance, this happens often when the camera focuses upon actors speaking in the front seat of a moving vehicle. The moving images that depict the street whizzing by are often a separate movie projected on the backdrop. In 3ds max, you can create animated backgrounds just as they do in the movies. (In fact, many filmmakers use 3ds max for just this purpose.)

Using animations as backgrounds

Although animation techniques and rendering procedures get a closer look elsewhere in the book (see Parts VI and VIII, respectively), you can use an animation for a background — it's as simple as using a single image. 3ds max accepts sequenced single frames (images that have a numbered extension), AVI movies, and QuickTime movies as background files. You select a movie file just as you would a single image, and configure it as a background in the same way, as shown in Figure 17-7.

If you have any AVI or QuickTime movies on your system, you can explore using them as backgrounds. (Meanwhile, watch the skies!)

Figure 17-7:
Scenes from an animation that shows a modeled flying saucer moving against an old film clip of the Old West. You can find this animation (Saucer_01. AVI) in the ANIMS folder on this book's CD-ROM.

Part V
Lights, Cameras, Action!

The 5th Wave   By Rich Tennant

THE GLACIER MOVEMENT PROJECT UPDATE THEIR WEBSITE

Camera ready? Wait a minute, hold it. Ready? Wait for the action...steady...steady...not yet...eeeasy. Hold it. Okay, stay focused. Ready? Not yet...steeeady...eeeasy...

In this part . . .

That's the first thing you do when you return to your home or apartment at night after opening the door? More then likely, you grope for the light switch. When the light comes on, your comfortable surroundings appear, and hopefully everything remains in the place that it was in when you left. Light and shadow also give us cues about where everything is in 3D space. Distant objects may look fuzzier and less detailed, while something approaching us from the distance calls for our attention as its details and purpose become clearer. When the light is too bright, we feel assaulted and seek the shade. When the light is too dim, we feel a bit fearful and seek safety. Sunlight, lamps, flashlights, candles . . . all cast their own enhancements on our world. 3ds max allows you to control all of the features of multiple light sources.

3D cameras in a virtual world allow you to travel anywhere, giving you views of your 3D scenes from any angle or distance. The camera is at once both an object and an extension of your eyes. You can peek into any crevice in a scene to capture still or moving images, then move on to another point of interest. This part of the book is about creating and using lights and cameras in 3ds max.

Chapter 18

Lights

3ds max has some great light and shadow features, which, if used correctly, can do far more than just make objects visible. Lighting adds drama and makes the scene more interesting to the viewer. Think of all the great movies you've seen that use light and shadow so effectively (like Citizen Kane), and maybe some other not-so-great movies. I bet lighting played a major role in all of them.

Lights and shadows have to be considered as carefully as you might think about the form of a 3D model, its texture, or the background elements in a scene. Just settling for a non-descript light cheats the viewer's sense of the underlying parts of a story, be it a major film or a short 3D animation. Lighting applied in the wrong way can make everything in a scene look pasty and bland. Lighting applied in the right way, especially in a 3D computer-animated scene, blurs the line between fantasy and reality. Your viewers can more easily accept what they're seeing, no matter how bizarre or fantastic.

Placing and Configuring Lights on the Scene

In some ways, the virtual world follows common sense no less than the real world. For example, you have to create content for a scene before you can apply light to it. You can find lights easiest by choosing Create⇨Lights from the Command Panel. You can also click the Lights icon (third from the left) under the Create tab. Two lights lists appear in the Lights Command Panel rollout — Standard and Photometric — as shown in Figure 18-1.

Figure 18-1:
The
Standard
lights and
Photometric
lights
rollouts
in the
Command
Panel.

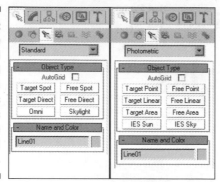

The Standard lights consist of Target Spot, Target Direct, Omni, Free Spot, Free Direct, and Skylight. The Photometric lights are Target Point, Target Linear, Target Area, IES Sun, Free Point, Free Linear, Free Area, and IES Sky.

Create a rectangular slab to act as a tabletop, and lathe an object to place on it. Figure 18-2 shows one possibility.

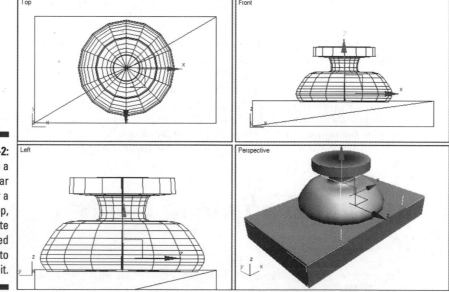

Figure 18-2:
Create a
rectangular
slab for a
tabletop,
and create
a lathed
object to
place on it.

Use a Standard Omni Light as an example. Do the following:

1. **Choose Create⇨Lights⇨Standard in the Command Panel, and then click Omni.**

2. **Click to place the Omni Light in the Front Viewport.**

3. **Switch to the Top Viewport to change its position so you get a well-lighted scene in the Perspective Viewport, as shown in Figure 18-3.**

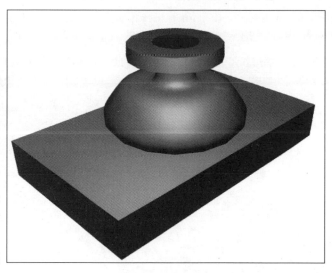

Figure 18-3:
After placing the Omni Light where you want it, you'll see the result in the Perspective Viewport.

If you did a render now (for a quick refresher on rendering a scene, spin through Chapter 24) your lighted scene would look similar to Figure 18-3, with no shadows.

4. **To create a more realistic lighted scene: With the Omni Light still selected, choose the Modify Command Panel.**

At the top of the Light modification commands in the Command Panel, a number of controls appear under General Parameters.

5. **Under Shadows, click in the On check box to place a check mark there.**

6. **Click the Exclude radio button.**

The Include/Exclude Panel appears. Use the Exclude/Include Panel to tell 3ds max which objects in the scene to affect with the selected light, and which ones not to affect. You have a lot of lighting control, and only 3ds max boasts this feature.

7. **Shift-select both items in the Scene Objects column.**

These objects serve as your tabletop and lathed object; they turn dark when selected.

8. **With both objects selected, click Include (instead of the default Exclude) at the upper right.**

9. **With both your tabletop and lathed objects still selected, click the right-pointing double arrows at the center of the panel.**

   Your object's name appears in the Include column at the right.

10. **Click OK to accept the changes.**

11. **Create a texture for both your tabletop and the lathed object, and use UVW Mapping commands to map them.**

If you render the scene now, it appears much more interesting and believable, with cast shadows where the Omni Light causes them to be, as shown in Figure 18-4.

Figure 18-4:
A scene with cast shadows, a Wood texture on the tabletop, and a Marble texture on the lathed object.

Other important light controls

The kind makers of 3ds max have included a number of other controls in a light's Modifier Command Panel. Some are for advanced users, and beyond the scope of this book, but you need to be aware of a couple.

Intensity/Color/Attenuation

Under Intensity/Color/Attenuation in the light's Modifier Command Panel (shown in Figure 18-5) are controls you should be aware of.

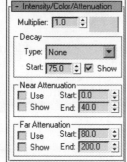

Figure 18-5:
The
Intensity/
Color/
Attenuation
rollout.

To fine-tune the look of your scene, you can adjust the following settings:

- ✔ **Multiplier and Color Swatch:** Leave the Multiplier at its default setting of 1, unless you want a much dimmer (values less than 1) or a much brighter (values more than 1) light. The Color Swatch enables you to set the light's color. Just click and choose the color you want from the Color Selector: Light Color Panel.

- ✔ **Decay:** You can investigate the subtle differences among these options in the Type List: None, Inverse, and Inverse Square. (I like to leave Show checked because it enables me to see the light's active area in any viewport.) The Start Value adjusts the size of the light's active area (the area affected by the light at maximum strength before any decay sets in).

- ✔ **Near/Far Attenuation:** Explore different values here to see how the light can be attenuated or dampened at different distances. When you're just beginning to use lights, leaving these values at their defaults is best.

Shadow Parameters

You also need to know how to configure the Shadow Parameters, given the following choices:

- ✔ **Color and Density:** Use the Color Swatch to set the Shadow's color, normally set to black. There's not much point raising the Density above 1.0. Lowering the density will enable textures in shadows to peek through, which can be effective as far as realism is concerned.

- ✔ **Map:** This is a neat option. If Map is checked and you click the button that by default reads "None," you can map a shadow with any texture option in the Material/Map Browser! Wouldn't a paisley shadow look keen?

- ✔ **Light Affects Shadow Color:** If your light has a specific hue, checking this option enables the light color to influence the shadow's color too.

She Lights Me, She Lights Me Not . . .

Selecting and placing the right type of lights can make all the difference in the world when it comes to presenting your best images and animations to your audience. Already having gone through the basic process for light placement, it's time to take a look at each of the Standard and Photometric light types to see how they differ.

The Standard lights

The Standard lights are Target Spot, Target Direct, Omni, Free Spot, Free Direct, and Skylight. They can be accessed in the Command Panel by going to Create⇨Lights⇨Standard. Here's what they offer you:

✔ **Target Spot:** You place the Target Spot by a click-and-drag movement, using the left mouse button. The click places the position of the light, and the drag movement enables you to place the position of the target. Both the light position and the target position can be moved with the Select and Move tool. The cone of the Target Spot can be either circular (the default) or Rectangular. Use the Rectangular option to project an image or texture, as shown in Figure 18-6.

Figure 18-6:
Using a Target Spot, you can center in on a specific part of the scene.

✔ **Target Direct:** The main difference between the Target Spot and the Target Direct Light is that the latter has a cylindrical light cone. The result is a subtle change in the way the light falls on targeted objects, as shown in Figure 18-7.

Figure 18-7:
Compare this Target Direct light with the Target Spot light effect shown in Figure 18-6.

✔ **Omni:** The Omni Light is often referred to as a *Lightbulb* because the light it casts is multidirectional. The result is a lack of targeted definition in the effect, as shown in Figure 18-8.

Figure 18-8:
The Omni light casts its rays in all directions.

✔ **Free Spot:** The difference between the Free Spot and the Target Spot is that the Free Spot offers you no target to manipulate. The Free Spot is a quick-and-dirty way to use a spotlight.

✔ **Free Direct:** The Free Direct, unlike the Target Direct, has no target point to adjust.

✔ **Skylight:** The Skylight serves to add overall light to a scene. It creates no shadows on its own, and has few controls. You can change its color and strength. Use the Skylight in combination with other lights to affect objects in the scene. The Skylight can be used by itself when used with the Advanced Lighting⇨Light Tracer command. Just choose Rendering⇨ Light Tracer, and then render the scene as usual.

Photometric lights

Photometric lights are best used to create light models that require precise effects. One of the features Photometric lights offer is that their color can be determined by a set of specific light types, including: Fluorescents, Halides, Incandescents, Mercury, and Xenon. In general, the Targeted and Free Photometric lights should be placed close to the object(s) affected by them. Photometric lights have built-in decay. *Point lights* act somewhat like the Standard Omni light; *linear lights* are like long fluorescent lights; *area lights* cast light as a flat plane. Here are some examples of effective Photometric settings:

✔ **Target Point/Linear/Area:** Target Point/Linear/Area lights offer you the chance to place both the light and the target. Placement should be in close proximity to the lighted object(s).

✔ **Free Point/Linear/Area:** The Free Point/Linear/Area lights are placed almost as if you were placing highlights on objects themselves, especially the Free Point lights. This way you can create exacting specular effects, as shown in Figure 18-9.

Figure 18-9: A number of Free Point lights were created by cloning a single Free Point light for this scene. The lights were then placed in close proximity to the objects.

Here comes the sun

The Photometric *IES Sun/IES Sky* options offer you the opportunity to light your worlds from a sun source. Though potentially a complex effect, IES Sun can be compared with the Standard Skylight option. The main difference is that IES Sun gives you a greater fine-tuning capability through the adjustment of its settings. The Daylight System (sun and sky) can also be created from the Create Systems icon.

IES Sun

By carefully positioning and adjusting the parameters of the IES Sun lighting option, you can create light and shadow effects for a scene that appear natural. Use the IES Sun light to illuminate outdoor scenes, or as a way of creating sunlight as seen through a window. The proximity from the IES Sun object to the objects to be illuminated is not important; the distance is assumed to be infinite. The angle of the light is important; it can be used to represent the angle of the sun at different times of the day. After placing the IES Sun light, you can adjust its parameters in the Modify Panel for intensity and shadow settings, and in the Motion Panel for time of day/time of year settings. The Intensity value is vital if you want to emulate sunlight at different times of the day. Values of 0 to 1.5 work best, with 1.5 being a high noon sun. Push the Intensity value too much above 1.5, and you'll create the blinding light of a nuclear explosion, washing out most of the textural detail in the scene, as shown in Figure 18-10.

Figure 18-10:
From left to right, the IES Sun intensity was set to .5, 1.0, and 1.5, respectively, as if sunlight was referenced from morning to noon.

IES Sky

IES Sky is meant to work in conjunction with the IES Sun light. After placing the IES Sky in a viewport, adjustments are made by going to the Modify Command Panel, with IES Sky selected, as shown in Figure 18-11.

Figure 18-11:
The IES Sky
Command
Panel
rollout.

Using the Sky Color swatch to set the overall hue of the sky effects how the IES Sun light will illuminate the scene. Setting a solid black Sky Color, for instance, blots out the sun; other hues tint the light. The IES Sun light is muted if you move the slider all the way to maximum Cloudy, with lower cloud settings muting the light less.

One way to try out these effects is to do a few designs for tourist posters touting hotels on the moon. People do weirder things all the time.

Chapter 19

Cameras

*E*very viewport in 3ds max represents a window into your 3D world. A Camera object is a window you can move around at will, while adjusting the scope of what you see through it. A camera also represents your eye. Just as your vision adjusts to your environment, so, too, can you tweak a 3ds max camera to frame what you look at. Your eyes work together to give you a sense of the 3D depth of the world you look at, but just one 3ds max camera is quite capable of providing you with a 3D appreciation of the virtual world all by itself.

Creating New Cameras

To create a new camera, choose Create⇨Cameras, and choose a Camera Type. Two camera types exist — *target* and *free,* which I cover in the following sections. Cameras are created so they point perpendicular to the viewport they are created in, so the Front Viewport is the most common place to create a camera. Click and drag to create a Target Camera's Camera and Target, and just click to create a Free Camera. You can reposition and rotate a camera in any viewport after you create it, and you can name a camera anything you want.

The Target Camera

The Target Camera offers you the best opportunity for fine-tuning settings to get exactly the image you want. You create a target camera by clicking and dragging the mouse. Clicking sets the position of the Camera in whatever viewport you're using, and dragging enables you to place the target exactly where you want the camera to point. You can reposition and/or rotate either or both the camera and its target point afterward if needed.

The Free Camera

The Free Camera doesn't have a target point, so it points in whatever direction it's aimed. You create it by a simple left-click in any viewport.

Setting Up a Camera Viewport

Until you tell 3ds max to look through the camera at your scene, the camera is just another object. You have to set up a Camera Viewport to see what your camera is pointed at. "Just how do you do that?" you ask with a nervous shrug. Here's how:

1. **Place a new camera in a scene. Name it whatever you like, or just accept the default name (**Camera_01**).**

2. **Make the Perspective Viewport active by left-clicking in it.** Right-clicking changes the active viewport while maintaining the current selection, this way the camera stays selected for further editing if needed.

   You can transform any viewport into a Camera Viewport, though the most common choice is the Perspective Viewport.

3. **Right-click the name of the Perspective Viewport (in the upper-left corner of the viewport).**

   The Camera menu pops up.

4. **Choose Views, and then choose the name of your camera.**

   What was the Perspective Viewport becomes a Camera Viewport, as shown in Figure 19-1. What you see there corresponds exactly to what the camera (with its present settings) is pointing at.

Positioning and Configuring Multiple Cameras

You're not limited to having just one camera in a scene, but can place as many as you need. Think of a major motion picture set, or even a TV broadcast studio. In most cases, at least three cameras are used at the same time. The director sits at a console, telling the camera operators to switch to one camera or the other. That way, each separate camera can be used for its own purpose — close-ups, side shots, or zooms — after which the stored frames can be edited together to form the finished piece. You can use your 3ds max cameras in the same manner. If you had three cameras, for example, you could use three separate viewports to see what each one was targeting, just like a director sitting at a multiscreen console.

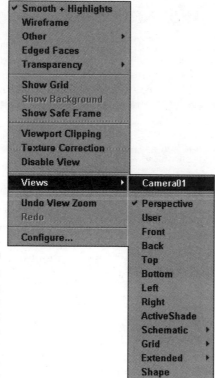

Figure 19-1:
The
Perspective
Viewport
becomes a
Camera
Viewport.

If you plan to use more than one camera in a scene, make sure each one offers a different view. One can be used for establishment shots (wide angle shots that take in everything in the scene), another for a close-in zoom, and perhaps another for a bird's eye view of the scene.

Making the most of a shoot

Another reason for using multiple cameras — especially in films — is to get every drop of image content possible out of an expensive shoot. Say you're filming an exploding building. When the pyrotechnics are set off, there's really no way to reshoot the scene again if something goes wrong. Plus, the explosion that you paid thousands of dollars to set up may only take seconds to happen. Filmmakers often shoot expensive effects scenes like this in slow motion, milking every penny they invested from the shot. They also use multiple cameras in many cases.

I'm sure you've seen movies where a car crash, explosion, or some spectacular stunt is shown three or more times in a row from different angles. This is the result of having several cameras on hand to capture the action.

Compositing multiple camera cuts together

Although we cover 3ds max animation in Part VI of this book, it's worth saying a word or two here about how to use your computer to make the best use of animations recorded separately from several camera vantage points. The process of stitching the animations together is called *post editing*. If this is a topic that interests you, check out Discreet Software's Combustion or two Adobe programs — AfterEffects and Premiere.

Adjusting a Camera's Settings

Camera settings can be adjusted in the camera's Modify Command Panel. You always have to make at least some minor adjustments, beyond positioning and rotating it, before you get a camera to do what you want it to do. All cameras are saved with a scene, so you don't have to worry about having to tweak them all over again after you set them.

Using Command-Panel Camera controls

Two groups of camera controls are available in the Command Panel: General Parameter controls (just called *Parameters*) and Depth of Field Parameter controls.

Parameters

Under the Parameter rollout in the Camera Modify Command Panel, you can adjust the following (see Figure 19-2):

- **Lens:** Cameras capture images through a lens. Lenses come in a variety of sizes, named according to their millimeter aperture. In the Parameter rollout, you can enter the millimeter size manually in the space provided, or choose one of the standard Lens sizes from the preset list provided. The smaller the lens size, the more data in the scene is captured (although ranges below 20mm actually distort the image). 35mm is a common size to use. Ranges higher than 35mm zoom the camera in for close-ups, with a 200mm setting representing an extreme close-up.

- **FOV:** The FOV (Field Of View) value determines how much of the scene you are forcing the camera to take in while maintaining a focus on the target. Think of your eyes. If you could negate your peripheral vision (the blurry image information seen out of the corner of your eyes), your vision could take in everything in front of you and to the sides. This would be a maximum of 180 degrees, comparable to an FOV setting of 180. The problem is that while you would have a wider field of view, the image would be distorted to accommodate that view. Normally, our eyes have an FOV range of something on the order of 40 to 60. In 3ds max, the Lens and FOV values are linked together to prevent distortions. The maximum FOV value available is 175 degrees, which automatically triggers a lens setting of about 10mm. Figure 19-3 shows what some FOV settings look like.

Figure 19-2:
The Parameters rollout in the Camera's Modify Command Panel.

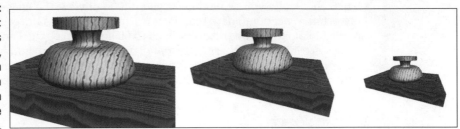

Figure 19-3:
Left to right:
FOV settings
of 40, 60,
and 90, with
the camera
remaining in
the same
place.

✔ **Orthographic Projection:** When Orthographic Projection is checked, the view is zoomed in on and distorted, and the true perspective is lost. Orthographic Projection is common among draftsman for rendering mechanical drawings.

✔ **Type:** Choose either the Free Camera or the Target Camera type. Check Show Cone to display the camera's viewing cone, and check Show Horizon to see where the horizon line is in a viewport.

✔ **Environment Ranges:** Show the Near and Far Environment Ranges to get a better sense of the range your camera can cover. You can adjust the default values of each.

✔ **Clipping Planes:** The Clipping Plane values are normally defaulted to the Environment Ranges. Objects closer to the camera than the Near Clipping Plane or farther away than the Far Clipping Plane will not be displayed in any of that Camera's Viewports. You can reset these values manually, keeping an eye on the Camera's Viewport(s) to see if any objects in the scene vanish.

✔ **Multipass Effect:** You have two available options here: Depth of Field (similar to LOD, or Level of Detail) and Motion Blur. If you check Enable for the Multipass Effect, the Depth of Field option will start to blur anything in the scene beyond the values set in Depth of Field Parameters, making the object(s) at the Target Distance sharper so they stand out. Motion Blur is an animation effect, adding blurred edges to moving objects in a scene.

✔ **Target Distance:** This is the distance from the camera to the Target Point when you are using the Target Camera. Altering this value moves the target point the camera is focused upon.

Depth of Field Parameters

Depth of Field controls the distance at which objects are seen clearly. Depth of Field Parameters are on their own rollout in the Command Panel, as shown in Figure 19-4.

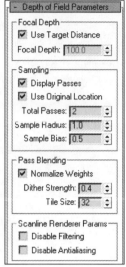

Figure 19-4:
The Depth
of Field
Parameters
rollout.

Each Depth of Field Parameter has its own function and settings:

- **Focal Depth:** By default, the Focal Depth value is the same as the Target Distance value, but you can override that and use your own value. Anything beyond that distance will get increasingly blurry if Depth of Field is activated.

- **Sampling:** The higher the Sample value, the higher the quality of the camera rendering, but the longer the rendering takes. Best to leave these values at their defaults until you're an old hand at 3ds max.

- **Pass Blending:** Pass Blending is an advanced topic beyond the scope of this book. For the time being, leave these values at their defaults.

- **Scanline Rendering:** This process is a faster way to create images, usually of poorer quality than what you get from a standard rendering.

Camera Control Icons

When you select a camera, the Camera Control Icons appear at the lower right of the 3ds max screen. These are interactive controls. After you choose one of them by left-clicking it, you can click and drag within any Camera Viewport to see them work on the view. From top-left to bottom-right, they are Dolly Camera Perspective, Roll Camera, Zoom Extents All, Field of View, Truck Camera, Orbit Camera (around the Target Point), and the familiar Min/Max Toggle. Spend some time tweaking each of these tools to get a feel for manipulating the camera.

The Miner's Helmet

 If you create a light (Omni or Target Spot), place it just above your camera facing the same direction as the camera, and then link the light to your camera, you can ensure that no matter where you move your camera relative to the objects in your scene, those objects will be well lit.

Part VI
Animation at Its Best

The 5th Wave   By Rich Tennant

"Is this really the best use of 3ds max animation on our e-commerce Web site? A bad wheel on the shopping cart icon that squeaks, wobbles, and pulls to the left?"

In this part . . .

Movement is the first seduction of the eye. When we were floating around as amorphous jelly in the primeval ooze (that's a nice thought, isn't it?) we developed an archaic eye spot early on. This ancient ancestor of the eye could not distinguish color at all, just shadow and light. If something moved in front of the eye spot that suddenly cut off the light, we had two choices . . . chase and eat or run to avoid being eaten. It was a toss-up. This is known as the *fight or flight* (or *eat or be eaten*) syndrome, and it remains deeply embedded in our active psyche. Movement remains unavoidably attractive to us, so much so that we can't turn away from moving objects. This is a big problem in urban areas of course, where there is so much movement that our eyes go bananas trying to adjust. Maybe blinders will be the next stage of evolution, our eye spots having come full circle.

Added to this, and important in the theory of animation, is our still echoing primitive belief that everything in the world is alive — animated (which literally means that everything has a consciousness). Within this primitive tradition it is quite possible for mice to talk and tables to walk, so when we see an animation that shows these impossible activities, something in us says "I told you so!" Walt Disney knew all of this, as does the modern computer graphics animator, which gives them instant access to our attention span. Anything in 3ds max can be set in motion, so animation is a vital part of the max learning curve. This part of the book guides you through the max animation tools and procedures, making it possible for you to hypnotically gather the attention of your audience.

Chapter 20

Making Friends with the Timeline

● ●

In This Chapter

▶ Using the Track Bar controls

▶ Creating keyframes

▶ Editing keyframes

▶ Creating keyframe animations

● ●

*M*ovement is the primary seduction of the eye. When we see something move, even in our peripheral vision, our archaic senses kick in. Is that something to eat? Is that something about to eat me? Friend or foe, meal or predator, we immediately ask ourselves what the movement is all about. Science tells us that the most primitive eye spots an organism can possess are devoted to sensing movement about image, color, or anything else. Because of this, we still harbor the suspicion that anything that moves is alive. The swaying branches of a tree in the wind, a bouncing ball, the movement of waves on the sea, some part of us, an old part, believes that anything animated possesses a form of consciousness. This is exactly what Disney and the rest of the early animators realized, and took advantage of. Intellectually, the audience may know that the movie cartoon is composed of nothing but ink, paint, or (these days) computer-generated lines and forms, but in those magic moments in the darkened theater, we surrender disbelief to talking dragons and clever animated mice with big plans. In this chapter, the timeline is the target for exploration.

I Was Framed!

An animation is composed of a series of single images, called *frames,* played back at a set speed so your eye interprets them as movement. Each frame may display an object at a different position, scale, rotation, or other transformation. The speed of the playback is counted in Frames Per Second (FPS). After you determine the FPS value, the finished rendered size, the file format to be used, and a folder on your computer where the animation will be stored, the movie file can be rendered. Rendering animations/movies is covered in Chapter 26.

The Track Bar

The Track Bar is the long horizontal display that covers most of the bottom of the 3ds max interface, as shown in Figure 20-1.

Figure 20-1:
The Track
Bar.

If you don't see the Track Bar, go to Customize⇨Show UI⇨Track Bar. The Ruler on the Track Bar ranges from 0 to 100 by default; 3ds max is set up initially for a 100-frame animation. Above the Ruler is a slider that can be moved horizontally, with a readout that tells you exactly what frame of the total frames it is currently at. By default, the slider is set to 0/100. Place your mouse pointer over the slider and (using the left mouse button) click and drag the slider to a new position over the Ruler. Release the mouse button and the slider displays the frame corresponding to its new location.

Using the VCR Controls

At the lower right of the Track Bar are the VCR Controls that control your navigation through the animation you're creating.

The row of buttons across the top of the VCR Controls indicates Go To Start, Previous Frame, Play Animation, Next Frame, and Go To End. The Play Animation button becomes the Stop Animation button when the animation is playing back. Click any of these buttons to move the slider accordingly, although you can also move the slider manually as you have already seen. The bottom row of the VCR Controls features the Key Mode toggle, Frame Feedback area, and the Time Configuration button. The Frame Feedback area has two purposes. It displays what frame you are currently at, and it can also be used as a type-in area to get to any specific frame. Clicking the Time Configuration button brings up the Time Configuration Panel.

The Time Configuration Panel

Before you create an animation, open the Time Configuration Panel to make sure the parameters are set the way you want them. Click the Time Configuration button to display the Time Configuration Panel, shown in Figure 20-2.

Figure 20-2:
The Time
Configura-
tion Panel.

Here's a list of parameters that you can adjust in the Time Configuration Panel:

✔ **Frame Rate:** The default Frame Rate (NTSC at 30 FPS) will suffice in most situations. If you are in Europe or another place on the globe that uses the PAL standard, then check PAL and set the FPS value to the common PAL FPS value.

When you check Film, always input suitable FPS values for the film format you're using (usually 24 FPS). Ticks are the actual timing adjustments for an animation (for example, 4800 ticks per second). Adjusting the frame rate has no effect on the actual timing of animated events.

✔ **Time Display:** As a default, the Time Display is set to Frames. The other options are there for professional editing.

✔ **Playback:** By default, the Playback rate is set to 1x. Selecting any of the other options will cause the Playback to be either slower or faster. Checking Active Viewport Only will enable the Playback to proceed only in the selected viewport. If Loop is checked, the animation will play back over and over again until you stop it.

✔ **Animation:** Under the Animation parameters, you can alter the length of your animation. By default, it's set to 100 frames. At an FTP setting of 30, 100 frames would equal a 3⅓-second animation. To change the total number of frames available to you in an animation, change the End Time value to the frames you want to use, and click the ReScale Time button.

✔ **Key Steps:** Leave everything checked under Key Steps.

Set Key Filters

If you right-click the Set Key Filters button in the Track Bar, the Set Key Filters Panel appears. Place check marks in every option on this panel so that you can animate everything in a 3ds max scene.

Revving Up the Time Machine

Before you create animation, start with the obvious: Add some objects to a scene. Start (for example) by adding a Standard Sphere in any viewport. Then click Zoom Extents All to center the sphere in all viewports.

The Data Readout

Below the Ruler in the Track Bar is a readout that displays the Position, Rotation Angle, or Scale of the selected object in a scene. The information it displays depends on the Transformation tool you have selected: Move, Rotate, or Scale, as shown in Figure 20-3.

Figure 20-3:
The Data
Readout
area
following
the Track
Bar.

Under non-animation circumstances, this is a useful display. When you are animating, it can be a vital helper. Why? Because it not only responds to your activities in a viewport, it also commands those activities. If you have selected the Scale tool for instance, you can alter the scale of the selected object on any of its axes by simply typing in a new value in the proper axis box in the Data Readout area. This gives you exacting control over the position, rotation, and scale of a selected object at any point (frame) in an animation.

Key á la mode

Before you become familiar with keyframing tools, know what keyframing is. A *keyframe* is an important (hence *key*) frame in a sequence or a frame in an animation where some attribute of the selected object changes definitively. All other frames between keyframes are called *in-betweens* (*tweens* for short).

For example, suppose you set up an animation with 60 frames. At the first frame, the size of your object is 10. (The first frame is always a keyframe because that's where everything begins.) At frame 30, the size of your object has reached its maximum, size 20. Frame 30 would be a keyframe because it represents a maximum value. In the last frame, the size of your object is 10 again. That frame also would be a keyframe because it represents an end-point value; all frames between the keyframes are tweens.

If you played the animation, you'd see the object starting at size 10, gradually increasing in size until it reached size 20, and then decreasing in size until it was size 10 again.

You find the keyframing tools at the right of the Data Readout below the Ruler (also called the *timeline*). Figure 20-4 shows the tools.

Figure 20-4:
The
keyframing
tools.

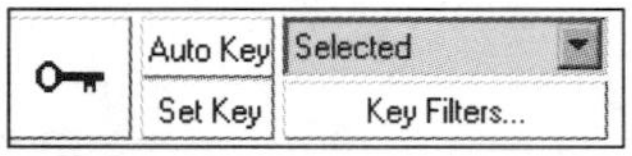

I explain the Key Filters button earlier in this chapter. That leaves three other buttons — the Key icon, Auto Key, and Set Key.

Setting up and creating keyframe animations

The Key icon works in conjunction with the Set Key button. The Auto Key button works as a standalone keyframe creator. Use either or both, like this:

✔ **The Set Key button:** If you click the Set Key button, it becomes active and lights up. If you move the slider to any frame position and click the Key icon, a keyframe is created at that point. A small vertical bar on the timeline at that frame represents the new keyframe. Clicking the keyframe on the timeline selects it. Hitting the Delete key on your keyboard removes that keyframe.

✔ **The Auto Key function:** Clicking the Auto Key button selects it, and it lights up. Moving the slider to a new frame position on the timeline selects a new frame for action. Using any transformation tools in any viewport on the selected object automatically creates a keyframe at that frame, so you don't have to click the Key icon.

✔ **Both:** If you like, you can switch between Auto Key and Set Key options to create an animation. Any time a keyframe is created, a keyframe indicator (the small rectangle) appears at that frame's location on the timeline.

Editing keyframes

The topic of editing keyframes in 3ds max is not something you will jump into at the start. Editing keyframes is a more advanced topic, but you still may want to know how to do it.

Introducing the expanded Track Bar

Keyframes are edited in the expanded Track Bar. To get to the expanded Track Bar, click the icon to the far left of the timeline ruler. The Track Bar expands, as shown in Figure 20-5.

In the list at the left of the expanded Track Bar, every item in your scene (objects, cameras, lights, and everything else) will be listed. To the right is the Track Bar. The length of the Track Bar shows your frame-number marks. The height of the Track Bar is based on a zero-line at the center.

Selecting an object's Transformation label at the left (Position, Rotation, or Scale) displays a curve in the expanded Track Bar at the right. Nodes on the curve represent keyframes, as shown in Figure 20-6.

Passing your mouse pointer over the tool icons at the top of the expanded Task Bar reveals their labels. You can elect to add more keyframe nodes to the curve, and/or move the ones already present. You can also delete any keyframes. Adjusting the curve in any way will effect how the selected object is transformed during the length of the animation, giving you complete editing control prior to rendering the finished animation, as shown in Figure 20-7.

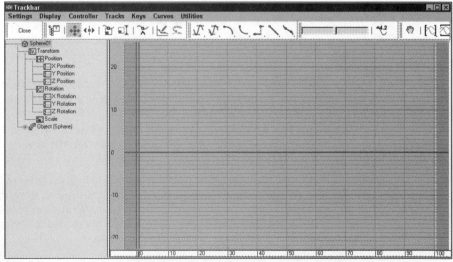

Figure 20-5:
The expanded Track Bar.

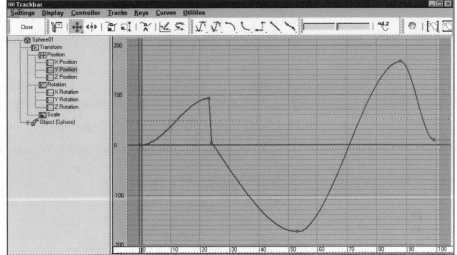

Figure 20-6:
The curve displays the Y position keyframes for a sphere that has been animated in a scene.

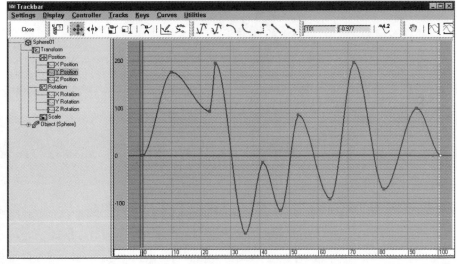

Figure 20-7:
Here, the Y position curve has been edited, resulting in a different animation.

Action!

Okay. Time to create some keyframe animation examples. These four examples should prepare you for the zillions of 3ds max animations you may want to create in the near future.

This animation explores keyframe movement (positioning) as its theme. Before you begin the keyframing process, place a lathed object on a flat slab in a scene. Place a sphere above the lathed object. Texture the objects any way you like, as shown in Figure 20-8.

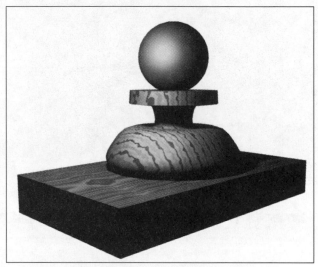

Figure 20-8:
Create a scene that looks something like this.

Virtual athletics, anyone? Here's how to make the sphere bounce on top of the lathed object:

1. **Activate Auto Key in the Track Bar.**

2. **Bring up the Time Configuration Panel, and make the Length of the animation 120 frames at 30 FPS.**

   These settings yield a 4-second animation.

3. **Click OK to accept the settings.**

4. **In the Front Viewport, create a keyframe at the first frame.**

5. **At Frame 40, move the sphere vertically on its Z-axis so it's about twice the height of the lathed object.**

6. **At Frame 70, return the Z position of the sphere to where it was at Frame 1.**

7. **At Frame 100, move the sphere upward on its Z-axis to about half the height it occupied at Frame 40.**

8. **At Frame 120, the last frame, position the sphere where it was at Frame 1.**

ON THE CD

That's it. Preview the movement by clicking the Play button in the on-screen VCR Controls. Save the project to disk for later rendering. For reference, you'll find the finished animation in the ANIMS folder on this book's CD-ROM. It's called SphereBounce1.avi, as shown in Figure 20-9.

Figure 20-9:
Frames from the Sphere Bounce1.avi animation.

Note: The animation SphereBounce1b in the ANIMS folder shows the same animation after the Z position curve has been edited a bit.

In this example, the sphere rotates around the other objects. You can use the same scene as in the previous example. Work in the Left Viewport.

1. **Delete all keyframes except for the keyframe at Frame 1.**

2. **With the sphere selected, choose the Hierarchy rollout in the Command Panel.**

3. **Click Affect Pivot Only, and move the sphere's Pivot Point in the Left Viewport down on its Z axis, so it is at the center of the rectangular slab.**

4. **Deselect the Affect Pivot Point Only button.**

   Because the sphere's Pivot Point is now at the center of the rectangular slab, it uses the newly placed Pivot Point as a center of rotation.

5. **With Auto Key on, rotate the sphere in the Left Viewport so it is 25% of the way around the X-axis at Frame 30.**

   Doing so creates a keyframe at this location.

6. **Rotate the sphere around its Pivot Point so it is at the 50% mark on the X-axis at Frame 60, which will be another keyframe.**

7. **Rotate the sphere so it is at its 75% rotation mark on the X axis at Frame 90, which will be another keyframe.**

8. **Return the sphere to its original position of rotation at Frame 120, moving in the same X-axis direction.**

   This keyframe is the last one in the animation.

9. **Check the position readouts to make sure that the sphere's position at Frame 1 and Frame 120 are the same, and adjust if necessary.**

That's it. Preview the movement by hitting the Play button in the VCR Controls. Save the project to disk for later rendering. For reference, you'll find the finished animation in the ANIMS folder on this book's CD-ROM. It's called SphereRotate1.avi. An edited version is also included as SphereRotate2.avi, as shown in Figure 20-10.

Figure 20-10:
Frames
from the
Sphere
Rotate
animation.

In this example, scaling is animated. You can use the same scene as in the other animations, just be sure to delete all keyframes except the first one. Work in the Front Viewport. Here's the drill:

1. **Make sure Auto Key is on.**

2. **If the sphere's Pivot Point is still located outside the sphere, move it back to the sphere's center.**

3. **Select the lathed object. Keyframe it at Frame 1. Move to the last frame, and scale it down as tiny as possible.**

4. **Select the sphere. Keyframe it at Frame 1. Move to the last frame and scale it up until it is sitting on the rectangular slab.**

That's it. Preview the movement by clicking the Play button in the on-screen VCR Controls. Save the project to disk for later rendering. For reference, you'll find the finished animation in the ANIMS folder on this book's CD-ROM. It's called SphereScale1.avi. An edited version is also included as SphereScale1b.avi. Figure 20-11 shows a sample of the animation.

Figure 20-11:
Frames
from the
SphereScale
animation
on the
CD-ROM.

Use all three transformation processes (movement, rotation, and scaling) to create some exploratory animations with objects of your own choice. (One such example in the ANIMS folder on the CD-ROM is called Mixed.avi.)

Doing a retake

If an animation looks strange when you preview it, try some of these options for correcting errors:

- ✔ Try to find the offending keyframe and delete it. Then make whatever corrections are necessary at that keyframe with Auto Key on.
- ✔ Delete the offending keyframe and create new keyframes on either side of the one you deleted.
- ✔ Click the keyframe in the timeline and move it left or right.
- ✔ Use the Set Key tool to create adjusted keyframes.
- ✔ Delete all the keyframes and begin again.
- ✔ Explore the use of Keyframe Editing in the Expanded Track Bar.

Making Post-Production Changes

If you plan to create a long animation — one that runs for minutes rather than seconds — create shorter animations that represent separate scenes in the story. Use some different camera angles in alternate scenes to create a more interesting look. Always create your longer animations in parts. That way you can stitch the parts together in post-production software such as Discreet Combustion, Adobe AfterEffects, or Adobe Premiere.

Chapter 21

Path Animations

In This Chapter

▶ Creating path animations

▶ Creating combined keyframe/path animations

▶ Animating lights

▶ Animating the camera

*1*n keyframe animation, the movement of a selected object results in a path that the object will take through 3D space. The path can be simple, like a straight line, or complex, like a skater's figure eight curve. In path animation, you create the path first, and then assign an object to it.

Object/Path Animating

In 3ds max, the object that every other 3D software developer calls a *path* is named a *trajectory*. The reason that max alters the name from path to trajectory is that max reserves the title *path* for a *lofting path,* part of the lofting modeling process. Too many developers think 3D users can't handle walking and chewing gum at the same time, and that calling an animation path by the same title that dozens of other 3D software uses will confuse the max user. In this chapter, I use the terms path and trajectory interchangeably, with a preference for *path* because it's the industry standard term.

Creating Animation Paths

In path animation, the path is set up first. An animation path is nothing more than a 2D spline shape. You can access 2D spline shapes by choosing Create⇨Shapes⇨Spline, and then choosing one of the options from the Command Panel list.

As detailed in Chapter 5, each of the Spline Shape options has its own extended parameter rollout where the shape you draw (in this case, an animation path) can be defined.

✔ The Line option, for example, can be sharp (angular) or smooth (rounded).

✔ The Star can have multiple points.

✔ The Rectangle can have a variable corner radius.

Anything you do to an animation path affects the movement of the object that travels on that path.

When an animation path is created in any viewport, you can move any of the control points on the animation path in any viewport. You do this by selecting the animation path and then choosing Modify⇨Object Space Modifier⇨ Edit Spline.

The easiest way to reshape an animation path is to choose the Vertex icon at the top of the Spline Modifier rollout. Then choose any viewport and click and drag on one of the control points of the animation path with the Select and Move tool. This enables you exacting control over the shape of the animation path. If the animation path requires less accurate control, but a more general modification, you can also use modifiers like Bend, Twist, and Wave to quickly warp the animation path. The following sections provide a couple of examples.

The figure eight

To create an animation path that looks like the classic figure eight, follow these steps:

1. **Choose Create⇨Shapes⇨Spline⇨Circle.**

2. **Draw a circle in the Front Viewport.**

3. **With the circle selected, choose Modify⇨Twist.**

4. **In the Twist Modifier's Command Panel rollout, use the following parameter: Angle = 90 on the X Twist Axis.**

5. **Choose the Non-uniform scale from the Scale flyout tool, then type a value of 0 in the Y type-in box below the viewport.**

Voilá! A perfect figure eight (see Figure 21-1).

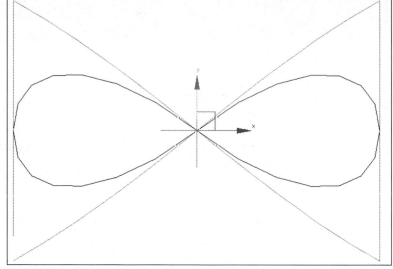

The "S" path

You can use any letter as an animation path. Here's how:

1. **Choose Create⇨Shapes⇨Splines⇨Text.**

2. **Choose Arial Black as the font.**

3. **Type the capital letter "S" in the Text area.**

4. **Click and drag out the letter shape in the Top Viewport.**

That's it. This shape can now serve as an animation path for an object, as shown in Figure 21-2.

Setting an object on a path

A path has no importance if no actors make use of its existence. A path is just a possibility waiting to happen. The task, then, is to let 3ds max know what objects in a scene will be selected to travel the animation path once you have created it. The process is pretty straightforward and easy to follow:

1. **Create an animation path, open or closed, as detailed earlier in this chapter.**

2. **Create or import an object to travel on that animation path.**

   The object can be placed anywhere in the scene, and does not need to be in proximity to the intended animation path.

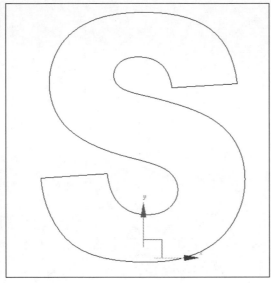

Figure 21-2:
Text can
serve as an
animation
path.

3. **With the object selected, choose the Motion rollout in the Command Panel (the Motion icon looks like a wheel in motion) and choose the Trajectories option (see Figure 21-3).**

4. **In the Trajectories parameter settings, check the settings titled Sample Range.**

   The Start and End time values should match the total frame length of your present project setup. You can change them so that a completed path animation is either faster or slower than your present animation length, by altering either or both of the Start and End values.

5. **Check to make sure the default value (10) is entered in the Samples area.**

   This is an important value when you are configuring a path animation. It represents the number of keyframes to be forced upon the animation path when your object is glued to that path. If the animation path is complex, you should raise this value. A value set too low for a complex animation path will force the object to adhere less closely to the shape of the path.

   There is no set rule for calculating what the exact Sample value should be. It all depends on the complexity of the path. If the value is too low and the path the object takes does not follow the animation path the way you want it to, simply choose Edit⇨Undo and recalculate the Sample value.

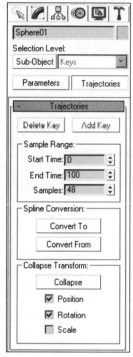

Figure 21-3:
The Motion
rollout in the
Command
Panel.

6. **With the object selected, choose Convert From under Spline Conversion and then click the animation path, once, in any viewport.**

   Your object is instantly transported to the first point (keyframe) on the animation path. If you look in any viewport, you'll see that the object is now attached to what appears to be a clone of the animation path. The original animation path is still there by itself, and should be left there. The animation path that the object is attached to shows nodes where the keyframes are, and the keyframe times are also displayed in the Track Bar's timeline.

7. **Click the Play button in the VCR Controls.**

   Your object zings along the animation path, as shown in Figures 21-4 and 21-5.

Linking object and path

Your first inclination may be to use the Link tool to attach the object to the animation path. Don't do it! Use the trajectory process as outlined previously. You can, however, link an object on an animation path to another object on its own animation path, and repeat that process as many times as necessary. This creates extremely complex animations.

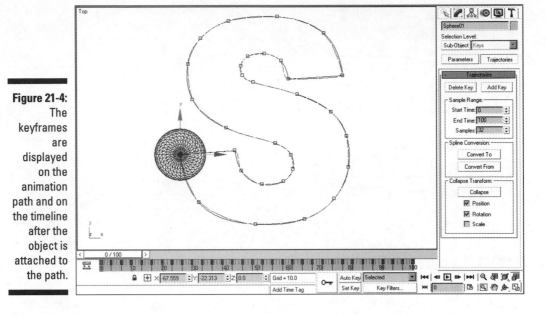

Figure 21-4:
The keyframes are displayed on the animation path and on the timeline after the object is attached to the path.

Figure 21-5:
The object moves automatically along the animation path, smoothly navigating from one keyframe to the next.

Timing is everything

After you have attached the object to an animation path, you will see that the intended number of keyframes (set by altering the sample value in the Motion Command Panel rollout) are indicated along the timeline. If you notice, they are all placed equidistant from each other, as much as possible. If you look at the corresponding nodes on the object's animation path, you will see (except in the case of a straight linear path) that they are not equidistant from each other.

The object moves through the same amount of time from one keyframe to the next. When the keyframe nodes are bunched up on the animation path, the object slows down. When keyframes are spaced farther apart, the objects speed up. Knowing this, you can delete intervening keyframes, or move them farther apart, to speed the object up at certain points. You can also add more keyframes at certain points along the animation path to slow down the object. You have control over the variations in timing while the object traverses the animation path.

Filming the action

When you set up a camera or cameras to film the action of the path-animated object, remember to do so from interesting viewports. The movement alone is not all that stimulating to the viewer — but tie it to interesting perspectives and viewing angles, and it gets a lot more intriguing.

Motion within Motion

Chapter 20 focuses on keyframe animations in the same detail that this chapter looks at path animations. You can combine keyframing and path-animation techniques to create uniquely interesting effects.

Using both path and keyframing elements

There is nothing to prevent you from creating an animation that contains a keyframe-animated object moving on an animation path. In fact, this is the only solution to many animation challenges. For instance, if you have a spaceship that has to be spinning on its directional axis, while at the same time making its way around asteroids, you would use both a keyframed directional spin for the ship and attach the ship to a path through the asteroids. If you want a 3D actor to walk through a patch of woods to Grandma's house, you would first keyframe-animate the various motions of the actor's walk cycle, and then set the actor on an animation path through the woods.

Keyframing the actor's movements

A zillion possible 3D objects could serve as animated actors — and they could follow another zillion possible animated paths. Follow these steps to keyframe actor movements:

1. **Create a basic actor.**

   In Figure 21-6, I create a teapot Primitive — in the Top Viewport.

2. **Create a rather tall, thin cylinder Primitive, and move its Pivot Point vertically to the top of the cylinder.**

   This cylinder will serve as a model for the top and bottom legs of the teapot.

3. **Clone three more cylinders.**

4. **Move the cylinders into place so each leg of the teapot character has two cylindrical legs, each composed of a top and bottom leg.**

5. **Link each bottom leg to its top leg, and each top leg to the teapot, as shown in Figure 21-6.**

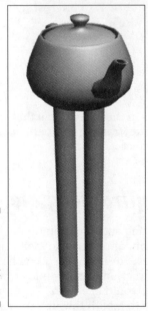

Figure 21-6:
The finished linked teapot character.

6. **Using your 100-frame default timeline, develop a walk cycle for your character. Make sure Auto Key is on.**

7. **Rotate the leg cylinders to create a keyframed walk.**

   This step may take a while; fortunately, keyframes can be deleted and moved. If necessary, you can clone a moving keyframe by holding down the Shift key while moving the keyframe (as shown in Figure 21-7).

8. **Create two same-size Primitive tubes and place them on a rectangular slab.**

   Make them large enough for the character to stand in.

Figure 21-7:
Develop a walk cycle for the teapot character.

9. **Place the character inside one of the tubes, facing toward the other tube.**

10. **Create a linear spline for an animation path.**

   Start in the tube where the character is, and extend it into the other tube. Move the animation path so it's as high as the character's head, and so it starts at the center of the head.

11. **With the Teapot head selected, choose the Motion Command Panel. Left-click Convert From, and then click the animation path in any viewport.**

12. **Preview your efforts, and make any alterations that are necessary.**

   The teapot character should walk from one tube to the next, as shown in Figure 21-8.

The finished animation can be found on this book's CD-ROM in the ANIMS folder. It's called Teawalk1.avi.

Setting up the camera view for the actor's movements

If you plan to set up a camera to film this action, think about interesting placements and angles. I show some in Figure 21-9.

Animating lights

In the world of 3ds max, a light is an object — and as an object, it can be keyframe- and path-animated.

What can be animated in a light

You can keyframe-animate a light's color, multiplier (intensity), attenuation, and shadow color and density.

Making lights breathe

One of the scariest effects in a horror movie is the pulsed dimming of a light. You can create this same effect in 3ds max by keyframe animating a light's brightness (intensity). You can also explore the keyframe animation of a light's color along with the dimming effect, so that it turns bluer as it dims. (Cue the ominous music here.) *Don't preview this effect alooonnne.*

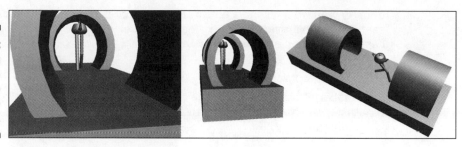

Figure 21-9:
Interesting camera views of the same animation.

Creating a parent light

Creating a series of linked lights necessitates that one of them will act as a parent for the other lights. If you want to set the lights on an animation path, use the Trajectories process to set the parent to the path. The other lights can be keyframe-animated on their own with any of the light parameters involved.

Cloning lights

If a light is already keyframe-animated and you clone it, you also clone all its keyframes. After you clone the lights, as long as Copy Cloning is used, you can alter the keyframed elements of the clones so that the lights have some randomized action, as opposed to doing whatever they do at the same time (unless you want that, of course).

Something spooky is moving there!

When you want to create the maximum scary situation, let the lights do the work. Subtly keyframe-animate their color and intensity so that they pulse slightly. Link Point lights to animated objects in an otherwise dark scene. Your viewers are frightened most when they can barely make out the shape of things, and only catch a fleeting, occasional glimpse of *something moving*.

Animating the Camera

A camera is more than a point of view — it's also an object. No less than any other object, it can be easily keyframe- and path-animated.

The camera as actor

Remember that in an animation, the camera is your eyes. Any actions it observes are actions you yourself feel that your eyes are witnessing. If the camera speeds through a scene or flies out a window, it is as if you had wings. If a camera peeks slowly around a corner to catch a glimpse of some monster, you will feel just a bit threatened. That's the magic of movies, at least well done movies. We don't feel like observers after a while, but react as if everything happening is quite personal.

Attaching a camera to a path

Cameras are attached to paths the same way that other objects are attached to paths — by using the Trajectories process. Here's an example of a camera path animation.

1. **Create a concentric ring of Torus Primitives standing on end, like a tunnel with breaks in it.**

2. **Create a splined circle to act as an animation path.**

   Make sure the path is positioned to pierce all the holes in the Torus Primitives at their center.

3. **Create a camera.**

4. **Use the Trajectories process to attach it to the circular path.**

5. **Keyframe-animate the camera's rotation.**

   Make sure the camera is always facing the direction the circular path is taking, and always facing the Torus Primitives it's traveling through. This is the ideal place to use the Path Constraint option. The Follow option canister allows the camera to always point in the direction of the path.

6. **Set some multicolored Omni lights inside the Torus tunnel.**

7. **Preview the animation in a Camera Viewport, as shown in Figure 21-10.**

The finished animation is on this book's CD-ROM in the `ANIMS` folder. It's called `TorusRide1.avi`. (You might want to take a pill for motion sickness before you view it.)

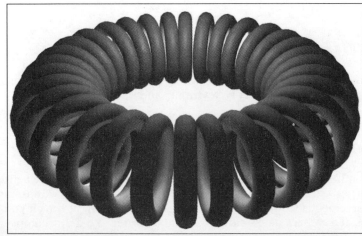

Figure 21-10: The Torus tunnel with a Camera-path animation inside.

Keyframing the camera

When you keyframe-animate the camera, you can animate both its position and rotation. (Altering its Scale has no effect; the camera is not a scalable object.) You can also animate some of the camera parameters in the Modify Command Panel — for example, lens and FOV settings, Near and Far Range, Clipping Planes, and Focal Depth.

Chapter 22

Materials That Won't Stand Still

● ●

In This Chapter

▶ Creating Bump channel animations

▶ Creating Diffuse channel animations

▶ Creating Opacity channel animations

▶ Creating Displacement channel animations

● ●

*F*rom the beginning of animated films in the late nineteenth century, artists soon realized the potential of the medium to visually show the bending and breaking of all accepted physical laws, blurring the distinction between reality and dream. Giving life, animated movement, to inanimate objects was the first step. The world was suddenly alive with singing rocks and trees, and characters that could do the impossible.

With the advent of computer graphics in the 1960s, animators started to apply their skills to more photographic scenes, instead of relying on the cartoon drawing of the past 75 years. Suddenly, it became possible to blend animated content with real actors on the screen, astounding the audience even further, making every viewer question the boundaries of reality. Initially, transferring the standard animation processes into the computer realm took all the time and energy of the computer animators, but computer animation presented possibilities that were otherwise impossible to realize.

Computer animation enables other explorations because of one factor — the shrinking of time. In a standard animation, every frame has to be created, one at a time, through the laborious task of the repetitive redrawing of each frames content . . . or at least most of it. Computer animators, on the other hand, just have to be concerned with keyframes, enabling the computer itself to calculate the *tweens*. What were computer animators to do with all this saved time, if not stretch their creativity even further? One area computer animators soon began to investigate was *morphing* — transforming one image into another in front of the audience's eyes. Complex morphing involves transforming one 3D object into another; the geometry of each object is involved. For the computer animator, however, morphing geometry can be as simple as creating one keyframe with the *source* object, and another keyframe with the *target* object. The computer than calculates all the tweens in seconds.

Yet a third type of morphing came about through the evolution of computer graphics — the transformation of an object's surface materials. Suddenly it became possible (easy, in fact) to create a 3D form that was wood at one moment, metal the next, and perhaps ended up constructed of smoke. To an audience, morphing an object's material substance seems almost impossible. But for you, an initiate into the secret society of computer animators, the task is a snap. At least it will be, with the help of the details in this chapter, which covers all the material channels and how you can morph their contents when needed.

Movies in Movies in Movies

Altering the surface materials of an object in an animation enables the computer animator to create movies within movies. In effect, the camera remains focused on a target object as the object moves on its own path, and, the surface of the targeted object can be going through its own animated changes. One example of this might be a planet orbiting in space, with the camera tagging along. The surface of the planet might be configured to resemble boiling lava, and the lava could be in constant, chaotic movement. You can create this effect, and many others, easily in 3ds max, which is why 3ds max is used so often in the production of major Hollywood films.

Swimming the Channel

Chapters 15 and 16 cover the methods of customizing the content in various Material Channels. You can find the Material Channel Mapping controls under the Maps rollout in the Material Editor, shown in Figure 22-1. Channel Mapping controls for all Channels — and for any selected Material — are there.

Clicking in the box next to any Channel's name activates that Channel for mapping configurations. Altering the value under Amount determines how strong that Channel mapping will affect the material. The next section offers a closer look at the qualities you can adjust for each Channel, pointing out how each Channel Map's contents affect the Material involved.

Material Channel mapping components

The Material Channels offer various settings that adjust the appearance of any Material you apply to an on-screen object. These settings affect color (Ambient, Diffuse, Filter Color), the hot-spot (Specular Color and Level), the Material's surface (Glossiness, Self-Illumination, Opacity, Bump), and how the Material reacts to light (Reflection, Refraction, and Displacement). This section of the chapter looks at each of these Channel settings.

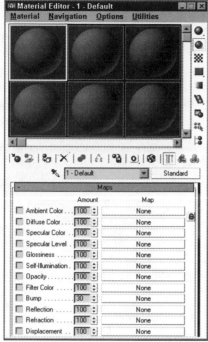

Figure 22-1:
Channel
Mapping
controls
under the
Maps rollout
in the
Material
Editor.

Ambient Color

Ambient Color is the color of shadowed part(s) of your object. (Usually Ambient Color and Diffuse Color are locked together. To unlock them, click the Lock icon at the right.) The amount of Ambient Color can range from 0 to 100%; this setting determines how strongly this color appears on parts of the material in the shadow. The value can be animated.

If a Map is applied instead of a color, the brightest areas of the Map create a stronger ambience; the darker areas show a reduced ambience. You can either program such a Map or base it on an existing bitmap. Animating the Ambient Color causes the hue (whether Color or Map based) used for the shadowed parts of the object to change in response to movement.

Diffuse Color

Diffuse Color is the Color of the object's surface as displayed when illuminated by a light. The amount can range from 0 to 100%, with 100% being maximum brightness. Content in the Diffuse Color Channel alone, when unmixed with other Channel content, is rather flat. This value can be animated.

If a Map is applied instead of a Color (procedural or bitmap), the pattern or image of the Map will become the observed surface pattern or image of the object's apparent surface. Animating the Diffuse Color content, whether

Color or Map based, will result in a changing color, pattern, or image on the surface of the targeted object.

Specular Color

Specular Color is the hue of the *hot spot* that appears when a light is aimed at a glossy object. The possible amount can range from 0 to 100%. A Specular Color setting of 100% results in a hot spot that obliterates other Channel content. This value can be animated.

If a Map is applied instead of a Color to this Channel, the hot spot will take on the content of the applied procedural or bitmap. Animating the Mapped content will result in a movie applied to the hot spot. If the light moves, the movie will appear in the moving hot spot.

Specular Level

Sometimes the hot spot is a subtle but highly effective means of adding realism to an illuminated scene. Specular Level ranges from -999 to 999, and it controls the strength of the Specular Level Map being applied to the targeted object's surface. This value can be animated.

The Map applied in the Specular Level Channel will be a mix of the Specular Color and the Mapped pattern or image. It will appear wherever a hot spot exists on the on-screen object.

Glossiness

This setting specifies a smooth and shiny quality for the object's surface. The amount ranges from 0 to 100%. Maps placed in this Channel control the brilliance of the pattern in a glossy hot spot. This value can be animated.

The procedural or image Map applied in this Channel overrides the overall glossiness of the surface of the targeted object, disregarding the Glossiness value as set under Basic Parameters in the Material Editor. Animating the Map data in this Channel gives the impression that the targeted surface is moving from a glossy to a non-glossy or partially glossy state.

Self Illumination

This setting makes the object glow. The amount value of Self Illumination ranges from 0 to 100%. A mapped procedural or bitmap image in this Channel is applied to the entire selected object's surface. This value can be animated.

Using a Map in this Channel overrides any numerical value for Self Illumination set under Basic Parameters. The surface will be illuminated at maximum strength where the Map has a white shade, and will remain non-illuminated where the Map has a black shade, with corresponding illuminated values at all lightness values in between. The effect is a lot like a light bulb with a burned and blotchy surface. Animating the contents of this Channel makes the surface resemble that of a fading or flickering light bulb.

Opacity

Values in the Opacity Channel range from 0 to 100%. Zero percent Opacity is totally transparent, while 100% is completely opaque. Values in between are partially transparent. This setting is usually left at 100% when applying a Map to the surface of the object. This value can be animated.

Using a procedural or bitmap Map as the Opacity Channel component, you can create objects that seem to have holes in them. The holes (called *drop-outs*) appear wherever the Map is black or 100% dark; 100% light areas appear as solid. An Opacity Map ignores all color data; the Map is read as a grayscale texture. Animating the Map contents of this Channel causes the transparent areas of the surface to appear and disappear.

Filter Color

The Filter Color Map alters the color data seen in the Diffuse Channel, as if you were using a color Gel over a light. The amount ranges from 0 to 100%, with 100% applying the maximum strength of the Filter Color Map. This value can be animated.

Animating the Channel contents here will result in subtle color shifts on the surface of the targeted object.

Bump

Bump Channel values range from -999 to 999. Bump Maps applied to a surface cause apparent alterations in the elevations and depressions of the surface. Maximum values, negative or positive, accentuate the apparent alterations caused by the pattern of the Bump Map. These alterations don't affect the geometry of the surface, only the Map. This value can be animated.

Animating the Map contents of this Channel cause apparent moving alterations in the elevations of the mapped pattern placed on the surface. Bump mapping uses only the intensity data of the map, not the hue data. The best Bump Map contents are grayscale images, not black-and-white images.

Reflection

Do not confuse a Reflection Map with a reflective object. A reflective object reflects all the other objects in a scene. An object that has a Reflection Map applied seems to be reflecting the contents of that Map. For instance, an object can be sitting in a room, while the Reflection Map of its surface may make it seem as if the object is reflecting a cloudy sky.

The value amount in this Channel ranges from 0 to 100%, measuring the strength of the apparent reflection. This value can be animated.

Animating the Reflection Map creates a surface that looks like it is reflecting moving environments.

Refraction

Refraction Maps are best used when some degree of transparency is already applied to the surface. This enables you to see through an object to appreciate the way it refracts the other contents of the scene made visible behind the object; refractivity bends light. The Refraction Map value ranges from 0 to 100%, with the Map applied at maximum strength (the highest value you can enable). This value can be animated.

There's not a whole lot of use in animating the contents of the Refraction Channel; the result would be subtle. The animation would result in a shimmer-like effect, perhaps useful in creating some liquid simulations (such as a streambed seen through water). With respect to the Map, only grayscale values are used. The lighter the content, the more refraction applied, and vice versa.

Displacement

Displacement Channel content warps the geometry. Although the value ranges from -999 to 999, you will seldom want to go beyond the range of -50 to 50; the distortion will be severe. This value can be animated.

Displacement Maps should be grayscale maps. The intensity of the light areas will create either elevations (when a positive value is used) or depressions (when a negative value is used). Animating a Displacement Map will result in the warping of the object's geometry over time.

Common Animated Channel Maps

Although you can animate the content placed in any Material Channel, four channels are more commonly targets for animated Maps — Diffuse Color, Bump, Opacity, and Displacement Channels.

Animating the Diffuse Color Channel

The most common Material Channel to animate is the Diffuse Channel; it results in moving patterns or movie frames whose color is preserved on the surface of the object. It is even common to select an AVI movie as the Map content for the Diffuse Channel. Reducing the amount value following 100% will result in a faded effect on the object's surface.

You can also animate the Diffuse Color Channel by using different colors on various keyframes, instead of using Map contents. This creates hues that blend into one another over time.

Mapping a Movie to the Diffuse Color Channel

Here's how to Map a movie file to the Diffuse Color Channel of a Material.

1. **Place a cube primitive in the scene.**

2. **Open up the Material Editor, and click an empty Material Preview slot.**

3. **Go to the Map rollout, and check the Diffuse Color Channel. Click the Map button.**

   The Material/Map Browser appears.

4. **Double-click the Bitmap option.**

   A path browser appears.

5. **Use the path browser to locate any AVI movie file on your system, and then click Open to load your chosen AVI movie.**

6. **Use the Modifier Command Panel to choose your cube, and then choose UVW Map Modifier⇨Box Mapping.**

7. **In your Material Editor, open the Bitmap Parameters rollout (if it's not already open), and under Cropping/Placement, click the View Image button.**

   The Specify Cropping/Placement panel appears. Moving the borders that surround the frame from the movie file, you can adjust the size and cropping of the movie. Figure 22-2 shows an example.

Figure 22-2:
Adjust the size and cropped image area of a movie frame, if needed.

8. **When cropping is complete, close the panel and make sure Apply is checked in the Material Editor under Specify Cropping/Placement.**

9. **Save this file for later rendering of the animation.**

Look in the ANIMS folder on this books CD-ROM for the file
AnimTxtr_01.avi to see an example of a movie created with this process.

Animating the Bump Channel

When you animate a Map in the Bump Channel of a Material, you create what
appears to be moving indentations on the surface of the targeted object. I say
"what appears to be" because Bump Mapping doesn't really affect the geometry
of the object at all. Here is one example.

1. **Place a sphere primitive in any viewport.**

2. **Select an empty slot in the Material Editor, and open the Maps rollout.**

3. **Click the Map button next to Bump.**

   The Material/Map Browser appears.

4. **In Browse From⇨New, choose the Cellular procedural texture.**

5. **Click OK to close the Browser and accept your choice.**

6. **Under the Coordinates rollout in the Material Editor, set XYZ Tiling
   to .02.**

   Doing so enlarges the size of the separate Cells in the texture.

7. **Under Time to keyframe, switch on AutoKey.**

8. **For the first frame, set the Amount value in the Material Editor for the
   Bump Channel to 345.**

9. **At a middle keyframe, set the Bump amount to -555.**

10. **On the last frame, create a keyframe for a Bump amount of 345 again.**

11. **Create rotation keyframes so the sphere rotates on its vertical axis.**

12. **Save this file to disk for later rendering.**

Note that you could also animate the Offset value, allowing the map to creep
across the surface.

An example of this animation is on the book's CD-ROM in the ANIMS folder.
It's called AnimBump_01.avi. Take a look at it to see what happens. Note that
you can animate any of the Bump Channel parameters, including the Tiling
sizes. Figure 22-3 gives you an idea of what to expect.

Figure 22-3:
Frames
from the
animation.

Animating the Opacity Channel

You can copy the Map data from any Channel to another Channel. Here's an example.

1. **Use the same steps as those for animating the Bump Channel (in the previous section).**

2. **Click and hold the Map button for the Bump Channel content. Choose Copy, Instance, or Swap.**

3. **Drag your chosen Bump Channel content to the Map button for the Opacity Channel and drop it there.**

Data in the Opacity Channel creates transparencies from Map data, dropping out all colors and leaving a grayscale map. Black becomes 100% transparent, and solid whites become 100% opaque. All the grays in between create partial transparencies. Figure 22-4 shows an example.

Figure 22-4:
Placing a
Map in the
Opacity
Channel can
create holes
in the
objects
surface,
as well
as other
levels of
transparency.

To really appreciate the changes in opacity created with this method, be sure to take a peek at the `OpacityAnim_01.avi` movie in the `ANIMS` folder on this book's CD-ROM.

Animating the Displacement Channel

Try copying the same Map to the sphere's Displacement Channel. Use an Amount value of -20 for the first keyframe, and 20 for the last keyframe. Save the file for later rendering. Displacement Maps radically alter the underlying geometry of an object. Values over 50 will replace the geometry with a chaotic mess of polygons in most cases. (At least now you know how to create a chaotic mess when you need one.)

Animated Channel Sandwiches

If you plan to use a single-image Map in multiple Channels, you may consider creating a series of separate Map versions first. Use an image editor like Photoshop from Adobe. Create a color pattern for the Diffuse Channel, and save it. Then create a separate Map based on the Diffuse Channel Map for the Opacity Channel, but make it a black and white image. Use the black part of the image as places where there will be holes in the surface, and solid white areas of the Map for areas where there will be a solid opacity in the color pattern of the Diffuse Map. Create a separate Bump Map of the same image by first making a grayscale image from the color data. Then invert the grayscale tones, and blur it about three times. See Figures 22-5 through 22-7 for some examples.

Figure 22-5: Map variations for the Diffuse, Opacity, and Bump Channels for a single Material.

Figure 22-6:
The three connected image maps applied to the Diffuse, Opacity, and Bump Channels of a Material.

	Maps	
	Amount	Map
☐ Ambient Color . . .	100 ⬍	None
☑ Diffuse Color	100 ⬍	Map #13 (5a.tif)
☐ Specular Color . .	100 ⬍	None
☐ Specular Level .	100 ⬍	None
☐ Glossiness	100 ⬍	None
☐ Self-Illumination .	100 ⬍	None
☑ Opacity	100 ⬍	Map #14 (5b.tif)
☐ Filter Color	100 ⬍	None
☑ Bump	777 ⬍	Map #15 (5c.tif)
☐ Reflection	100 ⬍	None
☐ Refraction	100 ⬍	None
☐ Displacement . .	100 ⬍	None

Figure 22-7:
The composited maps show UVW Box mapped to a cubic object, and a Torus UVW-tiled and Shrink-mapped. Each map's parameters can be animated separately.

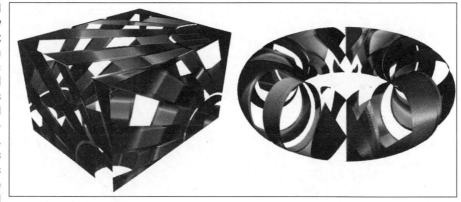

Part VII
f/x Are Us

The 5th Wave By Rich Tennant

"Mary Jo, come here quick! Look at this special effect I learned with 3ds max."

In this part . . .

There you are, sitting in front of your computer screen, admiring the close up view of a fish tank you just created in 3ds max. Suddenly, without warning, the screen dissolves, and a rush of fishy water winds up in your lap. Impossible? Or what about this scenario: You and a friend debate the correct way to break an egg. You claim the best way is to break the egg on its larger end, while your friend insists that the smaller end must be the recipient of the blow. The argument gets more and more heated. Your friend places his face close to yours, as if to shout loudly to win the debate. Instead, a flame escapes his lips, singing your eyebrows. Can this be true?

Well, in the everyday world, computer screens do not dissolve nor do flames leap from the mouths of our detractors. But in the realm of computer graphics and animation, all of this and more are possible. Many of these f/x (that's the word nerds use for *effects*) can be generated by using a common utility called a Particle System. In this part of the book, I look at 3ds max Particle Systems and other f/x phenomena.

Chapter 23

Particle Physics

· ·

· ·

Modeling 3D objects is one thing, but how do you model a *dynamic system* like an explosion, a snowstorm, billowing smoke, or a spray of water? Creating a realistic dynamic system is as important as creating a polygonal model in a scene — and sometimes even more important. Dynamic-system modeling goes way beyond traditional paint-and-ink animation processes, offering a wealth of effects to create in a professional 3D graphics and animation system such as 3ds max. The key to modeling such effects is the control of a *Particle System*. Traditional animators have nothing even remotely similar to a Particle System to call upon, which is a big reason why film effects make such extensive use of computer graphics and animation.

One timesaving way to create fire and explosion effects (though it lacks the full 3D capability of a Particle System) is to use an animated Map of an explosion or fire with the background dropped out. You put the Map on a flat plane in a scene, so the camera has to view the plane straight on for this to work. A company called ArtBeats (www.artbeats.com) markets dozens of high-quality animations of real fires and explosions, with the backgrounds already dropped out, for use in this manner. Chapter 22 details the methods for using an animated Map as a texture. Other than this flat-plane method, the best way to create animated dynamic-system effects (f/x) with 3ds max is to master the use of Particle Systems. Reading this chapter will enable you to start your own explorations in the magical world of Particle Systems.

Defining Particle Systems

A *particle*, in 3ds max terms, is simply a point in space; a particle is not, by itself, a 3D object. Although particles respond to their own creation controls — and can take on the *appearance* of 3D objects — a particle still has no actual dimensions. (Is that weird, or what?) Particles mainly identify on-screen places to apply specific animation settings — and places to apply the content of the Materials mapped to them.

As you use Materials on particles, the most important mapping option is the content of the Opacity Map. For that reason, it's a good idea to create a series of Opacity Maps in a 2D image-editing application like Adobe Photoshop. Opacity Maps play a strong role in defining the overall shape of a Particle, as well as the Particle's capability of showing soft edges.

Setting max Particle Systems

The six Particle Systems are Spray, Snow, Blizzard, PArray, PCloud, and Super Spray (see Figure 23-1). You can find them by choosing Create➪Geometry➪ Particle Systems. I detail each one in the following sections.

Figure 23-1:
The six
3ds max
Particle
Systems
in the
Command
panel.

Spray

Spray particles are emitted from a flat plane, emerging perpendicular to that plane. This *emitter plane* can be moved or rotated anywhere you need it in the scene. Create the emitter plane and its Spray particles by following these steps:

1. **Choose Create⇨Geometry⇨Particle Systems⇨Spray.**

2. **Create the emitter plane by using the left mouse button to click-and-drag in any viewport.**

   Use the Top Viewport if you want the particles to fall down from the top of the scene.

3. **After the emitter plane is created, keep it selected and choose the Modify Command Panel.**

   Doing so gives you access to the Spray Particle controls shown in Figure 23-2.

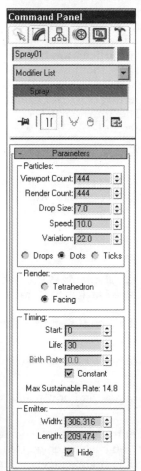

Figure 23-2:
The Spray Particle controls in the Modifier Command Panel.

Before you start tweaking the Spray Particle controls, preview the present Particle System settings by running a preview of the animation. To do so, simply click the Play button in the VCR controller, and watch the Particle System playback in any active viewport.

You can adjust the controls for the Spray particles in the Modify Command Panel. Under the Parameter heading are four groups of controls and commands: Particles, Render, Timing, and Emitter.

Particles

Render Count is the total number of Spray particles being emitted; the Viewport Count represents how many of the Spray particles will be seen in any viewport. Keep the Viewport Count the same as or less than the Render Count. Drop Size represents the surface area of a single Spray particle, and you can explore different sizes depending on the effect you want to create. The Speed value regulates how fast the Spray particles are traveling. Setting this value above ten will result in Spray particles that look more like linear trails than particles. Variation is a percentage value, representing how much the particle sizes vary from one another. A setting of 0%, for example, results in Spray particles that are all exactly alike. The Spray particles can also vary in shape, appearing in the viewports as Drops, Dots, or Ticks. Explore each.

Render

Spray particles can be rendered as one of two types: Tetrahedron or Facing. Use the Facing type if you plan to shape the Spray particle with an Opacity Map. Use the Tetrahedron type if you want to create streaks like those that cosmic rays create in a cloud chamber.

Timing

In an animation, even more than in the real world, timing is everything. Timing settings are the major tools that shape a Particle System:

- **Start:** This setting indicates the frame at which the emitter starts to spew out particles.
- **Life:** This setting indicates how many frames a Particle lasts before disappearing.
- **Birth Rate:** This setting determines how fast (and how many) new particles emerge on-screen.

The Birth Rate for particles is usually set to Constant — so new Spray particles are born at each frame — but you can switch off Constant and specify the length of the frames or the time that particles emerge.

Emitter

You can alter the Width and Length of the Spray Particle emitter plane here. Environmental effects like rain require a larger emitter plane; the spray from a hose or from a spitting cobra requires only a fairly tiny emitter plane. Choosing to Hide the emitter makes it invisible in the viewports. The emitter never appears in the rendered frames.

See the sample animation called `SprayAnim_01.avi` in the `ANIMS` folder on this book's CD-ROM for one example of a Spray Particle animation.

Snow

You definitely want to create the Snow Particle emitter in the Top Viewport, unless you want to use it to create an effect different from snow. The Snow Particle emitter is also a flat plane. After creating the emitter, you can visit the Snow Particle's controls in the Modify Command Panel, as shown in Figure 23-3.

At first glance, the Command Panel for the Snow Particle parameters looks much the same as that for the Spray particles detailed previously, but there are some important differences.

For example, under Particle Parameters you will find three new parameter commands: Flake Size, Tumble, and Tumble Rate. Flake Size refers to how big a snowflake shape you want to use. Unless you are exploring some strange particle effects, keep this value at or following 4.0. Snowflakes tumble as they fall, and both the Tumble and Tumble Rate values enable you to control the tumbling effect.

One additional new control is found under the Render heading. It's called Six Point. Clicking it to select it forces all the particles to assume the shape of a six-pointed polygon, just what you need for a snowflake simulation. Figure 23-4 shows such a simulation with the particles mapped in a solid white Diffuse Color; particles farther from the camera render in darker grays.

When zoomed in on, these six-pointed snowflakes look rather rudimentary, like confetti. They serve as basic examples here, but a fancier snowflake form is waiting at the end of this chapter. (**Hint:** Take a peek at the `SnwF1k1.avi` animation in the `ANIMS` folder on this book's CD-ROM.)

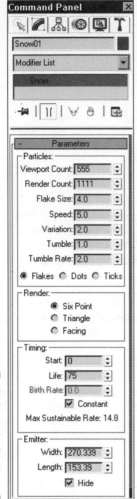

Figure 23-3:
The Modify
Command
Panel for
Snow
Particle
parameters.

Blizzard

A Blizzard Particle System emitter is usually created in the Top Viewport, though it's also possible to use other viewports for special effects. The emitter is a plane similar to the Spray and Snow Particle Systems. When you access the Blizzard Particle's Modifier Command Panel, however, things look different (as shown in Figure 23-5).

Figure 23-4:
Using a six-pointed snowflake-like shape for the Snow particles.

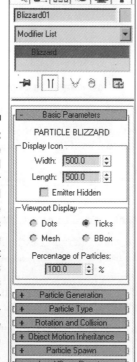

Figure 23-5:
The Command Panel for the Blizzard Particle System has far more rollout commands and controls than either the Spray or Snow Particle Systems.

Under the Particle Type rollout is a special feature that will thrill you to no end . . . the Instanced Geometry option. Farther down in the same rollout, which you can scroll to, are the Instanced Geometry controls shown in Figure 23-6.

Figure 23-6:
The
Instanced
Geometry
controls.

The most important control here is the button that reads Pick Object. Can you guess what it does? If you said "clicking this button enables me to select any 3D object in the scene and use it as a snowflake for a Blizzard Particle System," you must be either clairvoyant, or you read ahead. That's right. If you have any 3D polygonal or NURBS object in your scene, you can force the Blizzard Particle System to use it as a dynamic particle form! Here's how:

1. **Choose Create⇨Geometry⇨Hedra⇨Star1.**

2. **Click and drag in any viewport to create a 3D Star Hedra.**

3. **Open the Material Editor object, and select an empty preview slot.**

4. **Under the Shader Basic Parameters rollout, check Wire.**

   Doing so creates a Material which, when mapped to any object, forces the object to display only its polygonal edges, as if it were constructed from metal clothes hangers.

5. **Set the Diffuse Color/Ambient Color to a bright orange, and set Self Illumination to 50%.**

6. **Drag-and-drop the Material onto the Star1 Hedra in any viewport.**

   Choose Create⇨Geometry⇨Particle Systems⇨Blizzard, and click and drag a Blizzard emitter plane in the Top Viewport. Move it upwards in the Front Viewport.

7. **In the Blizzard Particle System's Modify Command Panel, choose the Particle Type rollout, and then choose Instanced Geometry.**

8. **Scroll down to the Instancing Parameters in the same rollout, and click the Pick Object button.**

9. **Click the Star1 Hedra object in any viewport.**

   The Star1 Hedra is now the particle to be used in the Blizzard effect animation, as shown in Figure 23-7.

10. **Save this project for future rendering.**

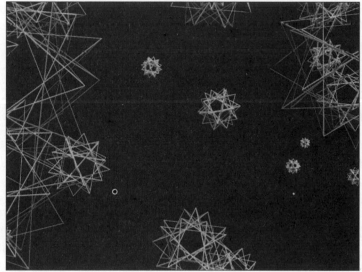

Figure 23-7:
The Star1 Hedra falls from the sky in a blizzard-like fashion when the project is animated.

You can see an example of this animation by opening the BlizPtl1.avi file in the ANIMS folder on this book's CD-ROM.

PArray

The PArray Particle System has such unique options and controls that two years of exploration would just scratch the surface of its capabilities. Think I'm kidding? Well, consider: The PArray is an *Object-Based Emitter* — you select a 3D object in your scene *other* than the Particle System icon to emit particles. That object can be just about anything. Opening the PArray Particle System's Modify Command Panel displays its wealth of commands and control rollouts, and so does Figure 23-8.

To get a handle on working with the PArray Particle System, use the following steps to modify a Torus Primitive:

1. **Place a Torus Primitive in a new scene.**

2. **Choose Create⇨Geometry⇨Particle System⇨PArray.**

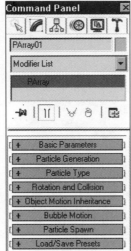

Figure 23-8:
The PArray
Particle
System's
Modify
Command
Panel
displays
numerous
rollout
buttons.

3. **Click and drag a PArray icon in the Top Viewport.**

4. **In the Basic Parameters rollout in the PArray Modifier Command Panel, click Pick Object and then click the Torus in any viewport.**

   The Torus is now the source of the animated particles that will be created. In the same rollout, you can select how the particles are emitted from the object.

5. **While still in the Basic Parameters rollout, choose Particle Formation⇨Over Entire Surface for the current example.**

6. **Under the Particle Type rollout, choose (for now) Standard Particles⇨Sphere.**

7. **Under the Particle Spawn rollout, choose Spawn Trails.**

   This option leaves the Sphere particle in place after rendering, creating a linear column of spheres over time. You can leave the other parameters at their defaults for now.

   You can always revisit the PArray Particle System later to experiment with a variety of values.

8. **Place any Material you like on the PArray icon, which will affect the particle spheres.**

9. **Place another Material on the Torus. Save the project for later rendering, as shown in Figure 23-9.**

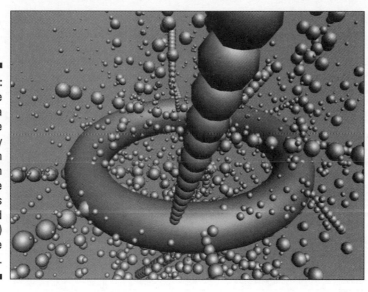

Figure 23-9:
This frame
from a
sample
PArray
animation
(which
follows the
parameters
outlined
here)
displays the
Trails effect.

Be sure to take a look at the `PArray1.avi` file in the `ANIMS` folder of this book's CD-ROM.

PClouds

The PClouds Particle System has some parameter control features that the other Particle Systems lack. Foremost among these is that the emitter can be selected from multiple options: Box, Sphere, Cylinder, or Object Based. This enables you to position the emitter more closely to an object it may be linked to, to create particle effects more closely related to specific objects in a scene. After you place your choice of PCloud emitter, you can adjust all the settings in the Modify Command Panel, shown in Figure 23-10.

Another interesting option is that you can set the vector (direction) of the particle spray along any XYZ axis combination. Some other controls are familiar compared to the Blizzard and other Particle Systems, but many give you far more detailed control over the particle effects. This is another Particle System that can keep you busy exploring until you retire.

Here's how you can use the PCloud Particle System to create some exhaust fumes from an object:

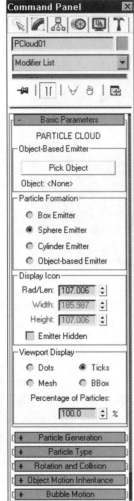

Figure 23-10:
The Modify Command Panel for the PCloud Particle System.

1. **Use the PCloud Particle System to create an emitter (for example, an object based on a Sphere primitive).**

2. **Create a Primitive Tube object, large enough so you can place the spherical emitter inside it.**

3. **Place the spherical PCloud emitter inside the Tube.**

4. **In the PCloud Modify Command Panel, select a Standard Particle Sphere as the particle type.**

5. **Use a Material on the particle that is 50% opaque with an orange Diffuse Color.**

6. **Try out different particle sizes until you find one that looks good.**

7. **Under Particle Generation in the Command Panel, choose Direction Vector and set the X,Y,Z values to 0, 0, -1.0. Set the Speed to 10 and the variation to 100%.**

   Setting Z to a negative value sends the particles down the Z (vertical) axis.

8. **Save the project for a later rendering, as shown in Figure 23-11.**

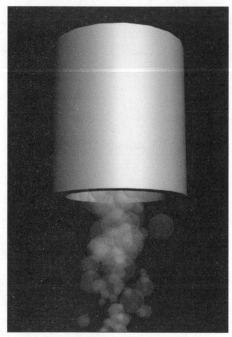

Figure 23-11:
A spray
of gases,
emitted from
the tube.

See the PCloud1.avi animation in the ANIMS folder on this book's CD-ROM.

Super Spray

The Super Spray Particle System is definitely the one to use when controlling the width and direction of a spray of particles is critical. The Super Spray Particle System emitter looks different from the others, displaying the clear directional arrow shown in Figure 23-12.

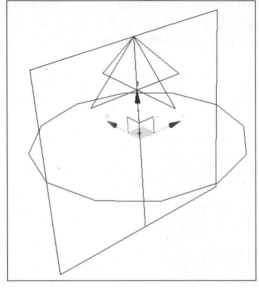

Figure 23-12:
The Super
Spray
emitter has
a directional
arrow.

You can use the Select and Rotate tool to point the arrow, and hence the particle spray, in any direction. It's also easy to Link the Super Spray Particle System to any object, and to scale and place it wherever it's needed. After placement, opening its Modify Command Panel exposes all the parameters adjustments, as shown in Figure 23-13.

The other controls match those of the other complex Particle Systems, except the controls for controlling the Spread of the emitted particles.

Here's a way to use the Super Spray Particle System to create a simple smoke effect:

1. **Create a surface with an object on it.**

   For example, you could create a rectangular tabletop with a sphere sitting on it.

2. **Use any Materials you like to add textures to both objects.**

3. **Create a Super Spray Particle System emitter with the arrow pointing upward.**

4. **Create a second object, about the same size as the first.**

   For example, create a Torus about the same circumference as the Sphere.

5. **Use the Instanced Geometry type in the Modify Command Panel for the Super Spray Particle System, and select a particle shape.**

   For this example, I selected the Torus particle shape.

6. **Use a brown Diffuse Color with a 50% opacity to map the second object with UVW Shrink Mapping.**

7. **Place the Super Spray emitter inside the upper portion of the first object (in this case, the sphere).**

   When the particles are animated, the resulting effect looks as if the first object is smoldering. The results with a sphere are shown in Figure 23-14.

Take a look at the `SupSpry1.avi` animation in the `ANIMS` folder on this book's CD-ROM.

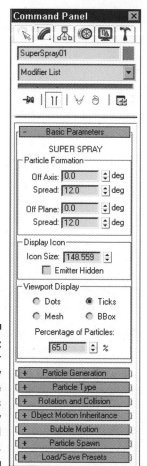

Figure 23-13: The Super Spray Particle System's Modify Command Panel.

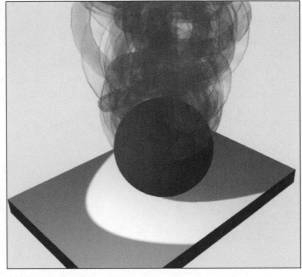

Figure 23-14:
A
smoldering
sphere.

Mapping Particles

Mapping particles is simple. Just drag and drop any Material you like on the targeted emitter. The single most important Mapping Channel for a Particle System is the Opacity Channel. If you use it with the right Map content, you can create particle shapes and objects that emulate many forms — stars, flames, smoke, water, and more. You'll need to have some skill in an image-editing program (like Adobe Photoshop) to create the Maps to have your own accessible library of Opacity Maps. If you set the Gradient Map to radial in the Opacity channel, you can create smoke effects on particles with facings.

The Snowflake

If you're working with the six-point Snow particle in the Snow or Blizzard Particle System, here's that "better snowflake" I promised earlier. What I did was to create a six-sided Opacity Map for the snowflake, as shown in Figure 23-15.

When this Opacity Map is used on a Material targeted to a Snow or Blizzard Particle System emitter, the result is a lot more pleasing than the standard six-point particle, as shown in Figure 23-16. Ah, progress.

Figure 23-15:
A snowflake
Opacity
Map
created in
Adobe
Photoshop.

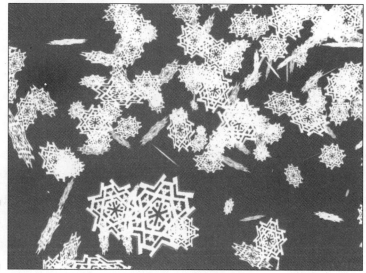

Figure 23-16:
The mapped
snowflakes.

The Opacity Map for the snowflake is included in the Textures folder on this book's CD-ROM. It's called Snwflk_01.tif. You can also take a peek at the animation called SnwFlk2.avi in the ANIMS folder on this book's CD-ROM. Wherever you are, whatever the sky is doing, and whenever the next holiday gets here, Happy Holidays!

Chapter 24

Traveling Through Space Warps

*I*f anything in 3ds max represents the latest technological edge in creating effects, it has to be Space Warps and Helpers. Using Space Warps and Helpers gives you the sense that you are Merlin reborn into the twenty-first century. Just think about it. A Space Warp gives you the ability to reshape the air, the atmosphere in a 3D environment. Any object that passes within a defined boundary of the 3D space where the Space Warp is will be . . . well . . . warped, disturbed, or affected in some magical way! This is another reason why 3ds max is used so extensively to create astounding effects in the movies. In this chapter you discover how to create and customize Space Warps.

Space Warp Transformations

A Space Warp is an energy field. Anything that comes close to that field is affected, or transformed. Some Space Warps are designed to affect polygonal models, while others reserve their power for particle systems. You can access Space Warps in two ways: Click the Space Warps tab in the Tab Panel to reveal the Space Warp icons. Click any icon to activate it and then click and drag in any viewport. You can also choose Command Panel⇨Create⇨ Space Warps to reveal the Space Warp category list.

Space Warps come in four categories, which I cover in detail in the following sections:

- ✔ Forces
- ✔ Deflectors
- ✔ Geometric/Deformable
- ✔ Modifier-Based

 When you place a Space Warp in a viewport, the placed Space Warp appears as what is called a *Gizmo*. Whenever you work with a Space Warp, the particle system(s) or object(s) affected by the Space Warp must be linked to it by the Bind To Space Warp process. You initiate this process by clicking the Bind To Space Warp icon in the toolbar, and then clicking and dragging a line from the particle system or object to the Space Warp.

Forces

The Forces Space Warps include Motor, Push, Vortex, Drag, Path Follow, PBomb, Displace, Gravity, and Wind. These are all particle-system specific Space Warps, except for Displace, which also works on modeled geometry. I talk about three of them here.

Displace

The Displace Space Warp works on either object geometry or particle systems. Here's an exercise that shows how it works on object geometry.

1. **Create a sphere in any viewport.**

2. **Choose Create⇨Space Warp⇨Forces⇨Displace.**

3. **Create a Displace Space Warp Gizmo in any viewport.**

4. **Choose the Sphere and then choose Bind To Space Warp.**

5. **Choose the Displace Space Warp's Modify Command Panel, shown in Figure 24-1.**

6. **Set the Strength to 12.0.**

7. **Click the Map button.**

   The Material/Map Browser opens.

8. **Choose Browse From⇨New, choose the Checker Map, and click OK to accept your choice.**

9. **In the Command Panel under Map, choose Spherical. Set the U, V, W Tiling to 3, 3, 3.**

   The Displace Space Warp is now complete.

10. **Use the Select and Move tool to move the sphere across the Displace Space Warp, and watch as it deforms.**

See the `DisSpW.avi` animation on this book's CD-ROM in the `ANIMS` folder.

Figure 24-1:
The Modify Command Panel for the Displace Space Warp.

Vortex

The Vortex Space Warp is meant for particle-system effects. A Vortex acts like a black hole, a gravitational field, or a drain. Here's how it works:

1. **In a new scene, choose Create⇨Geometry⇨Particle Systems.**

2. **Create a Blizzard Particle System in the Top Viewport.**

3. **Set the Size to 12, and then set Type to Standard Spheres.**

4. **Choose Create⇨Geometry⇨Particle Systems⇨Vortex, and create a Vortex Gizmo in the Top Viewport.**

5. **Choose the Blizzard Particle System, and then choose Bind to Space Warp.**

6. **In the Modify Command Panel, set Taper Length to 2 and the Taper Curve to 4.**

7. **Try out other Vortex parameters, as shown in Figure 24-2.**

   As you do so, click the Play button in the VCR Controller from time to time to see how everything moves. When you're satisfied with the way your Vortex works, save the project for later rendering.

See the `Vortex.avi` animation in the `ANIMS` folder on this book's CD-ROM.

Path Follow

Path Follow allows particle systems to follow a set path in the scene.

1. **In a new scene, choose Create⇨Geometry⇨Particle Systems, and create a Blizzard Particle System in the Top Viewport.**

2. **Set the Size to 5, and the Type to a Standard Sphere.**

3. **Choose Create⇨Splines⇨Circle, and create a circle in the Top Viewport so the Blizzard Particle System is on an edge of the circle.**

4. **Choose Create⇨Space Warps, and place a Path Follow Space Warp Gizmo in the Top Viewport.**

5. **Choose the Blizzard Particle System; then choose Bind to Space Warp.**

6. **Set Particles to a Use Total of 350, and the Stream Taper percentage to 99.**

7. **Select the Space Warp, and choose its Modify Command Panel.**

8. **Under Current Path, click the Pick Shape Object button; choose the Circle in any viewport, as shown in Figure 24-3.**

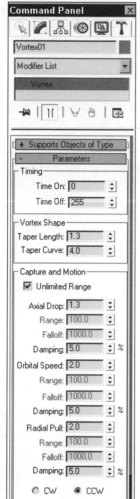

Figure 24-2:
Tweaking
the Vortex
parameters
in the
Modify
Command
Panel.

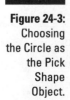

Figure 24-3:
Choosing
the Circle as
the Pick
Shape
Object.

You may have to tweak the timing a bit to get everything to look right. The result will be a stream of spheres following the circular path.

See the `PthFolw.avi` animation in the `ANIMS` folder on this book's CD-ROM.

Deflectors

A Deflector is a Space Warp surface that interferes with the movement of an object or particle. Objects and particles can bounce off of deflectors, or rest on them, but objects and particles cannot move through a deflector. 3ds max offers you nine Deflector Space Warp types. Two of them — PDynaFlect and POmniFlect — are typical examples.

PDynaFlect

PDynaFlect is a Particle System Deflector. Follow these steps to use it:

1. **Create a rectangular block created from a Box Primitive that can be used as a deflector surface.**

2. **Choose Create⇨Space Warps⇨Deflectors⇨PDynaFlect, and place a PDynaFlect Gizmo above the rectangular surface.**

   Make the Gizmo about 10 percent smaller than the surface, and leave a little space. The spherical particles in this example have their Pivot Points at their centers; an object's Pivot Point is what reaches the deflection plane.

3. **Choose Create⇨Geometry⇨Particle Systems⇨Blizzard, and place a Blizzard Gizmo above the rectangular block and the deflector.**

   Raise the Gizmo above the deflector at about viewport height, so the particles have a distance to fall before they hit the deflector.

4. **Set the Blizzard parameters.**

   For this example, use the following: Set the Particle Type to Standard Spheres. Use a total of 72 particles. Set Emit Stop to 2/3 of the way through your total animation frames, and set Display Until and Life to the same value as your total animation frames. Set Particle Size to 12. Under Rotation and Collision⇨Interparticle Collision, Enable and set the per-frame value to 2.0. Set Bounce to 22.

5. **With the Blizzard Gizmo selected, use Bind To Space Warp to connect to the PDynaFlect Gizmo.**

6. **With the Deflector Gizmo selected, choose the Modify Command Panel and change the Gizmo settings.**

   For this example, set Time Off to your last animation frame. Set Bounce to 0.2 and Physical Properties to 45 Grams. How a particle bounces depends somewhat upon how much it weighs and is affected by gravity.

7. **Run a test of the animation by clicking the Play button, and watch the results.**

   Tweak the parameters values as needed until you get an animation you like, as shown in Figure 24-4.

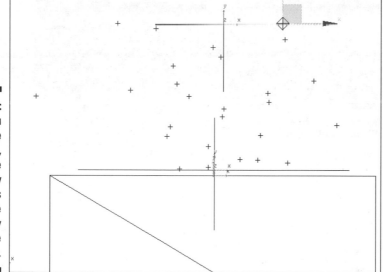

Figure 24-4: When you test the animation, you will see exactly how the particles bounce away from the deflector.

See the PdyFlact1.avi animation in the ANIMS folder on this book's CD-ROM.

POmniFlect

The POmniFlect deflection Space Warp is similar to the PDynaFlect option, but it has more parameter controls. One way to use it is to create an animation that forces the particle to stop at the deflector and stick there, as shown in Figure 24-5. To get this effect, simply set the Bounce parameter in the POmniFlect Modify Command Panel to 0. Everything else can be configured exactly as it is in the PDynaFlect section that precedes this one.

Geometric Deformable

Geometric Deformable Space Warps work on object meshes, not particle systems. You get seven types: FFD (Box), FFD (Cyl), Wave, Ripple, Displace, Conform, and Bomb. Three of them — Ripple, Conform, and FFD (Cyl) — provide a good idea how to use any of them.

Figure 24-5:
This time
the spheres
stay
attached
to the
deflector
surface.

Ripple

A Ripple Space Warp adds a wavelike ripple to any object in the scene that is bound to it as the object passes within proximity of the Space Warp. Follow these steps to use a Ripple Wave Warp effect:

1. **Choose Create➪Space Warp➪Ripple; then click and drag out a Ripple Gizmo in the Top Viewport.**

2. **In the Modify Command Panel, set the Ripple Space Warp parameters.**

   For this example, use these settings: Amplitude 1 and 2 at 32, Wavelength at 85, Circles 12, Segments 22, and Divisions 3. The Ripple Gizmo in your viewports will now look like Figure 24-6.

3. **Create an elongated sphere in the Top Viewport.**

   It should be something along the lines of a sandwich roll, with the long dimension on the X-axis.

4. **With the spherical form selected, use Bind to Space Warp and connect the object to the Ripple Gizmo.**

5. **Create an animation that passes the elongated sphere through the Ripple Gizmo from left to right over the length of the animation.**

   Figure 24-7 gives you an idea of what to look for.

6. **Preview your animation, alter as needed, and save to disk for later rendering.**

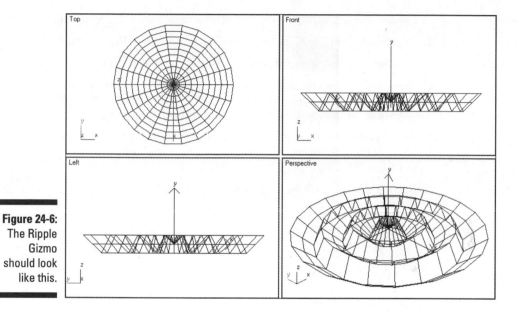

Figure 24-6:
The Ripple Gizmo should look like this.

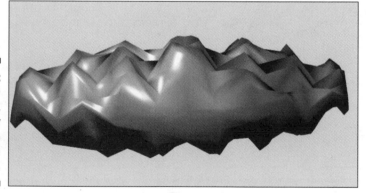

Figure 24-7:
The 3D mesh, deformed by the Ripple Space Warp.

See the `Rippler1.avi` animation in the `ANIMS` folder on this book's CD-ROM. With a dense mesh and the right texture, this is a great way to create an animated worm.

Conform

The Conform Space Warp transforms the geometry of a mesh by trying to force it into the geometry of another mesh. To use the Conform Space Warp, follow these steps:

1. **Create a cube, using a Box Primitive, with 8 x 8 x 8 segments.**

2. **Create a GeoSphere, and apply a Tessellate Modifier once.**

3. **Choose Create➪Space Warps➪Geometric/Deformable➪Conform.**

4. **Place a Conform Gizmo anywhere in the scene. In the Conform parameters Wrap to Object, click Pick Object and choose the Box object in the viewport.**

   The proportions and relative sizes of the objects (in this case, the cube and GeoSphere shown in Figure 24-8) affect the Conform operation, as does the direction of the space warp arrow.

5. **Bind the sphere to the Conform space warp.**

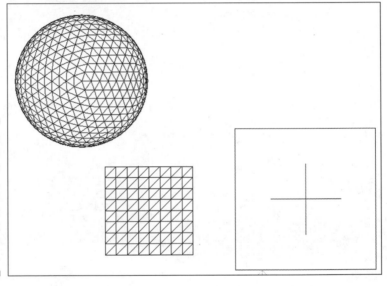

Figure 24-8:
Here's how the GeoSphere, cube, and Conform Gizmo look in the Top Viewport.

6. **Select the cube and choose Display➪Hide➪Hide Selected.**

   The cube can act as a Conform energy field even if it isn't visible.

7. **Use the Select and Move tool to move the GeoSphere over the area where the hidden cube is, and watch as it deforms.**

8. **Create an animation in which the GeoSphere moves through the invisible cube.**

   The cube is a stand-in for the Conform Space Warp shown in Figure 24-9.

See the Conform1.avi animation in the ANIMS folder on this book's CD-ROM.

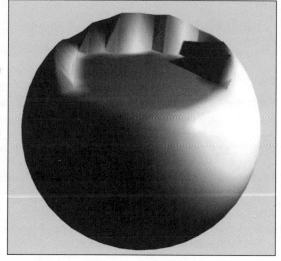

Figure 24-9:
The GeoSphere tries its best to become a cube when it passes through the Conform Space Warp energy field.

FFD (Cyl)

The FFD (FreeForm Deformation) Cylinder Space Warp creates the effect of a warped energy field. It works much like the FFD (Cyl) Modifier — you start with a cylindrical cage and then deform it to affect an object. The difference between the Space Warp and the Modifier is that the FFD (Cyl) Space Warp can be used dynamically in an animation — like this:

1. **Create a sphere with 128 segments.**

2. **Choose Create⇨Space Warps⇨Geometric/Deformable⇨FFD (Cyl).**

3. **Click and drag in the Top Viewport to create a FFD (Cyl) Gizmo. Ensure that the height of the Gizmo is as tall as the sphere.**

4. **In the Top Viewport, reshape the FFD (Cyl) by dragging its control points.** Be sure to drag a window across the desired control points, to ensure that the whole stack of points are selected.

   To activate and deactivate the control points, double-click the FFD (Cyl) heading in the Modify Command Panel to achieve the result shown in Figure 24-10.

5. **Select the sphere and Bind To Space Warp, connecting it to the FFD (Cyl) Space Warp.**

6. **Use the Select and Move tool to pass the sphere through the Space Warp to see what happens.**

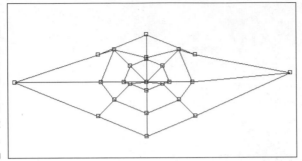

Figure 24-10:
Reshape the
FFD (Cyl)
cage in the
Top
Viewport
like this.

The effect varies in response to changes in the sphere's path through the Space Warp.

7. **Create an animation that passes the sphere through the Space Warp, and save the project to disk for later rendering.**

Modifier-Based

The strangest feature of Modifier-Based Space Warps is that their effects are inversely proportional to the distance between the deformable object and the Space Warp. (Sounds like Science Fiction Doubletalk 101, doesn't it?) In English, a Modifier Space Warp's effect is exaggerated when you move the affected object farther away (which is the opposite of how the other Space Warps work). You get six Modifier-Based Space Warps: Bend, Noise, Skew, Taper, Twist, and Stretch. I cover each of them here.

Bend

The Bend Modifier-Based Space Warp's Modify Command Panel looks the same as the standard Bend Modifier's Command Panel. The parameters are configured in the same fashion too, as shown in Figure 24-11.

When the object is centered on the Space Warp, any values you set apply to any object linked to the Space Warp. No matter how you move the object, its Pivot Point remains connected to the Space Warp. Moving the object creates distortions (more as you move it farther). Here's how to do the effect:

1. **Choose Create⇨Space Warps⇨Modifier Based⇨Bend.**

2. **Click and drag the Bend Gizmo in the Top Viewport.**

3. **Set the Bend parameters in the Modify Command Panel.**

   The current example uses Angle=180, Direction=0, and Bend Axis=Z.

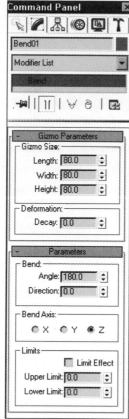

Figure 24-11:
The
Modifier-
Based Bend
Space
Warp's
Command
Panel.

4. **Create a cube in the scene.**

   For this example, use Length/Width/Height Segments of 12, 12, and 12.

5. **With the cube selected, use Bind To Space Warp to connect it to the Bend Gizmo.**

6. **Move the cube around the scene to see what the Bend Space Warp does to it.**

7. **Create an animation of the effect, and save the project to disk for later rendering.**

Take a look at the Bend1.avi animation in the ANIMS folder on this book's CD-ROM.

Twist

Twist is another Modifier-Based Space Warp that you can use to create some hypnotic animation effects. Here's how you use it:

1. **Create a Primitive (in this case, a teapot) in the Top Viewport; Change its Segments value to 12 to give it a denser mesh.**

2. **Choose Create⇨Space Warps⇨Modifier Based⇨Twist.**

3. **Click and drag a Twist Gizmo in the Top Viewport, away from the object.**

4. **Set the Twist angle to 270 with a Bias of 90 on the Z-axis.**

5. **With the object selected, use Bind To Space Warp to connect it to the Twist Gizmo.**

   Move the teapot around the scene to try out varying proximities to the Twist Space Warp Gizmo.

6. **Create a keyframed animation of the movement, and save the project to disk for later rendering, as shown in Figure 24-12.**

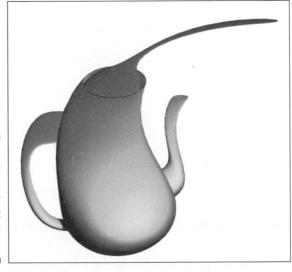

Figure 24-12: A teapot twisted like soft clay by the Twist Space Warp.

See the Twist1.avi animation in the ANIMS folder on this book's CD-ROM.

Stretch

The Stretch Space Warp pulls on a mesh like taffy, making it stretch out with a pinched mid-section. Explore the Stretch Space Warp by doing the following:

1. **Create a cube with Length/Width/Height segments of 12, 12, 12.**

2. **Choose Create⇨Space Warps⇨Modifier Based⇨Stretch, and click and drag a Stretch Gizmo in any viewport.**

3. **Set the Stretch parameters (in my example, I set Stretch=2 with an Amplify of 0 on the Z-axis).**

4. **Select the cube; use Bind To Space Warp to connect it to the Stretch Gizmo.**

   Now for the fun part: Move the cube around the scene in any viewport and watch what happens to it.

5. **Create a keyframe animation that uses the effect. Save the project to disk for later rendering.**

See the `Stretch1.avi` animation in the `ANIMS` folder on this book's CD-ROM.

Helping You Out

3ds max offers you some needed help with the Helper options. Access Helpers by choosing Create⇨Helpers to get a number of Helper categories. This section discusses two — Standard and Atmosphere Apparatus.

Standard Helpers

The Standard Helpers are located by going to Create⇨Helpers⇨Standard. You get six Standard Helpers: Dummy, Grid, Point, Tape, Protractor, and Compass. I take a closer look at three of them — Protractor, Dummy (now, *there's* a convenient name), and Points, as shown in Figure 24-13.

Figure 24-13: The Standard Helpers in the Command Panel.

Using the Protractor

Use the Protractor Helper to determine the angle from the Protractor Point to the Pivot Points of any two objects. Just place the Protractor Gizmo in the scene (preferably on an object so the angles can be determined), and then select the two additional objects. A readout of the angle appears in the Command Panel, as shown in Figure 24-14.

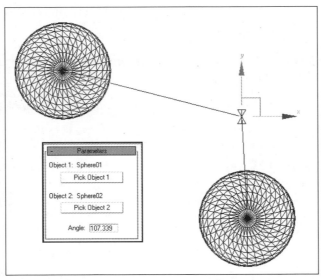

Figure 24-14: Use the Protractor to measure the angle between three points: the Protractor Point and any two objects' Pivot Points.

Constructing points

A 3ds max Point Helper is actually a substitute for the standard Dummy object, with more options. It's used the same way as a Dummy object is. A Point Helper has a total of four attributes, any of which can be switched off or on: Center Marker, Axis Tripod, Cross, and Box. You can also adjust the size of a Point Helper, as shown in Figure 24-15.

Figure 24-15: The Point Helper options are available in the Command Panel.

Atmospheric Apparatus

A very valuable Helper category is Atmospheric Apparatus. You get three choices: Box, Sphere, and Cylinder Gizmos. That's only the start of the fun — it's how you use these Gizmos that makes 3D life interesting.

Sphere of fire

You can create some stunning 3D fire effects with the Atmospheric Apparatus Helper.

1. **Place any two objects you like in a scene, with some distance between them.**

2. **Choose Create⇨Helpers⇨Atmospheric Apparatus, and select the Sphere Gizmo.**

3. **Click and drag a Sphere Gizmo so it encompasses part of each object in the scene. Then place some stuff inside the Sphere Gizmo.**

4. **With the Sphere Gizmo selected, choose the Modify Command Panel. Under the Atmosphere and Effects rollout, click Add.**

   The Atmosphere panel appears.

5. **Click Fire Effect, and then click OK.**

6. **Back in the Command Panel, select the Fire Effect text that appears in the Atmosphere and Effects rollout.**

7. **Click Setup.**

   The Environment panel appears, as shown in Figure 24-16.

Dummy objects? Why not?

You may think that AutoDesk, the developers of 3ds max, named this object after the *For Dummies* book series. Oh, that it were true. The truth is that *Dummy object* (an object that never renders, but that other objects in the scene are linked to) is a standard term in computer graphics and animation. In effect, the Dummy object is a control mechanism for other objects.

Suppose you wanted to have a series of diverse objects rotate around a single point (say, planets around a star). The simplest way to do it would be to create a Dummy object at that point and then link all the other objects to it. Rotate the Dummy object, and everything orbits the point. Neat, huh?

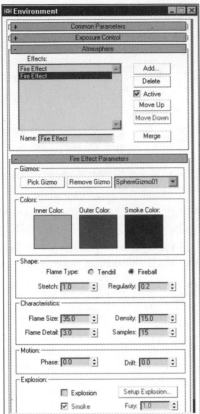

Figure 24-16:
The
Environment
panel.

8. **Shape the explosion in the Fire Effect Parameters rollout.**

   You can keyframe-animate the Shape, Characteristics, Motion, and Explosion parameters to produce an animation. Use whatever colors you like for the explosion.

9. **Keyframe the Fireball Characteristics.**

   For this example, have the Fireball start at a Flame Size of 0 and finish at a Flame Size of 50. Keyframe-animate the size of the Sphere Gizmo so it starts out small, gets huge in the middle of the animation, and vanishes at the end.

10. **Save the project for later rendering.**

   See the SphFire.avi animation in the ANIMS folder on this book's CD-ROM.

A foggy day

Using the Fog effect is a great way to create 3D fog and clouds.

1. **Place any two objects you like in a scene, with some distance between them.**

2. **Choose Create⇨Helpers⇨Atmospheric Apparatus, and select the Box Gizmo.**

3. **Click and drag out a Box Gizmo so it encompasses part of each object in the scene; place some fog inside the Box Gizmo.**

4. **With the Box Gizmo selected, choose the Modify Command Panel; in the Atmosphere and Effects rollout, click Add.**

   The Atmosphere panel appears.

5. **Back in the Command Panel, select the Volume Fog text that appears in the Atmosphere and Effects rollout; click Setup.**

   The Environment panel appears.

6. **In the Volume Fog Parameters rollout, set the controls for color.**

   You can keyframe-animate Shape, Characteristics, and Motion parameters. For this example, use the following settings: Color=light blue, Exponential Density=100, Step Size=5, Max Steps=75, and Fog Background checked. Under Noise, set the type to Turbulence. Set Levels to 5 and Size to 55. Set Phase to 0 and Wind Strength to 7, with a Wind from the Left.

7. **Create a keyframed animation from these parameters, keyframing the size of the Volume Fog Gizmo box as well (as shown in Figure 24-17).**

Figure 24-17:
A frame from a Volume Fog animation, with the fog made cloudlike.

Be sure to check out the VolFog.avi animation in the ANIMS folder on this book's CD-ROM.

Take a Snapshot

I'll bet you never thought of a Space Warp as a modeling alternative, but it sure can be used as one. Just choose any frame that displays an interesting warped alteration of an object. Select the object, and choose Tools➪ Snapshot to bring up the Snapshot panel.

You can Snapshot a single frame of the animated object or a series of frames for a collection of 3D objects. Select Mesh to create mesh objects, as shown in Figure 24-18.

Now go out and Snapshot your world!

Figure 24-18:
Diverse
bean-like
objects
created
from a
single
sphere
affected by
a Twist
Space
Warp,
using the
Snapshot
operation.

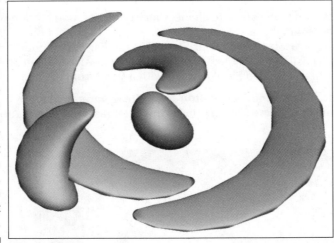

Part VIII
Pictures Perfect

In this part . . .

Remember how proud you felt when you brought a picture home from school, and your mom hung it on the fridge? Or perhaps your sense of personal value was underscored when you invited the neighbors over for dinner, and once they were too incapacitated to move after several courses of lasagna, you brought out the four hours of home videos you took of your vacation in the Florida swamps? We are all born storytellers, no matter the medium we use for self-expression. Getting your images on paper, film, or video is a necessary part of telling stories to others.

In this computer age, we can record our images, still or moving, to computer disks, videotape, CDs, DVDs, and perhaps one day soon, to some new media that will display our work hollographically in full 3D. 3ds max presents you with a number of options for recording your 3D masterpieces, and this part of the book shows you what they are and how to use them to your best advantage.

Chapter 25

Rendering Images

• •

In This Chapter

▶ Rendering with ActiveShade

▶ Using RayTracing and Radiosity

▶ Rendering backgrounds

▶ Using global lighting and exposure controls

▶ Generating render effects

• •

*R*endering is all about creating a means for others to see your work. You may think that when your scene is complete, all 3D objects have been modeled and tweaked to perfection, and all the textures are in place, your work is done. You're not done if you intend to show your work to others on something besides your personal computer. You have to consider what means you will use to store and display your work outside of your own workspace.

If you think your Aunt Millie would enjoy seeing what you're doing, it makes a difference if she has a computer or not, or a videotape player, or just a bare wall waiting for a poster. If you plan to send your work to a professional studio for consideration for employment, you have to make sure you understand the ways to get the images out there in a way that will be acceptable to whomsoever gets them.

If the lighting in your 3D scene needs some improvement to take your work from good to great, or you need to add some rendering effects, you'll want to know where to look in 3ds max to find the necessary tweaking tools and processes. The means for tweaking and rendering your work in 3ds max (or as we nerds say, "customizing the output") are located in specific menus and panels spread around the 3ds max GUI. This chapter is about locating and using these rendering output tools and processes.

Defining Rendering Types

You can render your work in a number of different ways, all of them slightly or grossly different. Sometimes you need to let your finished 3D scene remain out of view for a while, so you can come back to it and judge it with a fresh eye, and sometimes it may be worth your while to get the input of others before finalizing the work.

Render Scene

The Render Scene Panel is the mother of all global rendering controls because you can control all the rendering parameters within the panel. You can access this panel in one of two ways. Either choose the Rendering menu and choose Render, or use the render icons present in the Tab Panel. Notice the last four icons at the right under the Rendering tab. Clicking the first of those icons for the Render Scene brings up the Render Scene Panel. See Figure 25-1.

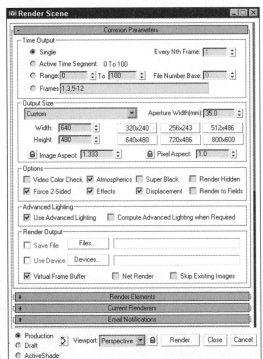

Figure 25-1: The Render Scene Panel.

As shown in Figure 25-1, I have left three of the rollouts in this panel closed (Render Elements, Current Renderers, and Email Notifications) because their parameters are for more advanced use and beyond the scope of this book. Everything you need to know to create the bulk of your rendering is contained in the Common Parameters rollout and the information and options at the bottom of this panel, so here's what's involved:

✔ **Time Output:** Choose to output a Single frame (an image). The other options are for animated output (I cover that subject in the next chapter). When you choose Single, the frame that's currently active in the Timeline becomes the rendered output.

✔ **Output Size:** Decide how large the output image is to be. To the right are six preset size buttons that cover standard image size output, though with a right-click on any one of the six buttons, you can customize the button to any size you prefer. In the Width/Height boxes, you can type in any additional size you want. Clicking the arrow next to the Custom window brings up a list of animation output sizes, covering standard (and not-so-standard) film sizes in use today. Until you've had a bit more hands-on time with 3ds max, leave the Image Aspect and Pixel Aspect values at their defaults.

✔ **Advanced Lighting:** Leave these settings at their defaults for now.

✔ **Render Output:** The only control that's especially relevant here is the Files button. Clicking it allows you to choose a name and destination for the storage of your image, in addition to File Type options. I recommend the TIF file format as the best stored File Type for images.

✔ **Render Controls:** At the bottom of the panel are the Render Controls. You can choose what quality the render should be, Production, Draft, or ActiveShade. In most cases, it's best to choose Draft or ActiveShade for quick previews, and Production for final renders. Choose which viewport to render from the list, and then click Render to set rendering in motion. The Production render takes place in a window of its own. At the top-left of the rendered image window is a disk icon. Click it if you forgot to specify the filename with the Files button before you rendered the scene. See Figure 25-2.

Figure 25-2:
After the image appears, click the disk icon at the upper-left to save the image to disk.

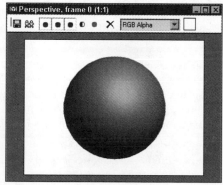

Without making any adjustments beforehand, this is the path to rendering an image in 3ds max.

Quick Render

Quick Render is activated by clicking the second teapot icon from the left in the Rendering Tab Panel. Quick Render skips over the Rendering Panel altogether, rendering the image with whatever the current settings are under Render Parameters, and renders the active viewport.

Render Last

Render Last renders the same viewport as the previous rendering, even though another viewport may be active. The speed is not different, nor is the exclusion of any scene changes.

ActiveShade

ActiveShade is a 3ds max exclusive, and is a super-fast way to preview a scene. Click the last teapot icon on the right in the Rendering Tab Panel, and *bam!* your preview of the scene is rendered with everything updated. All parameters you specified in the Render Scene Panel are taken into account.

What makes the use of shade "active" in this feature is its use of *lighting models* — consistent instructions to the computer that create a realistic interplay of light and shadow. The 3ds max options that provide these subtleties are Advanced Lighting, RayTracing, and Radiosity:

- ✔ **Advanced Lighting:** Although the Advanced Lighting options (Rendering⇨Advanced Lighting) are worth mentioning, this book doesn't delve into their details. Although these options won't singe you if you try them, the frustration level will be lower if you work with 3ds max for a few months beforehand.

- ✔ **RayTracing:** The RayTracing process is the simpler of the two most popular lighting models in current use (the other is Radiosity). The RayTracing model instructs the computer to render a scene by following how rays of light from your light sources affect scene content, and how they bounce off (and are absorbed by) various elements in the scene.

  If you use RayTracing in your rendering, you encounter two panels that adjust RayTracing parameters. One is for advanced users (Rendering⇨Raytracer Settings), and it brings up the Global Raytracer Settings Panel. For now, leave the defaults in this panel as they are. Come back to them later on, after 3ds max has become almost second nature to you.

If you want to get into RayTracing right away, choose Rendering⇨ Raytrace Global Exclude/Include. The panel that appears is called Exclude/Include for short. It works the same way as the Exclude/Include Panel for lights.

You can copy any scene content from the left column to the right column by clicking the double arrows and then choosing Include. Doing so applies Raytracing to only the included elements. Raytracing is especially effective on object surfaces configured to reflect and/or refract light. If you have only a couple of objects like that in your scene, then use Raytracing only on them.

✔ **Radiosity:** Radiosity computations are (initially, at least) a more complex and time-consuming approach. The computer must take note of not only the individual rays of light, but also of how object hues affect other objects in their vicinity (for example, when a shiny red ball reflects a dark blue cube).

After the Radiosity of a scene is computed (as long as you don't make changes to the scene elements), the rendering results are faster than those of RayTracing. In addition, most 3D artists and animators consider Radiosity a more realistic lighting model than RayTracing.

If you specify neither of the high-quality renderers, 3ds max uses the Scanline renderer as its default — resulting in good, but less accurate, lighting.

Be advised — radiosity parameters can be a real headache for a 3ds max beginner. If you've already had some experience with Radiosity in other 3D applications, then you can play around with these settings without resorting to the aspirin bottle. Access the Radiosity setting by choosing Rendering⇨Advanced Lighting, which brings up the Advanced Lighting Panel. Choose the Radiosity lighting model in the panel and tweak away.

Adjusting Render Settings

There are some important adjustments you can make before any final rendering to optimize your images for the uses you want them to serve:

✔ **Setting the output size:** When you want to create a high-quality rendered image, use an Output Size in the Render Scene Panel that is at least twice the size of the image you want to wind up with. When the image is rendered, copy it to a 2D image program like Adobe Photoshop and reduce it to the size you need. Everything will look much sharper than it would if you simply rendered to the output size in 3ds max.

✔ **Image options:** Save your images as Targa or TIF files if you're looking for maximum quality. Save the images as JPEG or PNG files if they are to be used on the Web. The BMP format is okay if you don't need to preserve the best image quality.

✔ **Render Elements:** Here's a potentially important — but not very well known — feature of 3ds max. In the Render Scene Panel is a rollout labeled Render Elements, shown in Figure 25-3.

When first opened, it looks blank. What it's waiting for is your selection of which elements — which aspects of an image — to render. Clicking the Add button at the upper-left of the rollout reveals a list of elements you can choose, as shown in Figure 25-4.

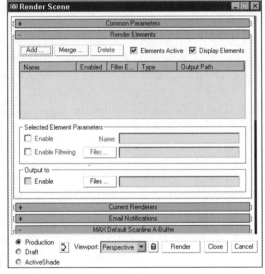

Figure 25-3:
The Render Elements rollout in the Render Scene Panel.

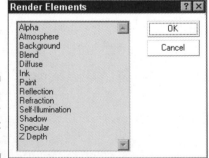

Figure 25-4:
The Render Elements list appears.

Choosing an element from the list (or several) allows you to render just the chosen elements of the image. Choosing Background renders just the background of a 3D scene. Choosing Reflection renders only the reflections in the scene. The same holds true for all other elements. The idea is to give you a chance to check certain elements of the scene by themselves — and even save out these renders as separate images.

Printing Your Images

To print your images, you'll need to open the saved image in software meant for that purpose, like Adobe Photoshop. There are so many high-quality printers on the market today for reasonable (and even downright cheap) prices, that most computer graphics users have at least one on hand. Some commercial facilities like Kinko's offer high-end printing from your removable disk or CD-ROM. Computer magazines are full of ads from companies who print your image files after you send the images online to their offices — which is especially good when you need oversized prints. The competition is keen, and the charges keep coming down. If you intend to display your print in a gallery or want to keep it for a long time, look for a service that uses archival-quality inks and paper. Standard inkjet printing fades over time, especially when it's exposed to light.

Render Environments

At the far left of the Rendering tab in the Tab Panel is button labeled Environments. Clicking this button brings up the Environment Panel. There are rollouts for Common Parameters, Exposure Control, and Atmosphere; other rollouts appear in response to choices you make.

Common Parameters

At the top of the Common Parameters rollout is an area for altering the content of your background. Click the color swatch if you want to choose a single background color. To choose an image for your background from the image types in the Material/Map Browser, check the Use Map box, and then click the horizontal button underneath.

Next are the Global Lighting parameters. Use the color swatch to tint the scene towards any hue, or choose the Ambient color swatch to change the global light's hue more strongly. Alter the brightness of the global lighting by raising or lowering the Level value.

Exposure Control

The Exposure Control reads None by default, but you can open a list of optional exposure controls. Choosing and modifying Exposure settings is a bit tricky, but it's worth spending some time to get a feel for how Exposure settings affect a 3D scene. Various rollouts appear with control parameters, depending on which Exposure option you choose from the list. Try choosing the Pseudo Color Exposure Control (for example), and then do a test render of a 3D scene. Pseudo Color radically alters how a scene is rendering, substituting posterized bright colors for all scene content. Pseudo Color is used for displaying light intensity in a scene, like a colored light meter.

Atmosphere

The Atmosphere rollout offers you the opportunity to choose any of four separate atmospheric effects to layer over your 3D scene: Fire Effect, Fog, Volume Fog, or Volume Light. The Fire Effect and Volume Fog effects require a Helper Atmosphere Apparatus Gizmo in the scene, something covered thoroughly in Chapter 24 of this book. The Fog Atmosphere is the simplest effect, and offers a minimum of parameters: Fog color and min/max distance settings. It creates a rather uniform swash of Fog (muted color) over the scene.

The Volume Light Atmosphere, however, is worthy of your exploration and use. When selected, a separate Volume Light Parameters rollout appears in the Environment Panel. See Figure 25-5.

You have to have at least one light in the scene to render this atmospheric effect. What actually happens is that the selected light acts like a projector that creates a 3D volume of atmospheric effects throughout the space where the light affects the scene. I like to use Omni lights here, but you can explore spotlights as well. The color and distance parameter controls are easy enough to understand, but if you plan to use this effect, don't pass up the chance to explore the use of the Noise parameters. Noise can create things like blotchy smoke or tendrils of creeping fog. Explore the use of different Noise values, and do some test renders. Figure 25-6 shows noise added to create a blotchy fog.

I prefer using the Volume Light Atmosphere effect over the Volume Fog Atmosphere effect because it requires no Gizmos in the scene, and seems to render a bit faster.

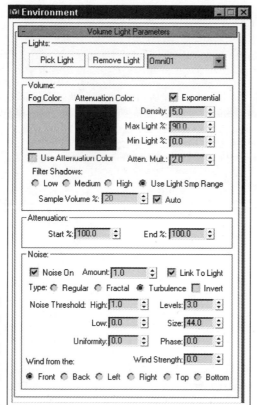

Figure 25-5:
The Volume Light Parameters rollout appears.

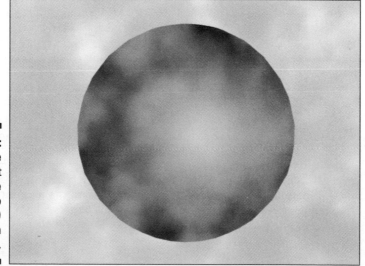

Figure 25-6:
A Volume Light Atmosphere targeted to a simple 3D scene with a sphere.

Render Effects

One more fancy list of options to cover in this chapter is Render Effects, which can add far more pizzazz to an otherwise dull scene. If you choose the Tab Panel and choose the Rendering tab, you will see a button at the left that reads Effects. Clicking it brings up the Effects Panel. After it opens, clicking Add displays a list of possible effects to be integrated with the rendering. You can choose as many as you like in whatever order, and they will all be processed when you render the image. See Figure 25-7.

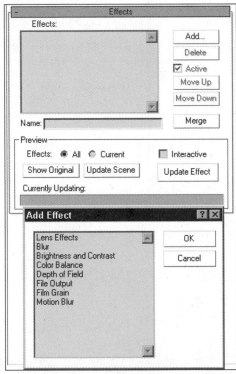

Figure 25-7:
The Add
Effect list in
the Effects
Panel.

In the Effects Panel, you can choose from the following options (choosing one of them brings up a parameter rollout for the particular option):

✔ **Lens Effects:** These effects mimic the quirks of light that have become familiar to filmgoers (for example a lens flare that puts a momentary streak of light in the image as the camera pans across a light source) — and the presence of such "flaws" actually enhances realism.

- **Blur:** Useful for suggesting motion, romance, or a dazed state of mind.

- **Brightness and Contrast:** These work like the familiar TV controls of the same names.

- **Color Balance:** This color-TV-style control changes the degree of dominance a particular color has in the scene.

- **Depth of Field:** This photography-inspired option will be an old friend to users of 35mm cameras — but remember that you need a 3ds max camera in the scene to use the option. DOF uses the camera's focal-length settings to enforce a background blur on parts of the scene, causing objects in the distance to interfere less with foreground content.

- **File Output:** This one is useful primarily if you are recording frames from an animation to an external device such as a single-frame recorder.

- **Film Grain:** You can use this one to suggest old, deteriorating film — or use its settings to either sharpen or soften the image details.

- **Motion Blur:** This option is also animation-specific; it mimics the inability of some cameras to freeze the motion of a moving object into a clear image. The result, oddly, is a motion sequence that looks more realistic.

Mimicking camera and eye

Have you ever looked up at the moon on a frosty night and observed a wide circular ring? Or perhaps you have squinted at a streetlight and seen starlike patterns emerging from it. These are *lens effects,* artifacts caused by the way light strikes a camera lens — or (for that matter) the lens of a human eye. Lens effects create beautiful content to certain images, and cause a greater suspension of disbelief by the audience when used with care.

To create Lens effects in a scene, you need to have a light or lights pointing at the camera. Omni lights work well, because they are always pointing in all directions at once. When you choose Lens effects in the Effects Panel, you are presented with a list of lens effect options. This includes Glow, Ring, Ray, Auto Secondary, Manual Secondary, Star, and Streak. Each of these types has its own parameter rollout where the color, size, and intensity of the effect can be adjusted (yes, you can animate all these parameters too by keyframing them). You can use different lens effects on a number of lights in a scene, or you can composite many lens effects on a single light. You need a dark background to appreciate lens effects. Try out different lens effect types and apply them to a light in your scene, doing test renders until you get the look you want. Figure 25-8 offers a glimpse of what's possible.

Figure 25-8:
Explore
applying
various lens
effects to
lights in a
3D scene.
Use a dark
background.

Remember that lens effects are applied to lights in the scene, so they affect objects according to their placement and their Include/Exclude parameters. Lens effects can be added to Materials as well; If you have a Material that you want to apply (for example) to a renderable spline as a piece of neon tubing, you can choose a specific Material Effect Channel. You can find the Material Effect Channel assignment icon just under the sample spheres in the Material Editor. Choose a non-zero number. In the Environment dialog box, add a Glow lens effect. Select Glow and move it to the right pane. Scroll down to find the Glow element options and place a check mark next to Effects ID and insert the same number you chose in the Material Editor. You can have up to 15 effects. Try the interactive option as well. Render effects are Post effects, and are added to the scene after it is rendered, and therefore do not affect nearby excluded or included objects in any way.

Chapter 26

Rendering Animations

Creating movement and watching as an image becomes animated is so exciting. When we observe the results of our keyframing and path-animating efforts as an object seemingly becomes conscious and goes through its scripted paces, it's hard not to think we've created life itself from those building blocks. Animators learn to appreciate every movement in the everyday world, studying them and trying to emulate them. This chapter is about getting your animated scenes into a format so others can appreciate the images you've brought to life.

Render Scene (Animation)

For the fidgety few who want the gist of this chapter in a single sentence, here it is: Animations are recorded from the Render Scene Panel, okay? You can go on to the next chapter now. For those who would like to hang out awhile to get a little more juice from this particular orange, read on.

Chapter 24 details the uses of the Render Scene Panel for recording images. Recording animations through the use of the same panel is a further extension of the same process, with a few more concepts to explore. You can access the Render Scene Panel by choosing Rendering⇨Render, or by clicking the first teapot icon in the Rendering tab of the Tab Panel. Either way, the Render Scene Panel pops up.

In the Common Parameters rollout of the Render Scene Panel, the default selection under Time Output is Single — the one option that won't work for recording an animation. Select one of the other three:

- ✔ **Active Time Segment:** Select this option if you want to record all the frames in succession, as indicated by the total frames represented in the Timeline. There is one change you can make when selecting this option. In the Every Nth Frame input area, you can select a number other than the default of 1. If you selected 2, for example, you would record the animation from the first to last frame represented in the Timeline, but the animation would skip over every second frame, resulting in an animation that would be half as long as recording every frame.

- ✔ **Range:** If you select this option, you can record starting at any frame number and ending at any frame number. Using a negative number for the start frame will record that value as a *pre-roll* segment, a segment of the animation that displays the scene in its first frame position for a specified hold time before everything starts to move (useful when you're editing segments together). The same is true for the last frame. Using a number larger than the total number of frames in the Timeline will record the additional frames frozen in their last frame positions.

- ✔ **Frames:** Select this option to record sporadic frames in the animation. Put a *comma* between numbers to record the single frames indicated by those numbers. Put a *dash* between numbers to record a continuous range of frames (from Frame X to Frame Y).

Saving rendered output

At the bottom of the Common Parameters rollout in the Render Scene Panel is an area titled Render Output. This is where you tell the computer that you want to save the animation, what its name will be, and in what animation format the animation will be saved. You start this process by clicking the Files button to bring up the Render Output File Panel.

1. **Type the name of your animation-to-be in the File Name area, choose the Save As Type option, and leave everything else at its default setting.**

2. **Click the arrow to open the Save As Type list.**

   This list presents an array of possibilities. In general, there are two ways to save an animation. The first is as a movie file. The second is as a sequence of single image frames. The advantage of saving as single frames is that the frames can be edited in an image-editing application like Adobe Photoshop. The disadvantage of single frames is that they take up far more storage space than a movie file. The most common movie formats are AVI and QuickTime. The standard Windows animation player can play AVI movies, but not QuickTime. The QuickTime player (from Apple Computing) can play both QuickTime and AVI movies. When you save in a movie format, a panel appears and asks you what compression format to use.

3. **Use whatever compression format comes up as the default.**

   Compression formats are the methods used to squash your saved movie down to the smallest possible space. The most common single-frame animation formats for Windows systems are BMP, JPEG, PNG, TARGA, and TIF, shown in Figure 26-1.

Figure 26-1: The list of animation format options.

Animation output size

In most cases, you'll probably use one of the preset sizes for your animation. You can always type in a size of your own as well. For those of you planning to work in the movie business, click to open the Custom list. There, you'll see output size options geared toward the film and broadcast industry. See Figure 26-2.

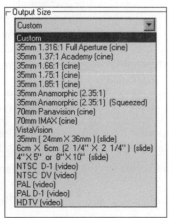

Figure 26-2: The list of custom sizes is meant for recording animation data for use in high-end film and broadcast environments.

After that, it's just a matter of selecting the render mode (Production, Draft, or ActiveShade), selecting which viewport to render from, and clicking the Render button in the Render Scene Panel.

Creating Rendering Level Animations

In most cases, the best approach is to create animations that display your fully textured objects against whatever backgrounds have been added to the scene — and see the fancy effects you've created in full blazing color. But what if you want to see your animation displayed with all the display options available to you in a viewport playback, and in addition, you want to see the light and camera icons in use in the scene? These display options are also known as *rendering levels*.

The most photographic Rendering Level is Smooth + Highlights — the option set for the viewport that uses the Perspective or Camera view. But try out the other Rendering Levels too, including Smooth, Facets + Highlights, Facets, Lit Wireframe, Wireframe, and Bounding Box. Can you create a playable animation file that uses *all* the viewport display options? Most certainly! Such animations are called *animation previews* in 3ds max. To create one, follow these steps:

1. **Choose Animations⇨Make Preview in the menu bar.**

   The Make Preview Panel appears. Some familiar parameter controls from the Render Scene Panel are repeated in this panel, with a few additional features:

   • **Image Size:** This value is tied to the value you used in the Render Scene Panel, though you may choose to use a percentage multiplier for that value. A separate button exists for applying a compression format.

   • **Display in Preview:** This list is to the right of the Make Preview Panel. Use any check box in the list to display items normally hidden in a Render Scene animation. This includes Shapes, Lights, Cameras, Helpers, Space Warps, Active Grid, Safe Frame, and Frame Numbers.

   • **Rendering Level:** You can specify how fully rendered the Preview appears.

2. **Click the Custom File Type radio button at the bottom of the panel.**

   A Make Preview panel appears.

3. **Use the Make Preview Panel to name the file, select the destination, and choose the animation format, as shown in Figure 26-3.**

Figure 26-3:
The Make
Preview
Panel.

4. **Click the Save button to create and save your new animation file.**

   Now you can play back your animation by using Windows Media Player or another suitable animation viewer.

Using the RAM Player

If you have enough memory (RAM) in your computer, you can use the 3ds max RAM Player to preview animations that you have already saved to disk. The RAM Player can actually play back two animations at the same time, displaying them side by side or at the top and bottom of the screen (Figure 26-4 shows a vertically split screen). You can compare animations, select one or the other as a better version, or get an idea of how to edit them together later on. The animations can be played back at variable frame rates (FPS), either forward or backward. To bring up the RAM Player, choose Rendering⇨RAM Player in the menu bar. The controls are simple to understand — they have pop-up labels that appear when you hold your mouse pointer over them.

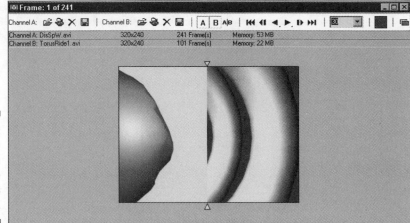

Figure 26-4:
The RAM
Player with
two
animations
loaded.

Animated Effects

Chapter 25 describes how to add a number of preset effects to images. Although any of these effects can be animated using the keyframe method, a couple of effects are designed specifically for a filmlike look (Film Grain and Motion Blur), so a quick look at them is in order.

Film Grain

Hairs, scratches, and smudges on a film are often annoying to watch; they distract your attention from the content of your movie. Another common film flaw is apparent graininess, as if the frames had sand embedded in them. Older films are especially vulnerable to these anomalies — and everybody knows it — so you can make your animation *seem* more antique (even more "historical") by adding such flaws. 3ds max doesn't yet have a hair/scratch/smudge creator for your animations, but you can increase the graininess of the rendering. Here's how:

1. **Load in an animation you have previously created.**

2. **Click the Effects button under the Rendering tab in the Tab Panel.**

   The Rendering Effects Panel opens.

3. **Click Add under the Effects rollout; choose Film Grain from the list.**

4. **Under Film Grain Parameters, input a value of 0.7.**

   This value creates a very grainy result.

5. **Render and preview the animation.**

Take a look at the `FilmGrain.avi` animation in the `ANIMS` folder on this book's CD-ROM. Notice that the sandy looking grains seem to jitter.

Motion Blur

If you hold your hand in front of your face and move it quickly, you see a blurred image as your fingers move. This effect is called Motion Blur; using it in a 3D animation adds to the believability of an animated scene. Follow these steps to create this effect in 3ds max.

1. **Create an animation that displays an object moving quickly on a path.**

   One way to do so is to move the object a bit farther from one keyframe to the next.

2. **Click the Effects button under the Rendering tab in the Tab Panel.**

   The Rendering Effects Panel opens.

3. **Click Add under the Effects rollout; select Motion Blur from the list.**

4. **Under the Motion Blur Parameters rollout, set the Duration to 100.**

5. **Render and preview the animation.**

Video Post

Video Post demands a book of its own, due to its features and complexity. Even as a 3ds max beginner however, there are some things you should know about it. Video Post is used to render effects to an animation after everything else is configured. It's especially useful for creating fast background and light effects. A quick blast through a typical Video Post project — a spacecraft in flight — shows off those capabilities (and isn't all that different from the way the pros do it in big-budget sci-fi movies).

Setting the scene

Think of Video Post as an ideal place to use the classic *lights-camera-action* sequence that movie directors know by heart. The first order of business is to set the scene. Here's what that looks like for the spacecraft-in-flight example:

1. **Access the Video Post Panel (shown in Figure 26-5) by choosing Rendering⇨Video Post.**

Figure 26-5:
The Video
Post Panel.

2. **Pass the mouse cursor over the top row of tools and options in the Video Post Panel.**

   A label appears over each tool. (Handy, isn't it?)

3. **Place an Extended Primitive Capsule in your scene to act as a spacecraft.**

4. **Place a camera in the scene, using the Front Viewport.**

5. **Place two Omni lights in the scene.**

6. **Change the Perspective Viewport to the Camera Viewport.**

7. **Create a keyframe animation so the lights move across the camera's view during the animation.**

8. **Keyframe the Capsule object so it too moves across the camera's view in the animation.**

   Make the object's movements different from those of the lights.

Using Add Scene Event

As most fans of Saturday morning cartoons know, only the cheapest animations freeze the entire scene and move only one thing (for example, a character's mouth). In the real world, lots of things are moving all the time — not just the item that's the center of attention. Adding a Scene Event makes your animation seem more like a real-world scene. Here's what that looks like in the spacecraft-in-flight example:

1. **Choose Rendering⇨Video Post to bring up the Video Post Panel.**

2. **In the top row of options, pass your mouse pointer over the tools and find the Add Scene Event tool.**

   No problem — just read the labels as they pop up.

3. **Click the Add Scene Event tool to bring up the Add Scene Event Panel.**

4. **Under the View heading, choose the Camera_01 option.**

   Doing so selects the camera as the effect-processing viewer for the scene.

5. **Click the Render Options button and configure the settings in the Render Options panel.**

6. **Close the Render Options panel, and then close the Add Scene Event Panel.**

Adding a lens flare

For the you-are-there realism everybody expects from a camera that's filming an actual scene, you can add a lens flare. Here's how:

1. **Click the Add Image Filter icon in the Video Post panel.**

   An Edit Filter Event Panel appears.

2. **Click the Setup button to open the Lens Effects Flare Panel (shown in Figure 26-6).**

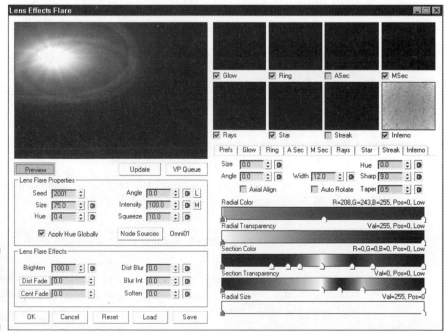

Figure 26-6: The Lens Effects Flare Panel.

3. **Click Preview to highlight the lens flare you are creating; check its appearance.**

4. **Click Node Sources on the left, and select your Omni01 light as the source of the new lens flare.**

5. **Click the tabs on the right; each represents an attribute of the lens flare.**

   Here you can experiment with the parameter values and play with the sliders, watching the preview window. As you alter the settings, the lens flare changes before your eyes.

6. **Click OK to accept your chosen settings for the Omni01 lens flare.**

Doing it again to enhance realism

You can reuse certain processes to refine the realism of your scene. Here's what happens to the spacecraft-in-flight scene when you reapply the Image Filter, the lens flare, and the lighting options:

1. **Repeat the Add Image Filter process again, creating another lens flare (different from the first) for the Omni02 light.**

2. **Add Image Filter Event again, this time choosing Star Field from the list.**

3. **Click Setup to enter the Stars Control Panel.**

   Use the following parameter values in the Stars Control Panel: Dimmest Star 77, Brightest Star 255, Logarithmic, Star Size 2.0, Motion Blur 0, Star Database Random, Count 12,777, and Background.

4. **Click OK to accept your settings.**

5. **Click the Add Image Output Event icon at the top of the Video Post Panel.**

   The Add Image Output Event panel appears.

6. **Click the Files button in that panel to create a filename, destination, and animation file format for the animation you are about to save.**

7. **Click Save to apply your information.**

8. **In the Video Post Panel, click the Execute Sequence icon (it looks like a running man).**

   Doing so starts the process of creating your animation and saving it where you told the computer to save it. Your Video Post Panel should resemble Figure 26-7.

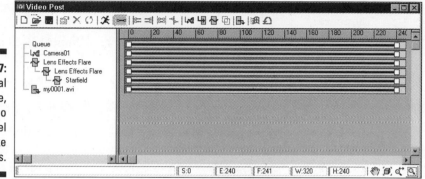

Figure 26-7:
In an ideal universe, your Video Post Panel looks like this.

Be sure to view the VidPost2.avi animation in the ANIMS folder on this book's CD-ROM.

This whole section of the chapter is only a taste of Video Post. If it has made you hungry for more, all I can say is, "Go for it — *bon appetit!*"

Part IX
The Part of Tens

The 5th Wave   By Rich Tennant

'Well shoot — I know the animation's moving a might too fast, but <u>dang</u> if I can find a 'mosey' function anywhere in the toolbox!

In this part . . .

It may be somewhat confusing that Part IX of this book is called the Part of Tens, but that's just the way that things worked out. All books in the *For Dummies* series have a section called the Part of Tens. This part of the book contains many of 3ds max's features that I didn't touch on in earlier parts. 3ds max is a huge piece of software, used by many filmmakers and TV broadcast artists and animators. Some of its features become useful only after you've spent some time, months or even years, getting the basics down. Although I don't have the space to go into exhaustive detail concerning all of these additional features, I can at least mention many of them so you are aware of where they are and have some sense of what they're used for.

Chapter 27

Ten Tips for Maximizing Your 3ds max Sessions

3ds max is like that famous pink bunny in the commercial — it keeps going and going and going. Even the most experienced max users keep discovering new features and better ways to do things, so it's no surprise that this book hasn't attended to every nook and cranny of 3ds max's potential. In an effort to provide you with more ways to lose sleep (and also to remind you to do some important stuff), here is another banquet of tasty information for your dining pleasure.

Remember to Save Frequently

Yeah, I know, nag, nag, nag. But if you want to prevent some expensive sessions with a psychiatrist, save your 3ds max work frequently. I recommend saving your scene every ten minutes or so during a work session. After all, all it takes is a quick Ctrl+S keyboard stroke. This is especially true when you are working on complex scenes with intricate elements. Computers aren't perfect, 3ds max isn't perfect, and your Windows operating system is way less than approaching perfection. Every once in a while, maybe just to test your emotional control, 3ds max may crash or freeze. If you've been going happily along before that point, neglecting to save your work, you may erupt into a burst of creative language that will wake the neighbors and start the dogs barking. Three cautions: Save, save, save!

Render Previews at Lower Resolutions

If you need a large-resolution rendering for either professional film or print use, don't apply the resolution you want until after you get your final rendering. Use lower-resolution renders as you put the project together. Doing so saves a lot of time, especially when you have to load the preview renders you make along the way.

Use the Spacing Tool

What if you have an object and a Splined path, and you want to create copies or instances of the object on that path? It could be a column that needs to be duplicated to form the multiple columns of a temple. Sounds like a job for the Spacing tool (trumpets sound a fanfare here!). Follow these steps to use it:

1. **Create a shape to form the cross-section for a column of your own design in the Front Viewport.**

2. **Move the Pivot Point to the end of the shape so you can lathe the shape.**

3. **Click the Modeling tab in the Tab Panel and Lathe the shape.**

4. **Choose Create⇨Shapes⇨Splines⇨Rectangle. In the Top Viewport, and create a square Spline the size that you want the temple to be.**

5. **Select the column object, and move its Pivot Point to its base.**

6. **In the Front Viewport, move the square Spline to the same vertical position as the column's Pivot Point.**

7. **Choose Tools⇨Spacing Tool.**

   The Spacing Tool Panel appears.

8. **Click the Pick Path button, and then click the square spline in the Top Viewport.**

   Use the following parameters: Click in the box next to Count to activate it. Input a Count value of 13 (the original column is counted). From the list, choose Divide Evenly, Objects at Ends.

9. **Under Content, choose Centers. Under Type of Object, choose Copy.**

10. **Click Apply to create the columns arranged in a square pattern.**

11. **Delete the original column. Add a roof of your own design.**

Work with the Light Lister

Sometimes you may want to tweak the parameters of several lights in a scene. You could select each one in turn and then choose the Modify Command Panel, but that would take some time (and wouldn't be much fun). The Light Lister is a quicker way to edit the parameters of any or all lights in your scene. To get to it, simply choose Tools⇨Light Lister. All parameter controls for the lights in your scene are in one convenient place: the Light Lister Panel.

Use the Schematic View

Sometimes a scene can get so complex that selecting one specific object to edit is nearly impossible. Fortunately, that's when you can use the Schematic View. Right-click the name of any viewport, and then choose Views⇨ Schematic⇨New. Your viewport is transformed into a schematic chart, displaying every object element in the scene — with all links clearly visible. Selecting any element in the schematic automatically brings up its parameters for quick editing in the Command Panel.

Create Morphed Geometry

Altering an object to resemble another object is called *Morphing*. The process requires a Source Object and at least one Target Object. Morphing can alter the shape of a character's expression in an animation, or magically transform one object into another. Morphing in 3ds max is a blast. Here's how:

1. **Create a sphere in a scene.**

2. **Press Shift and then click and drag to move the sphere to bring up the Cloning Panel, choose Copy, input 3 to create three duplicates, and close the Panel.**

3. **Move the three duplicated spheres off to the side.**

4. **Select one of the cloned spheres and apply a Taper Modifier to it.**

   Use the following parameters: Amount 1.3, Curve 10, Taper Axis Z/XY/Symmetry, Limits 0.0.

5. **Select a second cloned sphere and apply a Stretch Modifier to it (set the Modifier to 1.5 on the Z-axis).**

6. **Select the third cloned sphere and double its vertical scale. Apply a Ripple Modifier to it with the following parameters:**

   • Amplitude 1 to 20

   • Amplitude 2 to 15

   • Wavelength 0.1

   • Phase and Decay 0

   The three cloned objects become Morph Targets.

7. **Select the original object (Source).**

8. **Choose Modifiers⇨Morpher, and look in the Modify Command Panel for the Channel List rollout.**

9. **Right-click the first empty button, choose Pick From Scene from the list that appears, and click the first cloned sphere in any viewport.**

10. **Right-click the second empty button, choose Pick From Scene from the list that appears, and click the second cloned sphere in any viewport.**

11. **Right-click the third empty button, choose Pick From Scene from the list that appears, and click the third cloned sphere in any viewport.**

12. **Select all three cloned spheres, choose the Display Command Panel, and then (on the Hide rollout) click Hide Selected.**

    The cloned spheres are now configured as Morph Targets for the source sphere, so it's okay that they disappear at this point.

13. **Select the source sphere in any viewport.**

    In the Modify Command Panel, the first three slots in the Channel List are dedicated to the Target Morphs for the source sphere. Altering the values by clicking and dragging on the spinners next to each Target Morph will apply that target to the source sphere. You can mix and match the three Target Morphs to create interesting alterations to the source sphere's form.

If you like, you can keyframe-animate this process. You can even choose Edit⇨Snapshot to create any number of separate objects.

Merge Content

As you develop new scene content and save it, you may run into a situation where what you need in one scene has already been created in another. When this circumstance arises, you can combine two or more scenes into one, so that all of the content of both scenes is available to you. Just choose File⇨Merge to select another scene to add to the one presently loaded in max. When you locate the to-be-merged scene and select to open it, the Merge Panel appears. Using the options in the Merge Panel, you can choose what elements of the scene you want to merge with the present one. Lights and cameras, for example, are usually best not to merge, because they may interfere with the present scene elements.

The same process works if both your original and targeted merge files are animated, except you get a few more options in the Merge Animation Panel. Just choose File⇨Merge Animation.

Use the MaxScript Listener

Repetitive tasks are a drag — boring, time-consuming, and (in this case) unnecessary. To save your time and stimulate your imagination, 3ds max provides the MaxScript feature. MaxScripts are small bits of code that do a task from start to finish. All you have to do is to run the script by choosing MaxScript⇨Run Script and selecting a saved script from where it was stored. 3ds max comes with dozens of sample MaxScripts.

You may never have done any programming before, but don't let that stop you from creating some code with MaxScript. It's easy — try it out:

1. **Place a Torus Primitive in a scene.**

2. **Right-click the Left Viewport title, and choose Views⇨Extended⇨ MaxScript Listener.**

3. **Choose MaxScript⇨Macro Recorder from the menu bar.**

   This starts the recording facility.

4. **In the MaxScript Viewport, click in the pink area.**

   This is the Macro Recorder area.

5. **Use a series of Modifiers to alter the geometry of the Torus.**

   As you use the Modifiers, notice that a script is being automatically written in the Macro Recorder area.

6. **In the MaxScript Viewport, choose File⇨Save As, and name and save your MaxScript.**

7. **With the Torus selected, press the Delete key.**

   The Torus vanishes from the scene.

8. **Choose MaxScript⇨Run Script. Select the MaxScript you just saved, and open it.**

   Instantly a warped Torus is written into your scene.

There's a lot more depth to MaxScripting that can be learned from studying the MaxScript language, fully documented in the 3ds max Help files installed with 3ds max.

Use Connected Springs

Though you may only need it rarely, the Connected Springs modeling alternative really underscores the power of 3ds max. Here's the drill:

1. **Choose Create⇨Geometry⇨Dynamics Objects, and click the Spring button.**

2. **Click and drag in the Top Viewport to create a Spring.**

   The Spring's parameters appear in the Command Panel.

3. **Open the Modify Command Panel to adjust the Spring's parameters. Then enter values to specify the following settings:**

   - Bound to Object Pivots
   - Diameter 7
   - Turns 5
   - CCW
   - Automatic Segments
   - Round Wire with a Diameter of 0.7 and 6 Sides
   - Relaxed Height 1
   - Constant k of 3 Pounds Per Inch
   - Spring Works In Both

4. **Place a cube at either end of the Spring.**

5. **Select the Spring, open the Modify Command Panel, click the Pick Top Object button, and choose the top cube in any viewport.**

6. **Click the Pick Bottom Object button, and select the bottom cube in any viewport.**

   The Spring is now attached to each cube's Pivot Point on both ends. You may have to enlarge the cubes a bit if the Spring is showing through. You also will have to move the bottom cube's Pivot Point upward toward its top.

When you move the top cube down or up, it compresses or elongates the Spring, as does the bottom cube. (Great toy, isn't it? *Virtually* unbreakable!)

See the `Springer1.avi` animation on this book's CD-ROM in the `ANIMS` folder.

Trace Images

When you want to model something from a photograph, it's neat to trace the photograph inside of 3ds max to get a better idea about the shapes and proportions involved. To do that, you first look at the photo to decide which viewport (Front, Top, Side . . .) the image would be best traced in. The Front Viewport is used most often for this purpose. After selecting the needed viewport, choose Views⇨Viewport Background to bring up the Viewport Background Panel.

Click Files to select either an image or an animation (yes, this works with animations too!). It's best to select Match Bitmap under Aspect Ratio so the proportions are correct. Select Display Background in Active Viewport Only. Click OK, and your image is ready to be traced with Splines, or used as a template for 3D object creation. You can always use Layers to organize objects. Keep an eye on the Polygon Counter in the Utility Panel, which gives you feedback about polygon quantities.

Chapter 28

Ten or So Great Plug-ins

....

In This Chapter

▶ Great commercial plug-ins and vendors

▶ Great freebies and shareware

▶ Handshaking with max

*O*pen architecture — no, it doesn't mean buildings with no walls — is a computer-industry term for software that other developers can enhance by contributing their own special features *(plug-ins)* that you can (ahem) plug right in. Granted, 3ds max comes with an astounding array of on-board tools and Modifiers — but max is also an open (or *extensible*) architecture. You can extend its usefulness with plug-ins — and 3ds max has more plug-in developers than any other 3D software. Plug-ins can push software to do what it can't do on its own. As you become more experienced with 3ds max, you may want to explore the possibility of adding some plug-ins to it. Plug-ins come with their own instructions on what steps to take to install them. There are plug-ins of every type, though most address modeling in some way.

Please note that plug-ins have a way of disappearing from the market very quickly, and that some of the plug-ins mentioned in this chapter for your consideration may no longer be available by the time that you read this, or they may need to be upgraded to work with the latest version of 3ds max. The positive thing is that plug-in developers are always creating new plug-ins for 3ds max, so you will probably discover a whole new range of 3ds max plug-ins by visiting a 3ds max plug-in Web site.

Commercial Plug-ins and Vendors

A commercial plug-in is one that you pay money for. The number of commercial developers who create plug-ins for 3ds max only continues to grow. Most, however, instead of marketing their wares on their own, use a single plug-in clearinghouse for marketing purposes — Digimation. Digimation (www.digimation.com) is the largest commercial entity that both develops unique 3ds max plug-ins of their own as well as acts as a marketing and distribution center for many other 3ds max plug-in developers. Digimation's catalog ships with 3ds max, so you should have one too. There are dozens of commercial plug-ins listed in the Digimation catalog, and other commercial plug-ins not yet listed. Here are a few you may be interested in investigating.

Digimation's Particle Studio

The Particle Studio plug-in is an *event-based* particle system. You alter the way the particles are created at various keyframe points on the timeline, according to the particles' behavior at that point. If you want to freeze the particle motion, Particle Studio has a special Snapshot option in the 3ds max Utility panel. Custom Particles can be Object Instances, Copies, or Editable Mesh components. There are two ways to use Particle Studio. The first is to open its Event Map parameters panel.

You can use one of Particle Studio's preset Particle Systems or design your own.

Quick Setup Presets

Particle Studio Presets are ready-made animation templates that come in four categories: Streams, Transforms, Flocks, and Miscellaneous.

Streams

Streams are directional animations of particles, allowing the particles to target selected objects no matter where the target moves in the animation.

Transforms

Transforms are processes that allow you to create a Snapshot object from particles, or to animate the particles in a standard fashion. Either way, any selected Transform frame in the timeline can be translated into a mesh with the Snapshot option.

Flocks

Particle Studio has four Flock types: Grazing Herd, Flock of Birds, Swarm of Insects, and School of Fish. Be sure to use a low quantity when you use the Flock option; too many cloned objects can overwhelm your system.

Miscellaneous

Explode Object and Trail are the two alternatives in the Miscellaneous category. Trail creates streaks behind a moving object; Explode is obvious.

Shag Fur

Marketed by Digimation, Shag Fur creates fur, hair, and other fuzzy looks by using special lights. Shag Fur needs the Shag Render and Shag Fur components in the Environment panel and you must have a Camera Viewport active. Shag Lights are then added to the scene. The Shag Fur effects are not geometry related, so you can't expect the fur or hair to show if the object is saved to another format and exported from 3ds max.

Light Galleries

Marketed by Digimation, Light Galleries consists of a collection of lighting variation presets that can be quickly applied to any scene. The variations are almost limitless, but the steps are straightforward:

1. **Add your objects to the Include list for a light or lights.**

2. **Choose Utilities⇨Light Galleries.**

   The Light Galleries options appear in the Utilities rollout. The larger the X Rendering value shown in the rollout, the more lighting presets are offered.

3. **Click New to add a new Light Galleries preset.**

4. **Select any light in the scene and vary its position and angle, or use the Modify Command Panel to alter all attributes of the light.**

   Light Galleries uses the active viewport to create the alternative presets. The viewports display the lights placed at different preset positions.

5. **Use the Viewer button to see all the preset variations; click the Compositor button to start the final process.**

6. **In the Compositor, try out light transformations until you have the look you want.**

   For example, you can drag on the presets' thumbnails to interactively alter each light's brightness.

7. **Still in the Compositor, click Create These Lights.**

   The lighting you selected is written to the scene, as shown in Figure 28-1.

Visit Digimation on the Web at www.digimation.com to preview their huge collection of reasonably priced 3ds max plug-ins.

Figure 28-1:
Here are
some
scene-
lighting
variations
as they
appear in
the Light
Galleries
Compositor.

Freebies and Shareware

Freeware costs nothing, and many 3ds max Freeware plug-ins are out there.
Shareware comes with a plea from the developer that you contribute something. A new type of Shareware is *Charityware;* the developer asks you to contribute to a specific charity.

Polychop

http://www.bioware.com

This plug-in optimizes the number of polygons in a mesh. Polychop is more
functional than the internal 3ds max Optimize modifier; you can set boundaries and protect areas of your model from any reduction of polygons (for
example, Edge Length, Curvature, and Smoothing Zones). Most models can
be optimized by at least 25 percent without noticeable loss of detail.

Mountain

http://www.effectware.com

After installation, you can create a mountain in the Top Viewport if you
choose Create➪Geometry➪EffectWare Objects, and then click and drag. The
Mountain plug-in features a number of useful parameter options. Mesh Size
determines the sharpness or curvature of the peaks. The Fractal Dimension

value (0.0 to 4.0) affects general landscape contours and the number of peaks. Power Scale values higher than 1 tend to create craggy, separated peaks, as shown in Figure 28-2.

Airfoil

http://www.effectware.com

This is one of my favorite freeware plug-ins. After installing this plug-in, choose Create⇨Shapes⇨EffectWare Shapes. Airfoil creates a closed spline you extrude to form the surface of a dynamically accurate wing (based on the specs of real-world airfoils). Aeronautical engineers can find familiar parameter settings such as Chord, Chamber, Position, Thickness, and Node. Three types of scientifically accurate Airfoil cross-sections can be emulated: Joukowski, NACA 4-digit series, and NACA 5-digit series.

Helicoid Generator

http://www.effectware.com

The 3D form created by this plug-in looks a bit like a drill-bit with ends that can be reconfigured. You control the radius of tip and base, the quality of the mesh, and how many turns to put in your helix.

SuperQuad

http://www.effectware.com

After installation, choose Create⇨Geometry⇨Effectware Objects⇨SuperQuad. This plug-in creates both Ellipsoids and Toroids with modifiable U-Shape and V-Shape parameters.

Wing

http://www.effectware.com

Wing is another version of the Airfoil plug-in, capable of generating full 3D objects. It offers the same parameters as Airfoil, plus settings such as differential size (from root to tip) and extrusion value.

Figure 28-2:
Mapped
with bumpy
material, the
Mountain
plug-in
creates
realistic
scenery.

Decay Noise

www.blur.com

You can use this plug-in to move the center of the Noise effect anywhere in your scene, controlling parameter values such as intensity and influence perimeter. Use Decay Noise to give objects a bashed and battered look.

Twist-O-Rama

www.blur.com

After you install this plug-in, it shows up in the Modifier list *and* as a Space Warp. You can apply its effects at any distance by moving the Sub-Object Center; you control the area of influence. The Twist-O-Rama modifier works much like the standard Twist modifier, but with more variable controls.

Moebius

www.habwre.com

After installation, Moebius can be found by choosing Create⇨Geometry⇨ Fascination⇨Moebius. Then simply left-click and drag in any viewport to generate the object. You can even set the Number of Loops and their Angles (a normal Moebius Strip has just one loop).

SoapFilm

www.habwre.com

After installation, you choose Create⇨Geometry⇨Minimal Surfaces, and then choose one of the SoapFilm options: Helicoid, Catenoid, or Costa Surface. All three options are surfaces formed by real soap film.

Handshaking with max

Software that *handshakes* with other software establishes mutually agreed-upon communication practices such as a common file format. The 3ds object file format, for instance, is not only common to 3ds max, but dozens of other computer graphics and animation software packages are able to write and read it as well. This means that all those other software packages have a way to speak with, or handshake with, 3ds max. If a book were to be written with just one chapter for each of the 3D software applications that addressed the 3ds object file format, it would be a much larger book than this one.

There are more direct ways that one piece of software can handshake with another however. Software can be designed to handshake so closely with another targeted piece of software that the source package acts almost like a plug-in. Such relationships do indeed exist. Here are five very different and unique handshaking applications that address 3ds max in different ways, all worthy of exploration as you extend your max mastery.

Poser

www.curiouslabs.com

For creating and animating 3D characters of every type, Poser rules the roost. Poser has a wealth of character presets and character-related features. Poser handshakes with 3ds max by writing out full character-incorporated animation scenes and using a plug-in bridge between the two programs. Poser 5, the latest edition, contains groundbreaking advances in character design and animation technology — which its effective handshaking makes available to 3ds max users. Poser models can be exported as 3ds models (max artists and animators, rejoice!), and you can keyframe-animate any preset element in Poser by using the controls shown in Figure 28-3.

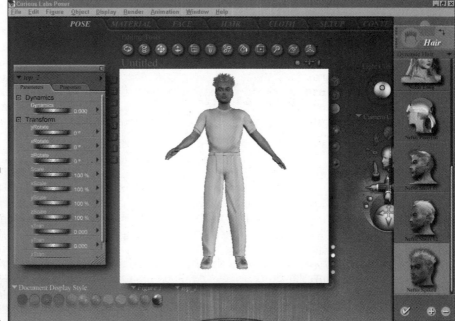

Figure 28-3:
The main Poser interface, or Room; parameter dial controls are on the left.

Poser does excellent materials, faces, cloth, hair, and fur. Poser may be a vital add-on for your 3ds max projects if you're planning to populate 3D worlds with virtual characters.

LifeForms

www.charactermotion.com

Credo Interactive's *LifeForms* is software dedicated to the creation of BVH and other movement file formats. These formats can be applied to characters in 3ds max and Poser to give superealistic motion to jointed characters. LifeForms has a large library of characters of its own that can also be ported to 3ds max. Preset movement scripts are also included, and you can order more character and animation files to add to your LifeForms resources, as shown in Figure 28-4.

Adobe Illustrator

www.adobe.com

Adobe Illustrator sets the standard when it comes to vector drawing software. You don't know what a vector is? Sure you do! A vector is a spline, the same thing as the splines you use in 3ds max to create shapes. 3ds max imports Illustrator vectors as spline shapes, which you can then extrude, lathe, make visible, or use as animation paths. Illustrator has a much wider array of tools for creating all sorts of splines, so Illustrator handshakes quite effectively with 3ds max. Illustrator is a must-have if your 3ds max work involves wide spline use.

Vue d'Esprit

When you need to create photorealistic backdrops of still or animated naturalistic environments for 3ds max, look no farther than Vue d'Esprit (pronounced Voo-Deh-Spree). With all the features needed to create 3D trees, water, clouds, landscapes, and more (as well as the ability to incorporate Poser animation projects), Vue is the perfect environmental complement to 2ds max. Vue's cloud and sky presets alone are worth the ticket, giving 3ds max users very high-quality natural backdrops. You can also use Vue's output to create still or animated Reflection and Diffuse Channel maps in max.

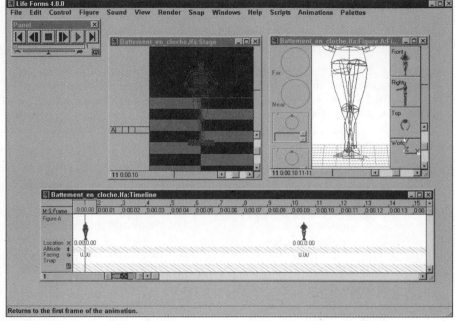

Figure 28-4:
Investigate
LifeForms
when you
need to
create
realistic
motion files
for 3ds max
characters.

Post-production plug-ins

Post-production effects are image effects applied to a project *after* it is rendered. (Effects created in the 3ds max Render Effects panel are post-production effects, as are Video Post effects.) Two excellent plug-ins are

- ✔ **Illusion:** This 2D particle-system application creates final touches for 3ds max animations. Illusion has been used to create professional effects for broadcast television shows including "The Starship Trooper Chronicles," "Star Trek Voyager," and Warner Brothers' "Max Steele," "Lexx," and "Superman."

- ✔ **Combustion:** This complete post-production effects package comes from AutoDesk, the developer of 3ds max; it handshakes with 3ds max on the fly! Using Combustion, you can layer animations and apply myriad effects, stitching everything together into one seamless whole. Combustion is used in major Hollywood and broadcast productions.

Why mention Illusion and Combustion in the same breath? The Illusion effects are folded into Combustion, and are available to all Combustion users. Combustion is included on its own CD-ROM in the 3ds max package, so if you have purchased 3ds max version 5, you also have the Combustion CD-ROM with the integrated Illusion effects. This is only a time-limited version of Combustion, which has to be purchased separately from Discreet, but when you are ready to create your first major animated films, Combustion will be there waiting for you.

Appendix

About the CD

••

*O*n the CD-ROM, you'll find:

- ✔ A 30-day trial version of 3ds max
- ✔ A folder with dozens of 3ds max animations that reference the text

System Requirements

Make sure your computer meets the minimum system requirements listed below. If your computer doesn't match up to most of these requirements, you may have problems in using the contents of the CD.

- ✔ Windows XT or 2000 Pro recommended.
- ✔ Intel or AMD based processor at 300 Mhz minimum (dual Intel Pentium 4 processor or dual AMD Athlon system recommended).
- ✔ 256MB RAM and 300MB swap space minimum (1GB RAM and 2GBswap space recommended).
- ✔ Graphics card supporting 1024 x 768 x 16-bit color (OpenGL and Direct3D hardware acceleration supported; 24-bit color, 3D graphics accelerator preferred).
- ✔ Windows-compliant pointing device (specific optimization for Microsoft Intellimouse)
- ✔ DVD or CD-ROM drive
- ✔ Optional: Sound card and speakers, cabling for TCP/IP-compliant network, 3D hardware graphics acceleration, video input and output devices, joystick, midi-instruments, 3-button mouse.

If you need more information on the basics, check out these books published by Wiley Publishing, Inc.: *PCs For Dummies,* by Dan Gookin; *Macs For Dummies,* by David Pogue; *iMacs For Dummies* by David Pogue; *Windows 95 For Dummies, Windows 98 For Dummies, Windows 2000 Professional For Dummies, Microsoft Windows ME Millennium Edition For Dummies,* all by Andy Rathbone.

Using the CD with Microsoft Windows

To install from the CD to your hard drive, follow these steps:

1. **Insert the CD into your computer's CD-ROM drive.**

2. **Click the Start button and choose Run from the menu.**

3. **Find the file called Setup.exe, or Install.exe, or something similar, and double-click that file.**

   The program's installer walks you through the process of setting up your new software.

To run some of the programs, you may need to keep the CD inside your CD-ROM drive. Otherwise, the installed program would have required you to install a very large chunk of the program to your hard drive space, which would have kept you from installing other software.

What You'll Find

Here's a summary of the software on this CD arranged by category:

Shareware programs are fully functional, free trial versions of copyrighted programs. If you like particular programs, register with their authors for a nominal fee and receive licenses, enhanced versions, and technical support. Freeware programs are free, copyrighted games, applications, and utilities. You can copy them to as many PCs as you like — free — but they have no technical support. GNU software is governed by its own license, which is included inside the folder of the GNU software. There are no restrictions on distribution of this software. See the GNU license for more details. Trial, demo, or evaluation versions are usually limited either by time or functionality (such as being unable to save projects).

Sample files from the book, from the author. *For Windows XT, 2000.* There is a folder of animations referencing specific items in the text. To run these animations, you need to have Windows Media Player installed. Simply double-click the animation you want to view and it should run automatically.

If You've Got Problems (Of the CD Kind)

I tried my best to compile programs that work on most computers with the minimum system requirements. Alas, your computer may differ, and some programs may not work properly for some reason.

The two likeliest problems are that you don't have enough memory (RAM) for the programs you want to use, or you have other programs running that are affecting installation or running of a program. If you get error messages like Not enough memory or Setup cannot continue, try one or more of these methods and then try using the software again:

- ✓ **Turn off any anti-virus software that you have on your computer.** Installers sometimes mimic virus activity and may make your computer incorrectly believe that it is being infected by a virus.

- ✓ **Close all running programs.** The more programs you're running, the less memory is available to other programs. Installers also typically update files and programs. So if you keep other programs running, installation may not work properly.

- ✓ **Have your local computer store add more RAM to your computer.** This is, admittedly, a drastic and somewhat expensive step. However, if you have a Windows 95 or later PC or a Mac OS computer with a PowerPC chip, adding more memory can really help the speed of your computer and allow more programs to run at the same time.

If you still have trouble with the CD, please call the Customer Care phone number: (800) 762-2974. Outside the United States, call 1 (317) 572-3994. You can also contact Customer Service by e-mail at techsupdum@wiley.com. Wiley Publishing Inc. will provide technical support only for installation and other general quality control items; for technical support on the applications themselves, consult the program's vendor or author.

Index

• V •